Table of Contents

Introduction

Tea drinking and the vessels for preparing and serving tea have a long and fascinating history in the West. Dutch traders from the Far East first imported tea to Europe in 1610 and for some time it was considered as much a medicinal herb as a refreshing drink. However, within a few decades, hot tea was being served all over Europe and in coffeehouses in England. Coffee, by the way, has a slightly longer history in the West, having come into Italy from Turkey and the Mideast in the 1500s.

Of course, the habit of drinking tea soon came to the British-American colonies by the mid-17th century and remained a popular, albeit fairly expensive, beverage for over a century. However, that seems to have all changed after the famous "Boston Tea Party" and the American boycott of tea imported from England. After the American Revolution tea never seemed to regain its popularity on this side of the pond, although it never completely went out of style.

Our new *Antique Trader Teapots Price Guide* will help you better understand and appreciate this history of tea drinking in the western world by providing a comprehensive overview of the teapot as it evolved from the 18th century through the end of the 20th. Early tea wares, including teapots, were quite choice items, often made of the finest porcelain and only available to the wealthy elite. It wasn't until the second half of the 18th century that teapots and accessories became more widely available and much less expensive. Fine porcelain gave way to fine earthenwares such as pearlware and Queensware, and sterling silver was superceded by Sheffield Plate in the late 18th century, and finally silver plate by the mid-19th century. The growth of tea cultivation also expanded tremendously by the late 18th century, which also helped to make tea a more everyday commodity.

As we know, hot tea remains the national drink of Great Britain where annually every person consumes about 7 pounds per year. That compares to less than a pound per person in the United States. I, like many Americans, still enjoy a relaxing cup of hot tea from time to time and find it less stimulating than coffee, even though it's reported that a cup of tea has about as much caffeine as a cup of coffee. I have a wonderful memory of my first cup of tea consumed in England. It was the fall of 1969 and I had just arrived in Dover from France with a carload of fellow American students. We had taken the late evening ferry and didn't arrive in Dover until nearly 11 p.m. Of course we had no idea of where to stay but fortunately caught the attention of a local constable who seemed to recognize we were a bit lost. He stopped our car and we explained our dilemma. He said he thought he could help and asked us to hold tight for a short while. We saw him pull up a nearby private driveway to a large brick house, and within a few minutes he returned to tell us the owners of this bed and breakfast did have room to put us up for the night. It was a bit embarrassing knowing we had roused these folks out of bed, but their welcome was warm and sincere and no sooner did we get in the door than the hostess offered us a cup of tea! I remember taking my steaming cup gratefully and adding just a bit of sugar (as I believe is the general habit in the U.S.). As soon as I lifted the cup to my lips, the hostess gave me a startled look and said, in all sincerity, "You mean you drink it BLACK!?" You see, the British almost invariably add cream or milk to their tea, and she was astonished anyone would drink the stuff "unadulterated." So, if you have the chance to travel in Britain, be sure and specify you want your tea "black." And please, don't ask for ICED tea unless you really want to appear to be rather uncouth. Of course, after 30 odd years, I'm sure the rules for foreign visitors have eased a bit and, yes, you can get a good cup of coffee in England.

I hope you'll enjoy our all-color compendium of all the major types of collectible teapots, from early porcelain and silver through the myriad of Victorian and early 20th century examples so widely available. Fortunately for collectors, there's a teapot for everyone's taste and budget and nice examples are still appearing on the market every year. Our new guide includes over 1,200 individual listings and nearly 1,000 color photos. The listings are arranged here according to the material of the teapot with the first section covering ceramic teapots, including porcelain, pottery and earthenware. Within this large category the listings are further arranged chronologically. The second major section is for metalware teapots, listed alphabetically by material such as brass, copper, graniteware, pewter and Silver. Then a miscellaneous section includes sections on teapots of glass and other materials and finally, just to round things out, chronological listings of tea sets of all types.

During the preparation of this guide, I had wonderful support from collectors and dealers around the country and in Britain. We have listed them in our "Special Contributors" section here. I must give special thanks to Louise Irvine, a leading English authority on Doulton and Royal Doulton wares, who also prepared our informative introductory feature on teapot collecting. Her enthusiasm and support were wonderful. Also, I must mention collector Mary Ann Johnston. I made contact with Mary Ann through other collecting friends, and she made material from her extensive teapot collection available to me most generously. In fact, thanks to her efforts, we have photos and descriptions of more than 150 teapots of all types and ages. I am deeply indebted to these remarkable ladies and so many other kind contributors. Finally, I am very grateful to Irish Belleek expert Del Domke, who not only supplied photos from his collection but also contacted noted Irish Belleek teapot collector Lady Marion Langham of England. Her ladyship graciously shared wonderful photos of pieces in her collection for our special bonus section - "Rare Irish Belleek Teawares," which is included at the end of our regular listing.

Even though the ritual of tea drinking may have waned for modern Americans, the teapot serves as an ageless reminder of the remarkable history of this wonderful, refreshing beverage. Now, brew up a nice hot cup of your favorite tea and sit back and enjoy our colorful tour of the beautiful world of teapots. Cheers!

Kyle Husfloen, Editor

TEAPOTS FOR COLLECTORS

By Louise Irvine

Teapots are no longer regarded merely as humble vessels for serving the popular beverage—they have been discovered by collectors. During the last 300 years, since tea was introduced to the West, teapots have undergone many fascinating variations in shape, material and decorative treatments, and they are widely appreciated around the world.

Tea first arrived in England in the early 17th century, having been shipped from Japan via Holland by the Dutch East India Company. Initially the beverage was promoted for medicinal purposes—a wonder remedy for colds, indigestion and many other ailments. In the 1660s it was made fashionable by Queen Catherine, wife of King Charles II, and the English aristocracy soon began to partake of a cup after dinner.

The East India Company began importing tea directly to England from China in 1689. Duty on tea became a lucrative source of revenue for the crown, and smuggling thrived. By the 18th century the American colonies refused to buy British tea because of the high taxes, and smuggled tea from Holland. Then, in 1773, the British government passed The Tea Act to force the colonists to buy their tea from the East India Company. The result was the famous "Boston Tea Party," when the Sons of Liberty dumped some 45 tons of tea overboard from British ships in Boston Harbor. The controversy over tea helped spark the American Revolution and eventual independence from Britain.

All the tea in China

Initially all the teapots and cups were imported from China—hence in England they were referred to as "china"—and they were packed underneath the consignments of tea, thus acting as ballast on the graceful tea clippers sailing from China. Soon the little red stoneware teapots made in China were being copied by potters in London and Staffordshire. Some Chinese teapots were modeled as animals, buildings and fruits, reflecting an ancient tradition of using mythological symbols to fashion everyday objects. The relevance of these designs may not have been appreciated by the new tea drinking British public,

Small early Meissen teapot, 1735-40.

Left: Chinese Export teapot, Canton-type with Famille Rose enameling, late 18th century.

but their novelty value certainly was. By the 18th century these teapots were being copied enthusiastically by English potters and, since then, designers have often sought inspiration from unexpected sources.

Admiration for Chinese porcelain tea wares stimulated European potters to emulate this beautiful white translucent body. At Meissen in Germany, the quest resulted in a hard-paste porcelain body, while English factories, such as Chelsea, Derby and Worcester, developed a soft-paste porcelain. Blue and white Oriental designs proliferated on teapots and at first were all hand-painted. However, the development of underglaze transfer printing in blue in the 1750s allowed more complex Chinoiserie designs to be created. The most popular of these printed designs became known as the Willow pattern, which depicts the story of the elopement of the star-crossed lovers Koongshee and Chang. There are a great many similar designs also featuring Chinese pagodas, temples and figures of mandarins.

By the late 18th century, tea was being enjoyed by a wider audience in England and Europe. Tea gardens became fashionable and allowed ladies to take tea in public. The beverage was still very expensive because of the high duty imposed on it, and in homes it was kept locked in tea caddies with the key closely guarded by the lady of the house. The new English tea wares were also expensive. One story relates that when avid tea drinker Dr. Samuel Johnson visited the Derby china works in 1777 he said, "The china was beautiful but ... too dear." For the same money he could have vessels in the same size made in silver, but he bought some Derby pieces anyway.

A few years later, in 1784, the duty on tea was lowered but the duty on silver wares increased, so there was more demand for ceramic teapots in which to brew the cheaper drink. Potters often copied silver shapes for their teapots as can be seen in Spode's new bone china designs and Wedgwood's Queensware, a fine cream-colored earthenware. The Josiah Wedgwood firm also used its Jasper Ware and Basalt bodies for teapots—the plain black of the basalt was thought to flatter the hands of the server.

The earliest English tea sets had tea bowls (sans handles) in the manner of the Chinese rather than with handles. Decorations also evolved in the late 18th century and began to reflect all the

Left: Rare early Staffordshire hexagonal teapot, ca. 1765.

Right: Early Blue Willow teapot, ca. 1807-13.

Small Limoges teapot with rose decoration, ca. 1892-1907.

fashionable tastes of the day including Neoclassical designs or the more ostentatious Regency style, which featured rich gilding. In complete contrast, many early wares featured floral posies, which echoed the sprigged muslin dresses worn by a hostess and her guests.

The cup that cheers

In the first half of the 19th century it was discovered that the tea plant also grew in India, and the development of British tea plantations in India brought the price down so much that it became Britain's favorite brew. The vociferous campaigns of the Temperance societies also helped to promote the beverage, proclaiming it "the cup that cheers but not inebriates."

The quest of novelty in teapot design continued to expand during the early Victorian era in England. The introduction of Minton's majolica wares in 1849 provided an ideal material for creating extravagant shapes in rich eye-catching colors. The image of tea spouting from a robin's beak seems quite absurd to us today, but in the 1870s it was a whimsical conversation piece. Recently, the growing popularity of these early Minton wares inspired the firm to

reintroduce some designs in limited editions, and these have become collectible in their own right.

Until the Victorian period, tea was generally served at breakfast and in the evening after dinner. By the 1840s, however, the dinner hour had moved so late that the gap between meals became uncomfortable. Ladies of leisure began to sustain themselves with tea and cakes in the afternoon, and this custom developed into the elaborate English ritual of afternoon tea served at 5 o'clock. Now the tea service was expanded to include side plates and serving dishes for cakes and sandwiches.

Victorian ingenuity

High tea, as it became known, evolved into the main evening meal for the middle classes and included cold meats, cheese and other savory dishes. Teapots grew bigger to accommodate these occasions and culminated in the introduction of Royle's Self Pouring teapot, introduced in 1886. It was promoted by the Doulton company as "a boon for mothers of large families." This labor saving invention did not need to be

Flow Blue Hong Kong pattern teapot, ca. 1840.

Two views of R.S. Prussia pedestaled teapot with overall floral decoration.

lifted since it worked on a vacuum principle, whereby a cup of tea gushed out of the spout when the top was raised and lowered.

The teapot also experienced many other "improvements" during this era. The "Simple yet Perfect" teapot design was an ingenious version invented by the Earl of Dundonald in the late 19th century and produced by the Josiah Wedgwood firm from 1905. It lies on its side while the tea is brewing and separates the tea leaves when it is turned upright.

Another amusing talking point was the "Cadogan" teapot, derived from the shape of a Chinese wine pot, which has no apparent opening on top. The secret is to turn the pot upside down so that the tea and hot water can be poured in through a hole in the base. This leads to a tube that spirals up the interior of the pot. When the pot is turned upright, the

Cadogan-style teapot by Royal Doulton, decorated in the Crows pattern, ca. 1907.

Right: Royal Doulton
Morrisian Ware
teapot, ca. 1900.

Right: Royal Doulton
Morrisian Ware
teapot, ca. 1900.

Left: Doulton-Lambeth
stoneware teapot, ca. 1894.

brewed tea enters the body of the vessel and can be served through the spout.

The famous Doulton company at the Lambeth, London factory, produced art pottery including tea wares in many different styles and techniques. These included salt glazed stoneware, faience, Marqueterie and Chine' Ware. Some examples have the added attraction of being one-of-a-kind pieces signed by famous Doulton artists such as Hannah Barlow or George Tinworth. The teapot was also called into service to commemorate important historical or royal occasions, and these examples also provide a fascinating field of collecting.

In the early 20th century "Doulton" became "Royal Doulton" and continued to show an astute awareness of popular taste. Many new and affordable tea ranges in robust earthenware were produced at its factory in Burslem in Stoke-on-Trent. Many of the designs featured nostalgic images of "Olde Worlde England," and continual favorites in the early years of the century were its various Series Wares.

Formal afternoon tea

Around the turn of the 20th century, afternoon tea had become one of the

Left: Royal Doulton
Series Ware teapot from
the Coaching Days Series,
introduced in 1905.

Right: Rare Watcombe Colored
Cockerel Motto Ware teapot by
Torquay Pottery.

Rare Noritake teapot in Lady & Bird in Garden pattern.

Left: Harker teapot in Zephyr shape and Red Apple pattern, ca. 1930.

major institutions of English country house life and was often attended by both sexes. Ladies dressed especially for the occasion in elaborate tea gowns, and their china reflected the pastel colors then in vogue. In fine weather tea might be held out on the lawn, perhaps accompanied by a game of croquet or tennis. A useful item was added to the tea service at that time. Known variously as a Tennis set, Croquet set or Party plate, it allowed the tea cup to rest on a little tray so that guests could stroll around while still enjoying their cucumber sandwiches.

The Jazz Age

After the trauma of World War I, the "bright young things" of the '20s were determined to enjoy life to the full. Tea dances became fashionable in the chic hotels up to and during the Second World War. After a quick fox trot around the Palm Court, the dancers could sip a refreshing cup of tea from one of the jazzy modern designs of the period. The names of those new patterns conjure up the atmosphere of the era: Tango, DeLuxe and Rialto. After dancing the night away socialites would awake to

Shelley China Art Deco-style Eve Shape teapot in Laburnum pattern, 1933-44.

Front and back views of a rare Royal Worcester Aesthetic Movement teapot, 1882.

"tea for two" served on a stylish early morning set.

Clarice Cliff at Wilkinson's Newport Pottery designed some of the most daring Art Deco shapes and patterns for tea wares in her Bizarre Ware line. Geometrically shaped teapots in dazzling patterns and bright colors became all the rage by the 1920s and 1930s. Various potteries produced triangular, hexagonal and faceted teapots, but the most successful shape of the period was the patented Cube teapot, which was leased to a large number of manufacturers. The streamlined spoutless Cube claimed to be a perfect pourer and the practicality of the cube for stacking and storage made it popular for hotel use and on the great passenger shipping lines such as Cunard.

Teapots with personality

Figural teapots are often thought of as a modern conceit, but even the Chinese contorted their gods into pot shapes. The Worcester factory produced a famous figural design in the 1880s inspired by Oscar Wilde. However, the full potential of the human body as a teapot was realized in the 1930s when firms such as Royal Doulton, John Beswick and James Sadler modeled several eccentric designs. Characters from the novels of Charles Dickens were especially popular for this treatment, verging as they do on caricature. Their forms were further parodied as matching sugar bowls and creamers. Royal Doulton has revived this humorous tradition in recent years with a series of character teapots for collectors.

Left: Attwell Pixie pattern child's teapot from Boo-Boo tea set, in Mushroom Shape, by Shelley China, 1930.

Right: Beach Tent Shape teapot, part of Shelley China's Children's line, introduced in 1927.

The 1930s also saw a vogue for teapots in the form of animals, often favorites for children to use. Serving tea in the nursery was an elaborate affair in Victorian and Edwardian England, with the nanny presiding and dispensing tea from a large china service decorated with appropriate children's themes. For example, the guests at the Mad Hatter's tea party from the popular book *Alice's Adventures in Wonderland* were featured on an extensive Royal Doulton nursery service in the early 1900s. After the First World War, however, life styles changed and families became smaller, so there was not as much demand for large children's tea services. Instead, each child had his or her own plate and mug. Nursery rhymes were a staple for toddler's tea times and, following the enormous success of Royal Doulton Bunnykins and Beswick's Beatrix Potter designs, there have been a host of anthropomorphic characters to enliven a child's mealtime.

Today the ubiquitous teabag, which can conveniently bypass the pot and go right into cup or mug, may have threatened the formal role of the teapot in our daily routine, but many ceramic manufacturers and studio potters continue to provide us with whimsical and humorous teapots specially designed to appeal to collectors. These new pieces can mix proudly with prized vintage teapots of the past in china cabinets around the world.

Group of Modernist American Teapots

Aladdin shape Hall China teapot in maroon.

Eva Zeisel Design teapot in Lyric pattern, 1965.

Russel Wright Casual China Restyled teapot with Mustard Gold glaze, mid-1950s.

Right: Eva Zeisel Design teapot from Tomorrow's Classic Dinnerware by Hallcraft, 1950.

Louise Irvine is an established lecturer and writer with a special interest in 19th and 20th century ceramics. She is an expert on the history of Royal Doulton, having written 15 standard reference books on this subject and numerous articles.

Of Scottish origin, Louise studied first at Edinburgh University, from which she graduated with an honour's degree in fine art. Later, she followed a post graduate course in museum studies at Manchester University, and it was during this time that she developed her special interest in ceramics.

After working for museums in Glasgow and London, she joined Royal Doulton in 1977 and became director of historical promotions, working on a wide range of projects. Foremost amongst these was The Doulton Story exhibition held at the Victoria and Albert Museum in 1979. During her career with Royal Doulton, she produced many other exhibitions for the company's London gallery, several of which traveled to North America and Australia.

Louise founded the Royal Doulton International Collectors Club, a worldwide organization for enthusiasts of the company's products. In her capacity as Director, from 1980 to 1990, she edited and wrote for the quarterly magazine and travelled extensively to lecture and broadcast on the subject in the United Kingdom and overseas.

Louise has been a teacher of ceramic history at North Staffordshire Polytechnic as well as at Christie's Education in London, and she is an approved speaker on the Index of the National Association of Decorative and Fine Arts Societies.

Louise lives in London with her husband and son and travels extensively to lecture and broadcast on ceramics in the United Kingdom and overseas, presenting lectures, arranging conventions for collectors and consulting on British ceramics.

For further details, phone Louise Irvine at 020-8876-7939 or e-mail louiseirvine@blueyonder.co.uk.

ROYAL DOULTON BOOKS
written, co-written or edited by Louise Irvine

Beatrix Potter Figures and Giftware edited by Louise Irvine, 2nd edition, published by UK International Ceramics, 1996.

Brambly Hedge Collectors Book by Louise Irvine, published by Richard Dennis, 1999.

Charlton Catalogue of Royal Doulton Animals by Jean Dale with introduction by Louise Irvine, 3rd edition, published by the Charlton Press, 2003.

Charlton Catalogue of Royal Doulton Bunnykins by Jean Dale and Louise Irvine, 2nd edition, published by the Charlton Press, 2002.

Charlton Catalogue of Royal Doulton Figurines by Jean Dale with introduction by Louise Irvine, 9th edition, published by the Charlton Press, 2004.

Charlton Catalogue of Royal Doulton Jugs by Jean Dale with introduction by Louise Irvine, 8th edition, published by the Charlton Press, 2004.

Charlton Catalogue of Storybook Figures by Jean Dale with introduction by Louise Irvine, 8th edition, published by the Charlton Press, 2004.

The Doulton Story by Paul Atterbury & Louise Irvine, published by Royal Doulton, 1979.

Gilbert Bayes, Sculptor by Louise Irvine & Paul Atterbury, published by Richard Dennis, 1998.

Limited Edition Loving Cups and Jugs with introduction by Louise Irvine, published by Richard Dennis, 1981.

Royal Doulton and Beswick Cartoon Classics by Louise Irvine, published by UK International Ceramics, 1998.

Royal Doulton Bunnykins Collectors Book by Louise Irvine, 2nd edition, published by Richard Dennis, 1993.

Royal Doulton Bunnykins Figures by Louise Irvine, 4th edition, published by UK International Ceramics, 2000.

Royal Doulton Figures by Desmond Eyles, Louise Irvine and Valerie Baynton, 3rd edition, published by Richard Dennis, 1994.

Royal Doulton Series Ware by Louise Irvine, Volumes 1-5, published by Richard Dennis, 1980-1998.

Snowman Collectors Book by Louise Irvine, published by Richard Dennis, 2004.

BOOKS ON TEAPOTS

The British Teapot. Salem by Janet and Tim Street-Porter, published by Merrimac, Publishers' Circle, New Hampshire, 1983.

British Teapots & Tea Drinking by Robin Emmerson, published by HMSO Publications Centre, London, England, 1992.

Collectible Teapots, A Reference & Price Guide by Tina M.Carter, published by Krause Publications, Iola Wis., 2000.

Instant Expert: Collecting Teapots by Leah Rousmaniere, published by House of Collectibles, New York, New York, 2004.

Contributors to Teapots Price Guide 2005

Abingdon

Elaine Westover
210 Knox Highway 5
Abingdon, IL 61410
(309) 462-3267

American 20th Century Dinnerware

Jo Cunningham
535 E. Normal
Springfield, MO 65807
e-mail: Hlresearcher@aol.com

American Painted Porcelain

Dorothy Kamm
P.O. Box 7460
Port Saint Lucie, FL 34985
e-mail: dorothykamm@adelphia.net

Amphora-Teplitz

O.S.A.R. Antiques Specializing in Amphora
Phil and Arlene Larke
1505 Black Oaks Pl.
Minneapolis, MN 55447
phone (763) 473-0394
fax (763) 404-0090
e-mail: imalark@aol.com

Banko

Arlene Rabin
P.O. Box 243
Fogelsville, PA 18051
e-mail: jwhelden@enter.net

Belleek

Lady Marion Langham
Claranagh, Tempo
County Fermanagh
Northern Ireland BT94 3FJ
44-288-954-1247
e-mail: marion@ladymarion.co.uk

Doulton & Royal Doulton

Pascoe and Company
253 SW 22nd Ave.
Miami, FL 33135
fax (305) 643-2123
e-mail:
sales@pascoeandcompany.com

Pascoe and Company is the world's largest retailer of Royal Doulton Antiques and Collectibles. The company was founded by Ed Pascoe in 1971 and was based in Philadelphia until 1979 when Ed opened a store on Madison Avenue in New York City. Ed moved his business to Miami in 1987 and it is now a thriving world-wide mail order and Internet company specializing in Royal Doulton and other fine art pottery.

Pascoe and Company promotes the Annual Doulton Convention and Sale in Florida and Ed exhibits regularly at antique shows all over the United States as well as at special events in Canada, Australia, the United Kingdom and South Africa.

Shop online from Pascoe and Company's fully illustrated inventory of Royal Doulton products at www.pascoeandcompany.com. Check out the great discounts on www.pascoedirect.com. Call Pascoe and Company's sales team for all your Royal Doulton needs – retired models, rare prototypes, new introductions – at (305) 643-2550 or toll free at 1-800-872-0195.

Flow Mulberry

Ellen R. Hill
P.O. Box 56
Bennington, NH 03442
(603) 588-4099
e-mail: MSMULB@aol.com

Franciscan Pottery

James Elliot-Bishop
500 S. Farrell Dr., S-114
Palm Springs, CA 92264
e-mail: gmcb@ix.netcom.com

Fry

JoAnne S. Autenreith
400 Fifth Ave.
Patterson Heights
Beaver Falls, PA 15010-3218
e-mail: jsaeea@comcast.net

Photos by David Bentley

Geisha Girl, Aladdin, Cloisonné

Elyce Litts
P.O. Box 394
Morris Plains, NJ 07950

Gonder Pottery

James R. and Carol S. Boshears
375 W. Pecos Rd., #1033
Chandler, AZ 85225-7405
(480) 899-9757

Graniteware

Jo Allers
2500 Greywolf
Hiawatha, IA 52233

National Graniteware Society
P.O. Box 9248
Cedar Rapids, IA 52409-9248

Harker

Neva Colbert
69565 Crescent Rd.
St. Clairsville, OH 43950
(740) 695-2355
e-mail: georgestreet@1st.net

Limoges

Limoges Antiques Shop
20 Post Office Ave.
Andover, MA 01810
(978) 470-8773
Web: www.limogesantiques.com and
www.collectinglimoges.com

Debby DuBay, Ret., USAF, USPAP
appraiser, member Appraisers Assoc.
of America, author of Living With
Limoges, Antique Limoges at Home
and Collecting Hand Painted Limoges
Porcelain Boxes to Vases. Visit
www.collectinglimoges.com.

Morton Potteries

Burdell Hall
201 W. Sassafras Dr.
Morton, IL 61550
(309) 263-2988
e-mail: bnbhall@mtco.com

Noritake

Janet and Tim Trapani
7543 Northport Dr.
Boynton Beach, FL 33437
e-mail: ttrapani1946@yahoo.com

Old Ivory

Alma Hillman
362 E. Main St.
Searsport, ME 04974-310
e-mail: oldivory@adelphia.net

Phoenix Bird and others

Joan C. Oates
1107 Deerfield Lane
Marshall, MI 49068
e-mail: koates120@earthlink.net

Quimper

Sandra A. Bondhus
P.O. Box 100
Unionville, CT 06085
e-mail: nbondhus@pol.net

R.S. Prussia & Related Wares and Royal Bayreuth

Mary McCaslin
6887 Black Oak Ct. E.
Avon, IN 46123
(317) 272-2776
e-mail: maryjack@indy.rr.com

Russel Wright Designs

Kathryn Wiese
Retrospective Modern Design
P.O. Box 305
Manning, IA 51455
e-mail: retrodesign@earthlink.net

Shawnee Pottery

Linda Guffey
2004 Fiat Ct.
El Cajon, CA 92019-4234
e-mail: Gufantique@aol.com

Shelley

Mannie Banner
12650 S.W. 15th St.
Pembroke Pines, FL 33027

David Chartier
1171 Waterside
Brighton, MI 48114

Bryan Goodlad
44 Long Meadows
Bramhope
Leeds LS169DS
England

Edwin E. Kellogg
4951 N.W. 65th Ave.
Lauderhill, FL 33319

Gene Loveland
11303 S. Alley Jackson Rd.
Grain Valley, MO 64029

Curt Leiser and Gene Loveland
National Shelley China Club
12010 38th Ave. N.E.
Seattle, WA 98125
(206) 362-7135
e-mail: curtispleiser@cs.com

Tea Leaf

Dale Abrams
"Mr. Tea Leaf"
960 Bryden Rd.
Columbus, OH 43205
(614) 258-5258
Web: www.tealeafclub.com

Torquay Pottery

Lee Graham
214 N. Ronda Rd.
McHenry, IL 60050

Uhl Pottery

Lloyd Martin
1582 Gregory Ln.
Jasper, IN 47546

White Ironstone

Bev Dieringer
75 Sport Hill
W. Redding, CT 06896

WICA, Inc.
P.O. Box 536
Redding Ridge, CT 06876

Willow Ware China

Jeff Siptak
4013 Russellwood Dr.
Nashville, TN 37204
(615) 383-7855
e-mail: willowware@aol.com

Zeisel (Eva) Designs

Pat Moore
695 Monterey Blvd., Apt. 203
San Francisco, CA 94124
e-mail: evazeiselforum@pacbell.net

PART I - CERAMIC TEAPOTS

Porcelain - 1750-1850

Early Japanese Arita Ware Teapot

Arita Ware, squatty bulbous hexagonal form w/a short conforming neck & matching domed cover, paneled upturned spout & squared C-form handle, Imari-style decoration painted in bold colors of cobalt blue & iron-red, mounted w/European gold fittings including a chain connecting the ball finial to the cap on the spout & band on the handle, teapot from Japan, ca. 1700, gold mounts possibly 18th c. Dutch, overall 6 1/4" l. (ILLUS.)... **$5,875**

Small Chinese Teapot with Piercing

Chinese Export, a footed spherical double-walled style w/the outer layer pierced overall w/a delicate green vine w/orange blossoms, a light blue shoulder band & the matched domed & pierced cover w/a button finial, a C-form handle & a straight angled silver spout, unmarked, late 18th - early 19th c., chips & repairs on cover, small chip on base rim, 6" h. (ILLUS.).......... **230**

Colorfully Decorated Chinese Teapot

Chinese Export, a round foot below a low flaring base below a wide slightly concave body band below a wide slightly rounded shoulder centering a short gold neck, a serpentine spout & C-scroll handle, the high domed cover w/a gold ball finial above a scene of a woman & a cartouche of a man above a band of flowers & birds, the wide shoulder painted overall w/colorful birds, flowers & butterflies, the body band decorated w/continuous scenes of Chinese ladies, ca. 1840, restoration to rim & spout, chip at pot mouth, wear to cover gilt, 9" h. (ILLUS.) **690**

Colorful Chinese Famille Rose Teapot

Chinese Export, Canton-type w/Famille Rose enameling, spherical body w/C-form handle & serpentine spout, each side painted in color w/a large Chinese landscape within a scrolling blue border, the yellow ground painted overall w/delicate Famille Rose florals, the spout & handle painted overall w/blue tendrils, the small cover w/abstract leaf design & acorn finial, China, late 18th c., overall 12" l. (ILLUS.).. **2,070**

Small Famille Rose Teapot

Chinese Export, Famille Rose decoration, footed squatty spherical body w/straight spout & C-form handle, domed flanged cover w/pointed knob finial, h.p. w/Chinese figures in a landscape, 19th c., 5 1/2" h. (ILLUS.) **288**

Chinese Export, Famille Verte decor, spherical body w/serpentine spout, C-form handle & small cover w/knob finial, painted w/a stylized Chinese urn flanked by various symbols on a white ground, Kangxi era (1662-1722), 4" h. (small chip on spout, cover possibly replaced)............... **660**

Chinese Export, tall tapering cylindrical body w/a straight angled spout & twisted strap handle, the flanged domed cover w/a knob finial, decorated for the American market w/a rusty orange design of an American eagle w/floral-decorated

shield, similar to a design used by the Nichols Family of Salem, Massachusetts, late 18th - early 19th c., two small hairlines w/dings, overall 10" h. (ILLUS., top of next column) **920**

American-market Chinese Teapot

Meissen, bulbous tapering body w/a foliage-molded wishbone handle & bird's-head spout, the body w/a yellow background painted on each side w/a black-outlined cartouche containing a waterway landscape scene of merchants at various pursuits by barrels, sacks & figures on horseback & boating, low domed cover w/pale red figural strawberry finial flanked by cartouches, further gold, puce & iron-red trim on the spout & handle, blue crossed-swords mark & impressed number, ca. 1740, 3 5/8" h...................... **4,183**

Small Early Meissen Porcelain Teapot

Meissen, nearly spherical slightly tapering body decorated w/a robin's-egg blue ground, the flat cover w/a gold knob finial, short curved shoulder spout & pointed arch handle, each side centered by a h.p. color scene of merchants haggling at quayside within a gold border, the cover w/two smaller views, "indianische Blumen" design under spout & on handle, blue crossed-swords mark, 1735-40, overall 4 1/4" l., 4 1/4" h. (ILLUS.)............. **4,780**

Meissen Teapot with Landscape Scenes

Meissen, slightly squatty nearly spherical body w/a molded fish-form spout & London-shape handle w/shell design, h.p. on each side in color w/a landscape w/cow & sheep framed by trellis & blossom bands, blue crossed-swords mark, ca. 1795, hairline in base (ILLUS.).............................. **748**

Sevres-style, cylindrical body w/flat shoulder centering a short neck & low domed cover w/pointed knob finial, curved rim spout & C-scroll handle, turquoise blue ground decorated on one side w/a vignette in color of a barefoot boy playing

Sevres-Style Decorated Teapot

the flute w/a dog at his feet, the other side w/a colorful bouquet of flowers within a gilt scroll border, teapot 18th c., the decoration added later, spurious blue Sevres interlaced Ls mark, 5" h. (ILLUS.)............... **598**

Porcelain - 1850-1950

Lovely American-painted Porcelain Teapot & Sugar Bowl

American-painted porcelain, teapot & matching cov. sugar bowl, each w/a round foot & knop stem below the bulbous ovoid body tapering to a flat rim & domed cover w/molded upright gold finial, serpentine spout & ornate gold scroll handles, the cover & upper body painted in pale green around the upper third above an undulating band of delicate gold scrolls & pink roses & green leafy stems on the lower white body, gold base bands, artist initials, unmarked blanks, ca. 1880-1910, teapot 6 1/4" h., 2 pcs. (ILLUS.) **$100-150**

Fancy Bavarian Porcelain Teapot

Bavarian porcelain, a flaring ruffled foot below the squatty bulbous ribbed body tapering to a flaring ruffled neck & domed cover w/knob finial, serpentine spout & fancy C-scroll handle, overall delicate scrolling vine decoration, Jollio, Bavaria, Germany, early 20th c. (ILLUS.) **60**

Canton porcelain, oval cylindrical form w/angled spout & entwined strap handle, inset cover w/fruit finial, worn gilt trim, China, 19th c., 5 1/2" h. **770**

Chinese Export, Rose Medallion patt., a round flaring foot supporting a wide urn-form body w/a serpentine spout & C-scroll handle, the high domed cover w/a gold ball finial, the cover, shoulder & body all decorated w/h.p. cartouches featuring birds, flowers & butterflies or Chinese figures, gold trim, ca. 1860, 11" l., 10 1/2" h. (ILLUS., top next page) **920**

Austrian Porcelain Fancy Teapot

Austrian porcelain, ruffle-footed ribbed baluster-form body w/a domed cover & ring finial, serpentine spout & ornate C-scroll handle, gold trim, Imperial Crown China, Vienna, Austria, ca. 1890s (ILLUS.) **45**

DuBarry Pattern Chintz Teapot

Chintz China, DuBarry patt., Diamond
    shape, James Kent, Ltd. (ILLUS.)...... **950-1,000**
Chintz China, Joyce-Lynn patt., Ascot
    shape, Royal Winton (ILLUS., middle of
    page)... **1,300-1,500**
Chintz China, Summertime patt., Ajax
    shape, Royal Winton (ILLUS., bottom of
    page)... **950**

Colorful Rose Medallion Teapot

Joyce-Lynn Ascot Shape Teapot

Royal Winton Summertime Pattern Teapot

Copeland-Spode Buttercup Teapot

Copeland-Spode, Buttercup patt., squatty ribbed body w/concave ribbed shoulder & low domed cover w/blossom finial, straight ribbed spout & C-form handle, England, early 20th c. (ILLUS.)..................... **85**

Czechoslovakian Porcelain Teapot

Czechoslovakian porcelain, footed widely flaring squatty octagonal body w/a wide shoulder tapering to the pointed cover w/button finial, serpentine spout & angled handle, Victoria Porcelain Factory, ca. 1920s (ILLUS.)... **30**

Lovely Dresden Porcelain Teapot

Victorian English Bone China Teapot & Undertray

Dresden, squatty bulbous body w/a flat rim, shaped spout & C-form handle, the low cover w/a pointed knob finial, h.p. w/colorful bouquets of flowers including roses, tulips & pansies, burnished gold trim, decorator's mark for Donath & Co., Dresden, Germany, gilder's mark for Grossbaum & Sons, Dresden, Germany, ca. 1893-1916, 6" h. (ILLUS., bottom previous page) **150-200**

English bone china, teapot & undertray, the pot w/four small tab feet supporting the wide squatty molded body w/an overhanging domed cover w/blossom finial, serpentine spout & ornate C-scroll handle, matching round tray, each in white decorated w/green transfer-printed panels of scrolls & blossoms alternating w/small h.p. gold blossom sprigs, second half 19th c., undertray 8" d., teapot 7" h., pr. (ILLUS., top of page) **201**

Toy Size Geisha Girl Porcelain Teapot

Geisha Girl Porcelain, child's size, spherical body w/wide flat rim, short angled spout & C-form handle, low domed cover w/knob finial, Bow B stenciled patt., scalloped cobalt blue border, gold lacing, these were sometimes packaged w/candy, first quarter 20th c., overall 5 1/2" l., 3 1/2" h. (ILLUS.) **25**

Geisha Girl Porcelain, Dragonboat patt., red & cobalt blue border w/gold lacing, swirl ribbed body **40**

European Porcelain Child's Teapot

European porcelain, child's size, baluster-form body w/a short angled spout & ornate scroll handle, domed cover, white w/a h.p. center band in pale yellow w/gold trim & stylized orange florals, possibly Germany, late 19th c., 3 5/8" l., 2 3/4" h. (ILLUS.) **35**

Geisha Girl Porcelain, Battledore patt., apple green border **35**

Geisha Girl Porcelain, Bow B patt. in reserve on floral backdrop, cobalt blue border w/gold striping, gold upper edge & spout rim **45**

Individual Size Geisha Girl Teapot

Geisha Girl Porcelain, individual size, bulbous melon-lobed body w/serpentine spout & ornate scroll handle, lobed domed cover w/loop handle, Garden Bench C stenciled patt., cobalt blue & red border, marked "Japan," overall 7" l., 4 1/2" h. (ILLUS.) **35**

Miniature Geisha Girl Porcelain Teapot

Geisha Girl Porcelain, miniature premium-type, squatty bulbous body w/straight spout, C-form handle, inset cover w/knob finial, Geisha in Cards patt., scalloped blue border, base stamped w/advertising "Café Martin New York," first quarter 20th c., 2" h. (ILLUS.)... **35**

Painted Miniature Geisha Girl Teapot

Geisha Girl Porcelain, miniature, squatty bulbous lobed form w/tiny spout & handle, Court Lady hand-painted patt., red border, first quarter 20th c., overall 3 1/2" l., 2" h. (ILLUS.) **15**

Geisha Girl One-Cup Teapot

Geisha Girl Porcelain, one-cup size, nearly spherical body w/a serpentine spout & C-form handle, tapering to a flat cover w/pointed knob finial, Cloud B patt., red border w/cherry blossoms, unusual steam hole in center of finial instead of on the lid itself, first quarter 20th c., 4" h. (ILLUS.).. **25**

Ikebana in Rickshaw Geisha Girl Teapot

Geisha Girl Porcelain, squatty bulbous body w/a short spout & upswept scroll handle, domed cover w/knob finial, Ikebana in Rickshaw patt., scalloped cobalt blue border, gold lacing, first quarter 20th c., overall 8" l., 4" h. (ILLUS.)........................ **38**

Bamboo-handled Geisha Girl Teapot

Geisha Girl Porcelain, squatty bulbous body w/serpentine spout, inset domed cover & bamboo swing bail handle, Foot-bridge A patt., red border, red background stencil of vine & flowers w/a pale red wash, marked on base in Japanese "Nihon" w/Mt. Fuji logo, first quarter 20th c., overall 8" l., 5 1/2" h. (ILLUS.).................. **40**

Fancy Ribbed Geisha Girl Porcelain Teapot

Geisha Girl Porcelain, squatty bulbous melon-ribbed body, shaped spout & ornate ring handle, low domed cover w/knob finial, Fan Silhouette of Hoo Bird patt., bluish green border, gold lacing, marked in Japanese on the base "Dai Nihon Tashiro tsukuru," first quarter 20th c. (ILLUS.).. **55**

Geisha Girl Teapot with Unusual Design

Geisha Girl Porcelain, standard size, spherical body w/low domed cover, serpentine spout, C-form handle, unusual That Way, Mon stenciled patt., brown edging w/h.p. cranes around the rim, base marked in Japanese "Dai Nihon Tashiro tsukuru," first quarter 20th c., overall 7 1/4" l., 5" h. (ILLUS.)........................ **55**

Garden Bench Q Geisha Girl Teapot

Geisha Girl Porcelain, standard size, squatty bulbous body w/serpentine spout & loop handle, Garden Bench Q h.p. patt., red, pine green, mint green & gold border, base marked w/"T" in a cherry blossom & "Japan," first quarter 20th c., overall 8" l., 4 1/2" h. (ILLUS.)........................ **35**

Tall Geisha Girl Pointing D Pattern Teapot

Geisha Girl Porcelain, tall ribbed body flaring at the base, serpentine spout & ornate C-scroll handle, domed cover w/arched scroll handle, Pointing D patt., red border, gold lacing, overall 6 1/4" l., 6" h. (ILLUS.) **45**

Ornate Dresden, Germany Teapot

Squatty Haviland Porcelain Teapot

German porcelain, wide tapering bulbous ribbed lower body tapering to a tall swirled & gently flaring neck w/arched rim, ornate conforming cover w/fancy gold scroll finial, tall molded serpentine spout, very ornate C-scroll handle, decorated w/bands of green trimmed in gold around the top & base, a large cluster of green & white lily-of-the-valley on the sides, Dresden, Germany, ca. 1900 (ILLUS., bottom previous page) **125**

Haviland china, wide squatty bulbous tapering sides w/a flat rim, low domed cover w/arched finial, upright serpentine spout & C-scroll handle, white w/gold trim & thin yellow leaftip bands around the rim & cover, double Haviland mark, ca. 1900 (ILLUS., top of page) **75**

Hexagon Pattern Belleek Teapot

Irish Belleek porcelain, Hexagon patt., large size, D407-II (ILLUS.) **600**

Belleek Harp Shamrock Teakettle

Irish Belleek porcelain, Harp Shamrock teakettle, overhead handle, large size, gilt trim, D1359-III (ILLUS.) **660**

Lace Pattern Belleek Teapot

Irish Belleek porcelain, Lace patt., medium size, D800-II (ILLUS.) **1,000**

Limpet Shape Irish Belleek Teapot

Irish Belleek porcelain, Limpet shape, coral-form handle & finial, ca. 1927-41 (ILLUS.).. **300**

Child's Lustre & Floral Japanese Teapot

Japanese porcelain, child's size from a snack set, squatty tapering body w/serpentine spout & angled handle, blue lustre body band & cover, h.p. colorful floral sprig, marked "Made in Japan," ca. 1920s-30s, 4 3/4" l., 3" h. (ILLUS.)................. **15**

Gold Lustre Child's Japanese Teapot

Japanese porcelain, child's size from a tea set, footed bulbous body w/flat shoulder & wide mouth, shaped spout & angled loop handle, domed cover w/knob finial, gold lustre background painted w/large stylized flowers, marked "Japan," ca. 1920s-30s, 3" l., 3 1/8" h. (ILLUS.)................. **15**

Japanese Mr. Pickwick Teapot

Japanese porcelain, figural Toby-style in the form of the Dickens character Mr. Pickwick, brightly decorated, "made in Japan" mark, ca. 1930s (ILLUS.)................. **35**

Large Flying Turkey Pattern Teapot

Japanese porcelain, Flying Turkey (extra-large) patt., footed spherical body w/serpentine spout & ring handle, flattened cover w/knob finial, marked w/six Japanese characters, ca. 1920s-30s, 9" l., 5 3/4" h. (ILLUS.)... **65**

Melon-lobed Flying Turkey Teapot

Japanese porcelain, Flying Turkey patt., squatty bulbous melon-lobed body on tab feet, short spout, D-form handle, domed cover w/knob finial, marked w/six Japanese characters, ca. 1920s-30s, 8" l., 5" h. (ILLUS.)... **85**

Flying Turkey (Style A) Pattern Teapot

Japanese porcelain, Flying Turkey patt. (Style A, fatter bird), footed squatty bulbous body w/shaped spout & C-form handle, low domed cover w/knob finial, marked "Made in Japan," ca. 1920s-30s, 7" l., 3 3/4" h. (ILLUS.) **35**

Flying Turkey, Style B Teapot

Japanese porcelain, Flying Turkey patt., Style B, skinny bird, footed squatty wide bulbous body w/C-form handle & serpentine spout, low domed cover w/knob finial, marked "Japan" w/three Japanese characters, ca. 1920s, 6 5/8" l., 4 1/2" h. (ILLUS.).. **35**

Flying Turkey (Style B) Pattern Teapot

Japanese porcelain, Flying Turkey (Style B) patt., scalloped flaring foot, bulbous ovoid body w/a flared scalloped rim, serpentine spout & fancy C-scroll handle, domed cover w/ring finial, marked w/six Japanese characters, ca. 1920s-30s, 6 5/8" l., 5 3/8" h. (ILLUS.) **65**

Japanese Howo Pattern Small Teapot

Japanese porcelain, Howo patt., tea-for-two size, bulbous tapering body w/short spout & squared handle, low domed cover w/button finial, marked "Sometuke - Nippon," Japan, early 20th c., 6 1/4" l., 4 1/4" h. (ILLUS.) **35**

Phoenix Bird Teapot Found in Three Sizes

Japanese porcelain, Phoenix Bird patt., bulbous body w/a narrow shoulder & wide flat rim, long serpentine spout & angled D-form handle, low domed cover w/knob finial, marked "Made in Japan" within a double circle, largest of three sizes, 8" l., 5 1/2" h. (ILLUS.) **35**

Rattan-handled Phoenix Bird Teapot

Japanese porcelain, Phoenix Bird patt., bulbous body w/a serpentine spout, over-

head woven rattan swing bail handle
(ILLUS.)... **35-55**

Phoenix Bird Wicker-handled Teapot

Japanese porcelain, Phoenix Bird patt.,
bulbous body w/serpentine spout &
domed cover w/knob finial, overhead
swing bail handle of blue bands of wicker
woven w/uncolored wicker, marked w/six
Japanese characters, ca. 1920s-30s,
5 1/4" h. (ILLUS. with liner) **45**

Extra Large Phoenix Bird Teapot

Japanese porcelain, Phoenix Bird patt.,
extra large nearly spherical body w/up-
right serpentine spout & a D-form handle
molded to resemble bamboo, originally
came w/a liner, unmarked, ca. 1920s-
30s, 9 1/2" l., 5 3/4" h. (ILLUS.)...................... **35**

Bulbous Phoenix Bird Pattern Teapot

Japanese porcelain, Phoenix Bird patt.,
footed bulbous body w/a serpentine spout

& heavy ring handle w/small thumbrest,
low domed cover w/knob finial, marked
"Made in Japan," ca. 1920s-30s, 7 1/2" l.,
4 1/2" h. (ILLUS.)... **30**

Extra Large Phoenix Bird Teapot

Japanese porcelain, Phoenix Bird patt.,
footed bulbous lower body & wide tapering shoulder w/a non-traditional design,
long serpentine spout, angled handle
w/small thumbrest, inset tapering cover
w/knob finial, marked w/an "S" enclosed
in a bulb above "Made in Japan," ca.
1920s-30s, extra large size, 10" l.,
6 1/2" h. (ILLUS.) **70**

Large Ovoid Phoenix Bird Teapot

Japanese porcelain, Phoenix Bird patt.,
footed tapering ovoid body w/serpentine
spout, C-form handle & domed cover,
various Japanese marks, found in three
sizes, largest 8" l., 8" h. (ILLUS. of larg-
est of three matching teapots) **60-70**

Japanese porcelain, Phoenix Bird patt.,
footed tapering ovoid body w/serpentine
spout, C-form handle & domed cover,
various Japanese marks, found in three
sizes w/largest size illustrated, medium
size, 7" l., 6 5/8" h. **45-55**

Japanese porcelain, Phoenix Bird patt.,
footed tapering ovoid body w/serpentine
spout, C-form handle & domed cover,
various Japanese marks, found in three
sizes w/largest size illustrated, small
size, 6" l., 6" h. **35-45**

Two Phoenix Bird Individual-sized Teapots

Long Squatty Phoenix Bird Teapot

Japanese porcelain, Phoenix Bird patt., footed wide squatty bulbous body w/high serpentine spout & long D-form handle, low domed cover w/angled loop handle, marked w/three Japanese characters over double flowers & "Japan," ca. 1920s-30s, 8 1/2" l., 4 3/8" h. (ILLUS.)........... **45**

Heavy Phoenix Bird Pattern Teapot

Japanese porcelain, Phoenix Bird patt., heavyweight footed bulbous body w/a wide shoulder tapering to a flat rim, serpentine spout, D-form handle w/thumbrest, flat cover w/button finial, not original cover, marked "Made in Japan" in three lines, ca. 1920s-30s, 9" l., 4 1/2" h. (ILLUS.)...................... **65**

Japanese porcelain, Phoenix Bird patt., individual-size, bulbous body w/a wide flat mouth, short angled spout, D-form handle, domed cover w/knob finial, originally came w/a round-bottomed strainer, marked "Made in Japan," ca. 1920s-30s, 5 1/4" l., 4" h. (ILLUS. left with other individual teapot, top of page)............................ **25**

Japanese porcelain, Phoenix Bird patt., individual-size, bulbous body w/a wide flat mouth, short angled spout, D-form handle, domed cover w/knob finial, originally came w/a round-bottomed strainer, marked "Made in Japan," ca. 1920s-30s, 5 1/4" l., 3 5/8" h. (ILLUS. right with other individual teapot, top of page)...................... **25**

Phoenix Bird - Morimura Bros. Teapot

Japanese porcelain, Phoenix Bird patt., large bulbous body w/long upright serpentine spout & wide D-form handle, low domed cover w/knob finial, Morimura Brothers mark & "Japan," ca. 1922, largest of four sizes, overall 10" l., body 6" d., 5 3/4" h. (ILLUS.) **35-40**

Squatty Phoenix Bird Pattern Teapot

Japanese porcelain, Phoenix Bird patt., low foot & wide squatty bulbous body, short serpentine spout, large ring handle, low domed cover w/angled ring handle, blue band around foot, unmarked but matches pieces w/the "T" inside flower & "Japan" mark, ca. 1920s-30s, 7 1/2" l., 4 1/4" h. (ILLUS.) **45**

Small HO-O Border Phoenix Bird Pot

Japanese porcelain, Phoenix Bird patt., nearly spherical body w/flattened cover & knob finial, C-form handle, short serpentine spout, unusual steam hole in cover finial, HO-O heart-like border variant, unmarked, 5 1/2" l., 4" h. (ILLUS.) **35-40**

Phoenix Bird Pattern with Variant Border

Japanese porcelain, Phoenix Bird patt., overall geometric design w/variant of Border K, ovoid body tapering to a flat rim, serpentine spout, D-form handle, low domed cover w/knob finial, marked w/a star, two crossed flags, six Japanese characters & "Trade Mark - Japan," originally came w/a strainer, ca. 1920s-30s, 6 3/4" l., 5 5/8" h. (ILLUS.) **55-60**

Phoenix Bird Pattern Ovoid Teapot

Japanese porcelain, Phoenix Bird patt., ovoid body tapering to a domed cover w/a pinched flower finial, smooth C-form handle, upright serpentine spout, marked w/a rising sun above four Japanese characters, ca. 1920s-30s (ILLUS.) **65-75**

Delicate, Quality Phoenix Bird Teapot

Japanese porcelain, Phoenix Bird patt., scalloped round foot supporting the wide squatty bulbous body w/a short spout & large ring handle, inset cover w/squared loop handle, delicate & fine quality, unmarked, ca. 1920s-30s, 7 3/4" l., 4 3/8" h. (ILLUS.) **55**

Phoenix Bird HO-O Border Teapot

Japanese porcelain, Phoenix Bird patt., squatty bulbous body w/low domed cover & knob finial, ring handle & short spout, w/HO-O heart-like variant border design, unmarked, 7 1/2" l., 4 3/4" h. (ILLUS.) **45-50**

Phoenix Bird Teapot with Less Vinework

Japanese porcelain, Phoenix Bird patt., squatty bulbous body w/low domed cover & knob finial, long serpentine spout, C-form handle, less vinework in the background design, originally came w/a strainer, unmarked, 7 3/4" l., 5" h. (ILLUS.).. **35-45**

Wicker-handled Phoenix Bird Teapot

Japanese porcelain, Phoenix Bird patt., squatty bulbous body w/serpentine spout, early overhead swing bail handle in woven wicker, marked w/three small triangles, each enclosing a Japanese character w/three additional characters below, originally came w/strainer, 6 3/4" l., 5" h. (ILLUS.) **45-55**

Phoenix Bird Stack-set Teapot

Japanese porcelain, Phoenix Bird patt., stack-set, squatty bulbous pot w/a long serpentine spout & C-form handle, stacked top w/a creamer topped by a cov. sugar, mark of a small flower w/a "T" inside & "Japan," ca. 1920s-30s, overall 5 3/4" h. (ILLUS.) **65**

Japanese porcelain, Phoenix Bird patt., tall tapering waisted body w/upright shaped spout & pointed loop handle, low domed cover w/button finial, marked w/a four-petaled flower on stem & "Japan," ca. 1920s-30s, 6 3/4" l., 5 1/2" h. (ILLUS. left with matching smaller teapot) **35**

Two Upright Waisted Phoenix Bird Teapots

Japanese porcelain, Phoenix Bird patt., tall tapering waisted body w/upright shaped spout & pointed loop handle, low domed cover w/button finial, marked w/a four-petaled flower on stem & "Japan," ca. 1920s-30s, 6 1/4" l., 4 1/4" h. (ILLUS. right with matching larger teapot).................. **40**

Finely Decorated Phoenix Bird Teapot

Japanese porcelain, Phoenix Bird patt., tapering waisted cylindrical body w/upright serpentine spout & high loop handle, low domed cover w/small loop finial, fine overall decoration, marked w/three Japanese characters above "Japan," ca. 1920s-30s, overall 7" l., 5 1/8" h. (ILLUS.).. **65**

Phoenix Bird with Circle-Border K Teapot

Japanese porcelain, Phoenix Bird patt. w/Circle-Border K, bulbous body w/a flat rim, serpentine spout, C-form handle, domed cover w/knob finial, unmarked, originally came w/strainer, ca. 1920s-30s, 8 1/4" l., 6 3/4" h. (ILLUS.)...................... **40**

"M in Wreath" Marked Teapot

Japanese porcelain, Phoenix Bird patt., wide squatty bulbous body w/serpentine spout & D-form handle, low domed cover w/knob finial, "M in Wreath" Morimura Bros. mark & "Japan," ca. 1930s, 7 3/8" l., 3 3/4" h. (ILLUS.) **20**

Hand-painted Japanese Porcelain Teapot

Japanese porcelain, spherical body h.p. w/a Dutch windmill landscape scene, serpentine spout, ring handle & small cover w/knob finial, Takito Porcelain, ca. 1930s (ILLUS.).. **35**

Japanese Porcelain Teapot with Pink Floral Design

Japanese porcelain, spherical footed body, applied loop handle, short serpentine spout, slightly domed cover w/knob finial, body & lid decorated w/large pink roses & green leaves, handle, spout, finial & rim highlighted in silvery grey, marked "Made in Japan," ca. 1930s, 5 1/2" h. (ILLUS.) **35**

Ovoid Thousand Faces Japanese Teapot

Japanese porcelain, Thousand Faces patt., tall ovoid body w/serpentine spout & C-form handle, orange trim, "Made in Japan" mark, ca. 1930s, 6 3/4" l., 6" h. (ILLUS.).. **65**

Japanese Thousand Faces Teapot

Japanese porcelain, Thousand Faces patt., tall waisted body w/serpentine spout & pointed angled handle, black trim, rising sun & "Made in Japan" mark, ca. 1930s, 7 3/4" l., 8 1/8" h. (ILLUS.).. **75**

Japanese Twin Phoenix Pattern Teapot

Japanese porcelain, Twin Phoenix patt., squatty ovoid body w/serpentine spout & C-form handle, low domed cover w/arched handle, band of decoration around top & cover, marked "Sometuke, Nippon," Japan, early 20th c., 7 3/4" l., 4 1/2" h. (ILLUS.) **45**

Twin Turkey Teapot on Tiny Figure Feet

Japanese porcelain, Twin Turkey patt., squatty bulbous body raised on five tiny figural Buddha-like feet, serpentine spout, long C-form handle, cover w/knob finial, unmarked, ca. 1920s-30s, 8" l., 5" h. (ILLUS.) **110-125**

Japanese Teapot with Painted Landscape

spout, C-scroll handle, h.p. w/a landscape scene of a cottage next to a lake, early 20th c., Takito Porcelain, Japan (ILLUS.) **45**

Colorful Takito, Japan Teapot

Japanese porcelain, wide cylindrical body w/rounded shoulder to a low domed cover w/loop finial, serpentine spout & C-form handle, h.p. w/large colorful stylized flowers, Takito, Japan, ca. 1930s (ILLUS.) **35**

Japanese porcelain, wide swelled cylindrical body w/a curved shoulder & flat rim w/inset cover & knob finial, serpentine

Decorated Japanese Tall Teapot

Japanese porelain, footed tall, gently flaring cylindrical body w/narrow shoulder to a domed cover w/knob finial, long serpentine spout, C-scroll handle, h.p. Japanese landscape design, marked "Futani (?) - Hand Painted Japan," ca. 1930s (ILLUS.) **20-30**

Fine Lotus Ware Porcelain Teapot

Geisha Girl Teapot with Unusual Pink Background

Knowles, Taylor & Knowles, Lotus Ware, Valenciennes shape, Fish Net patt., East Liverpool, Ohio, 1890s (ILLUS., bottom previous page) **350**

Kutani Porcelain, pedestal base supporting the wide squatty body w/a short wide neck, serpentine spout & C-scroll handle, low domed cover w/pointed finial, Fan Dance A & Flower Gathering A patterns in reserves, unusual pink background, gold border, signed "Kutani," Japan, first quarter 20th c., 5" h. (ILLUS., top of page) **95**

Footed Kutani Teapot in So Big Pattern

Kutani Porcelain, three-footed squatty bulbous body w/serpentine spout & C-form handle, low domed cover w/knob finial, hand-painted So Big patt., geometric pine green & red border w/gold trim, signed "Kutani," Japan, late 19th - early 20th c., overall 8" l., 5" h. (ILLUS.) **60**

Decorative Japanese Kutani Teapot

Kutani Porcelain, round scalloped foot below the wide ovoid body tapering to a short neck w/high domed cover w/figural butterfly finial, serpentine spout, ornate C-scroll handle, completely hand-painted w/Japanese Geisha, red & gold borders, signed "Watayasu Sei," Japan, late 19th - early 20th c., 6" h. (ILLUS.) **75**

Tressemann & Vogt Limoges Teapot

Limoges porcelain, bulbous tapering ovoid body w/long serpentine spout, high C-form handle & low domed cover w/loop finial, white w/simple trim, mark of Tressemann & Vogt, Limoges, ca. 1900 (ILLUS.) **200**

Ornately Decorated Limoges Teapot

Limoges porcelain, bulbous tapering ribbed body w/wide domed cover w/fancy loop finial, gold serpentine spout & C-scroll handle, star mark of the Coiffe factory & Flambeau China mark of decorating firm, also a Haviland & Co. mark, France, early 20th c. (ILLUS.) **100**

Limoges Elite - France Porcelain Teapot

Limoges porcelain, footed squatty bulbous body tapering to a domed cover w/arched finial, serpentine spout, C-scroll handle, marked w/Bawo & Dotter "Elite - France" mark, ca. 1900 (ILLUS.) **30**

Miniature Rose-decorated Teapot

Limoges porcelain, miniature, ribbed & slightly tapering cylindrical body w/a scalloped rim, domed cover w/gold knob finial, short spout & C-scroll handle, h.p. w/pretty roses, initials of artist on the base, factory mark of Bernardaud & Co., Limoges, France, ca. 1914-30s (ILLUS.) **400**

Small Rose-decorated Limoges Teapot

Limoges porcelain, single-cup size, squared bulbous body w/a short flared & scalloped rim, domed cover w/squared loop finial, angular scroll handle & beaded serpentine spout, h.p. w/large roses, factory mark of Tressemann & Vogt, Limoges, France, ca. 1892-1907 (ILLUS.)...... **300**

Studio-decorated Limoges Gold Teapot

Limoges porcelain, slightly tapering cylindrical body w/flat cover w/arched loop finial, C-form handle & long serpentine spout, overall gold-etched decoration, signed by American decorating studio artist "Osborne," blank marked by Jean Pouyat Company, Limoges, France, 1891-1932, small size (ILLUS.)................... **300**

Limoges-style Rose-painted Teapot

Limoges porcelain, squatty bulbous body
w/a flaring scalloped rim, domed cover
w/gold loop finial, short spout, C-scroll
handle, h.p. w/large roses, unmarked, Limoges-style, late 19th - early 20th c.
(ILLUS.)... 200

Fine Factory-decorated Limoges Teapot

Limoges porcelain, squatty bulbous body
w/low domed cover w/gold loop finial,
gold serpentine spout & fancy C-form
gold handle, factory-decorated w/large
roses, underglaze factory mark for Mavaleix, P.M., ca. 1908-14, overglaze decorating mark "Coronet - George
Borgfeldt," ca. 1906-20, 4" h. (ILLUS.)......... 600

Pretty Tressemann & Vogt Teapot

Limoges porcelain, squatty bulbous footed
body w/domed cover w/double-loop gold
finial, serpentine spout, gold C-form
handle, h.p. w/swags of roses, factory
mark of Tressemann & Vogt, Limoges,
France, ca. 1892-1907, 4" h. (ILLUS.) 400

Bernadaud & Co. Limoges Teapot

Limoges porcelain, tall cylindrical body w/a
long serpentine spout, C-form handle &
domed cover w/knob finial, decorated
w/an oval reverse & a border band of
grapevines, Bernadaud & Company,
France, early 20th c. (ILLUS.) 85

Simple Limoges Porcelain Teapot

Limoges porcelain, wide bulbous body w/a
long gold spout & C-form handle, domed
cover w/pointed disk finial, marks of B &
H Limoges, France & Legrand,
Limoges, ca. 1920 (ILLUS.) 50

Guerin Gold & White Limoges Teapot

Limoges porcelain, wide flat bottom w/ta-
pering cylindrical sides & flat rim, slightly
domed cover w/pointed disk finial, angled
handle, serpentine spout, white w/gold
bands & scrollwork around the neck & a
gold finial, spout & handle, marks of Wm.
Guerin & Co., Limoges, France, ca.
1891-1932 (ILLUS.) 150

Fancy Roses & Gold Limoges Teapot

Limoges porcelain, wide squatty bulbous
body tapering to a small domed cover
w/twisted loop finial, serpentine spout,
twisted loop handle, unusual decoration
of h.p. roses framed by heavy gold &
w/gold on the interior, gold cover, spout &
handle, artist-signed on the bottom "KLR
- 1890," Limoges factory "AK" mark (Lan-
denberg Mark 3), France, ca. 1880s-90
(ILLUS.)... 800

White & Gold Limoges Teapot

Limoges porcelain, wide squatty bulbous body w/low domed cover & knob finial, C-form handle, serpentine spout, white w/gold bands on the spout, rim & handle, marks of Tressemann & Vogt, Limoges, France, ca. 1907-1919, four-cup size (ILLUS.)......................... **150**

Early Maling-Ringtons Tea Teapot

Maling (C.T.) & Sons porcelain, upright waisted squared body w/small rim spout, angled handle & low domed cover w/button finial, Blue Willow style decoration, produced for & marked by Ringtons, Limited, Tea Merchants, England, ca. 1930s (ILLUS.)....................... **225**

Nippon Teapot with Birds in a Tree

Nippon porcelain, bulbous ovoid body w/a serpentine spout, C-scroll handle & low

domed cover w/gold loop finial, decorated w/colorful birds in a blossoming tree, "M [in Wreath]" mark, ca. 1911 (ILLUS.)........ **40**

Noritake-Nippon Porcelain Teapot

Nippon porcelain, footed wide squatty bulbous body w/a high domed cover w/button finial, short spout & C-form handle, decorated around the top & cover w/ornate gold scrolls & delicate roses, early Noritake-Nippon mark, ca. 1910-20 (ILLUS.)......................... **50**

Crinoline Lady Noritake Teapot

Noritake China, Crinoline Lady patt., bulbous slightly tapering body w/C-form handle & long serpentine spout, domed cover w/knob finial, Victorian lady in a garden against a blue background, Noritake mark "38.016 DS," 5 1/2" l., 3 3/4" h. (ILLUS.)......................... **175**

Figural Noritake Oriental Man Teapot

Noritake China, figural, model of a short stocky Oriental man wearing a blue robe, one arm extended to the side forming the spout, the other hand holding the end of a brown branch that continues to form the handle, black hair w/topknot forms the cover, Noritake mark "M1J," 8 1/2" l., 5 3/4" h. (ILLUS.) **40**

Noritake Teapot with Stylized Flowers

Noritake China, footed bulbous ovoid body w/angled green shoulder & domed cover w/oval loop finial, C-scroll handle & long serpentine spout, large stylized blossoms on a slender leafy tree, in shades of blue, purple, green & brown, Noritake mark "27.1 DS," 8 1/4" l., 5 3/4" h. (ILLUS.) **45**

Noritake Pattern #16034 Teapot

Noritake China, Gold & White Pattern No. 16034, squatty bulbous body w/long spout & pointed angled handle, domed cover w/pointed handle, band of gold decoration around upper half, marked "Noritake - Made in Japan - #16034," ca. 1920s-30s, 8 1/4" l., 4 1/2" h. (ILLUS.)...... **30-35**

Noritake China Howo Pattern Teapot

Noritake China, Howo patt., spherical body w/serpentine spout & hooked loop handle, domed cover w/knob finial, marked

"Noritake - Made in Japan," ca. 1930s, 9 1/2" l., 6 1/2" h. (ILLUS.) **85-95**

Squatty Noritake Howo Pattern Teapot

Noritake China, Howo patt., squatty bulbous body w/serpentine spout & C-form handle, low domed cover w/arched loop handle, marked "Noritake - Howo - Made in Japan," ca. 1930s, 8" l., 4 1/2" h. (ILLUS.).. **55-65**

Noritake Indian Pattern Teapot

Noritake China, Indian patt., wide squatty bulbous body w/small rim spout, inset red cover w/cylindrical finial, bent bamboo swing bail handle, the white sides decorated w/Native American-style stick-like figures, Noritake mark "50.3DS," 6" l., 3 1/2" h. (ILLUS.) **95**

Lovely Noritake Iris Pattern Teapot

Noritake China, Iris patt., Art Deco style, tall gently flaring body w/angled handle, tall angled spout, angled shoulder & peaked cover w/open diamond-shaped finial, blue iris & green leaves design, Noritake mark "54DS," 7 1/4" h. (ILLUS.) 130

Rare Noritake Lady & Bird Teapot

Noritake China, Lady & Bird in Garden patt., tall footed urn-form body w/long serpentine spout, tall arched black-trimmed blue handle, domed cover in red w/black urn-shaped finial, dark blue background w/an Art Deco-style scene of a crinolined lady holding a bird in one hand w/a birdcage in front of her, in shades of yellow, green, black, white, light blue & orange, Noritake mark "27.1 DS," 6 3/4" l., 6 1/4" h. (ILLUS.) 645

Deep Red Oriental Scene Teapot

Noritake China, tall footed urn-form body w/long serpentine spout, tall arched gold handle, domed cover w/gold urn-shaped finial, dark red background w/an Oriental scene decoration w/a figure standing looking out to a sailing ship & island, panel w/stylized florals, in shades of black, white, turquoise blue & gold, Noritake mark "27.1 DS," 6 1/2" l., 6 1/4" h. (ILLUS.) 160

Occupied Japan Decorated Teapot

Occupied Japan porcelain, bulbous tapering body molded w/bright colored stylized flowers, serpentine spout, C-scroll handle & low cover w/knob finial, 1945-52 (ILLUS.) 35

Old Ivory Teapot Decorated in Beige

Old Ivory porcelain, Alice blank, bulbous body tapering to neck w/short lip, angled handle, short curving spout, domed lid w/finial, decorated w/line decoration & roses in shades of beige & brown, Hermann Ohme, Germany, 7" h. (ILLUS.) 500

Child's Old Ivory Alice Teapot

Old Ivory porcelain, child's, Alice blank, bulbous body tapering in to neck w/slightly flaring lip, short foot, angled handle, slightly curving spout, inset domed lid w/finial, body decorated w/pale pink roses & green leaves, clear glaze, marked "Alice," Hermann Ohme, Germany, 4" h. (ILLUS.) 75

Two Sizes of Old Ivory Deco Teapots

Old Ivory Clairon Teapot

Old Ivory porcelain, Clairon blank, almost spherical ovoid body on short quatrefoil base, C-form handle w/separate thumbrest applied to body above it, short curved spout, domed lid w/cutout trefoil finial, the body decorated w/sprigs & garland of pink roses & green leaves, line decoration highlighting the shoulder, foot, handle, spout & finial, Hermann Ohme, Germany, 8" h. (ILLUS.) **250**

Old Ivory porcelain, Deco blank, nearly cylindrical body on short foot, w/tapering shoulder, angled handle, graceful curving spout, flat lid w/finial, Hermann Ohme, Germany, different sizes, each (ILLUS. of two, top of page) **500**

Small Deco Variant Teapot

Old Ivory porcelain, Deco Variant blank, cylindrical body on short foot, short tapering shoulder, angled handle, curving spout, flat lid w/cutout angled finial, decorated w/line decoration & daisies in shades of white, beige & brown, Her-

mann Ohme, Germany, 5 1/2" h. (ILLUS.) **450**

Deco Variant Teapot Decorated in Brown

Old Ivory porcelain, Deco Variant blank, Mold #24, cylindrical body on short foot, short tapering shoulder, angled handle, curving spout, flat lid w/cutout angled finial, decorated w/line decoration & roses in shades of brown, marked "24," Hermann Ohme, Germany, 7 1/2" h. (ILLUS.) **600**

Old Ivory Eglantine Teapot

Old Ivory porcelain, Eglantine blank, lobed bulbous body on scalloped foot, asymmetrical scalloped rim, peaked lid w/floral finial, ornate angled handle w/animal head thumbrest & serpentine spout w/applied decoration & animal head opening, the body & lid decorated w/sprigs of delicate pale green ribbons, flowers & leaves, gold highlights on foot, rim, spout & handle, Hermann Ohme, Germany, 7 1/2" h. (ILLUS.) **200**

Old Ivory Etoile Teapot

Old Ivory porcelain, Etoile blank, lobed ovoid body w/ruffled scalloped base w/embossed decoration & ruffled cutout rim, inset domed lid w/C-scroll finial, embossed C-scroll handle & serpentine spout, the body w/panels of embossing, the body & lid decorated w/pink-centered cream-colored roses & green leaves, line decoration on rim, marked "Old Ivory," Hermann Ohme, Germany, 7 1/2" h. (ILLUS.) **850**

Small Old Ivory Louis XVI Teapot

Old Ivory porcelain, Louis XVI blank, footed ovoid body, applied cut-out C-scroll handle, serpentine spout, tapering shoulder w/scalloped ruffled beaded rim, domed lid w/finial, decorated on body & lid w/delicate lavender flowers & vining green leaves, silver line decoration on spout, handle, foot & finial, clear glaze, Hermann Ohme, Germany, 5 1/2" h. (ILLUS.) **100-125**

Old Ivory Melon-shaped Teapot

Old Ivory porcelain, melon-lobed bulbous body on short quatrefoil foot, short flaring neck, domed lobed lid w/finial in the shape of a melon/gourd stem, C-form handle, serpentine spout, the body & lid decorated w/delicate blue & yellow floral designs, the spout & rim w/gold line decoration, Hermann Ohme, Germany, 7 1/2" h. (ILLUS.) **250**

Old Ivory Mignon Teapot

Old Ivory porcelain, Mignon blank, lobed bulbous body on ruffled foot, short flaring neck w/ruffled rim, peaked lid w/ornate cutout finial, ornate C-scroll handle w/thumbrest & serpentine spout, the body & lid decorated w/embossed decoration & sprigs of delicate green flowers & leaves, gold highlights on foot, rim, spout & handle, Hermann Ohme, Germany, 8" h. (ILLUS.) **135**

Old Ivory Rivoli Teapot

Old Ivory porcelain, Rivoli blank, hexagonal body on short foot, angled handle, long curved spout, slightly domed lid w/cutout pointed finial, clear glaze, handpainted decoration of purple violets & green leaves, gold highlights, Hermann Ohme, Germany, 7 1/2" h. (ILLUS.) **475**

Old Ivory Swirl Teapot

Two Unmarked R.S. Prussia Teapots

Old Ivory porcelain, Swirl blank, footed bulbous body w/delicate swirled ribs, flaring lip, domed lid w/finial, applied ribbed scroll loop handle w/thumbrest, serpentine spout, clear glaze, the body decorated w/large wine-colored floral design, the lid & spout w/wine-colored floral sprigs, the finial, rim, handle & base highlighted in gold, Hermann Ohme, Germany, 8 1/2" h. (ILLUS.) **250**

Old Ivory Worcester Teapot

Old Ivory porcelain, Worcester blank, waisted lobed body w/ruffled scalloped base & rim, inset domed lid w/cutout shell finial, C-scroll handle, serpentine spout, clear glaze, the body & lid decorated w/delicate flowers in shades of pale pink & orchid, heavy gold decoration highlighting base, handle, spout & rim, Hermann Ohme, Germany, 7 1/2" h. (ILLUS.) **245**

R.S. Poland Teapot with Oak Branch Decoration

R.S. Poland porcelain, squatty bulbous shape tapering to rim, short foot, angled handle, slightly serpentine spout, peaked cut-out lid, double-marked "RS Poland," decorated w/oak branch w/leaves & acorns & shadow leaves, line decoration on spout, handle, foot, rim & lid (ILLUS.) **375**

R.S. Prussia porcelain, egg-shaped body on a round pedestal foot, decorated w/dainty white flowers & green leaves on pastel green, pink, beige & white ground, unmarked, 7" d., 6 1/4" h. (ILLUS. left, top of page) **135-150**

R.S. Prussia Medallion Teapot

R.S. Prussia porcelain, Medallion mold (Mold 631), waisted paneled body w/ruffled scalloped rim, four short feet, angled handle, serpentine spout, lid w/cut-out finial, cobalt blue base w/gold vining decoration, body w/scene of sailing vessel on water w/cliffs rising on either side, gold beading at rim & finial, gold line decoration on handle & spout (ILLUS.) **350-450**

R.S. Prussia porcelain, Mold 474, Laurel Wreath patt., exotic form w/squatty bulbous bottom tapering to a tall narrow trumpet neck w/scalloped rim, tall shoulder spout, angular openwork handle, domed cover w/pointed finial, 8 3/4" h. (ILLUS., top next page) **800-1,400**

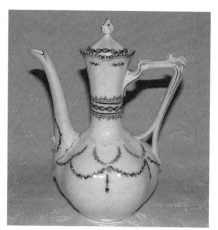

Unusual R.S. Prussia Mold 474 Teapot

R.S. Prussia Mold 616 Teapot

R.S. Prussia porcelain, Mold 616, tall inverted pear-shaped body on a ribbed & paneled pedestal base, ornate C-scroll handle, long spout, domed cover w/pointed finial, decorated w/a large bouquet of pink roses, gold trim, 7 1/4" h. (ILLUS.)... **800-1,400**

R.S. Prussia Young Lovers Teapot

R.S. Prussia porcelain, spherical body w/flaring ruffled rim & short foot, C-scroll handle, slightly serpentine spout, peaked inset lid, decorated w/gold filigree & line decoration & central scene of lovers holding hands in pastoral landscape, a large deep pink rose above them & leafy garlands cascading on either side (ILLUS.)... **200-250**

R.S. Prussia porcelain, squatty bulbous body w/wide shoulder raised on a square pedestal foot, decorated w/pink roses & green leaves on a pastel green ground, unmarked, 7 1/2" d., 5 3/4" h. (ILLUS. right w/unmarked egg-shaped teapot, top page 45)............................ **135-150**

R.S. Prussia Sweet Gum Ball Teapot

R.S. Prussia porcelain, Sweet Gum Ball mold, lobed bulbous body on short feet, tapering in at shoulder to flaring cut-out ruffled neck, cut-out angled handle, slightly curved spout, domed inset lid w/finial, decorated w/shadow leaves in shades of green & blue/green & embellished w/embossing & line decoration, rare mold (ILLUS.) **475**

Rare Royal Doulton Bone China Teapot

Royal Doulton Ware, bone china, handpainted w/images of exotic birds & heavy gilt scroll trim, painted by Joseph Birbeck, ca. 1910 (ILLUS.)...................... **2,000**

Royal Doulton Bone China Teapot with Gilt Floral Decoration

Royal Doulton Ware, bone china, wide squatty bulbous body w/a long angled spout, forked C-form handle & low domed cover w/button finial, decorated overall w/floral gilding, ca. 1923 (ILLUS.)..... **500**

Royal Doulton Ware, Bunnykins Series, model of a large rabbit, designed by Charles Noke, introduced in 1939 (ILLUS., next column) **3,000**

Royal Doulton Ware, Bunnykins Series, wide short cylindrical body w/angled spout & angled handle, Casino patt., introduced in 1937 (ILLUS., bottom of page) **750**

Figural Royal Doulton Bunnykins Teapot

Early Bunnykins Casino Pattern Teapot

Rare Royal Worcester Aesthetic Movement Figural Teapot

Royal Worcester, Aesthetic Movement figural design, molded on one side as a late Victorian Aesthetic dandy wearing a large sunflower, one arm & bent wrist forming the spout, his other arm the handle, the reverse modeled as his female counterpart wearing a large lily, each wearing a dark green shirt w/white collar & a dark pink hat in the spirit of Oscar Wilde, inscribed on the bottom "Fearful consequences, through the laws of natural selection and evolution of living up to one's teapot," signed "Budge," marked & w/date code for 1882, 6" h. (ILLUS. of both sides).. **11,163**

Rare Reticulated Royal Worcester Pot

Royal Worcester, spherical white body w/an elaborate overall reticulated outer layer composed of fine honeycomb, diamonds & rings, the low domed cover, C-form handle & shaped spout all w/further reticulation, the cover w/a spire finial & applied pale turquoise beaded chain trim also used on the handle & spout, crafted by George Owen, impressed factory mark, ca. 1890 (ILLUS.).......................... **4,780**

Fine Royal Worcester Dragon Teapot

Royal Worcester, Oriental design w/squared block-style body in turquoise blue molded on the sides w/a flying bird in green, yellow, tan & pink w/pink & green floral bands, the flattened shoulders w/an impressed Greek key design, flat square cover w/pyramidal finial, squared curved corner spout w/the end opening formed by the head of a black dragon whose slender body arches across the top to form the handle, late 19th c., minor professional repair to spout, 7 1/2" h. (ILLUS.)........................... **3,360**

Attwell Boo-Boo Teapot in Mushroom Shape

Shelley China, Attwell Pixie patt., from Boo-Boo tea set, Mushroom shape w/scene of Boo-Boo on side, 1930 (ILLUS.)........... **550-850**

Shelley Old Sevres Teapot in Bute Shape

Shelley China, Bute Shape, Birds - Old Sevres patt., decorated in color w/images of exotic birds below a scrolling border band enclosing florals, 1890-1935 & 1949-1963 (ILLUS.).............................. **250-350**

Shelley China, child's size, spherical body w/domed cover, C-form handle, serpentine spout, brown floral decoration, overall 5 7/8" l., 4 3/8" h. (ILLUS.)................ **150-250**

Shelley Child's Teapot with Florals

Cowham Beach Tent Teapot

Shelley Begonia Teapot in Dainty Big Floral Shape

Rare Dainty Floral Shelley Teapot with Molded Blossoms & Trim

Shelley China, children's line, Beach Tent Shape, part of the Beach set by Hilda Cowham, introduced in 1927 (ILLUS., previous page) **1,700**

Shelley China, Dainty Big Floral Shape, Begonia patt. No. 13427, from the Best Ware group, 1943 (ILLUS., bottom previous page) **180-280**

Shelley China, Dainty Floral Shape, Chintz Maytime patt. No. 0105, from the Seconds group, 1943 (ILLUS.)............. **1,500-2,000**

Shelley China, Dainty Floral Shape, not usually seen w/the printed flowers on the brown & green panels, 7 1/2" l., 4 5/8" h. (ILLUS., top of page)......................... **700-1,100**

Shelley Dainty Pink Teapot in Dainty Garland Shape

Dainty Floral Pink Panels Teapot

Shelley China, Dainty Floral Alternate Shape, Pink Panels patt. No. 11993, from the Best Ware group, 1919 (ILLUS.).. **800-1,000**

Shelley China, Dainty Garland Shape, Dainty Pink patt. No. 051/P, from the Ideal group, 1938 (ILLUS.)......................... **350-450**

Dainty Floral Chintz Maytime Teapot

Shelley Dainty Orange Teapot in Dainty Garlands Shape

Shelley Regency Teapot in Dainty Plain Shape

Shelley China, Dainty Garlands Shape, Dainty Orange patt. No. 051/8, from the Ideal group, 1932 (ILLUS.).................... **350-450**

Shelley China, Dainty Kettle Garlands Shape, Trailing Violets patt. No. 9056, shaded style, from the Best Ware group, 1897 (ILLUS.)...................................... **180-380**

Shelley China, Dainty Plain Shape, Regency patt. No. 785, from the Special group, 1945 (ILLUS., top of page)................... **150-250**

Shelley China, Dainty Repeat Shape, Rosebud patt. No. 13426, from the Best Ware group, 1943 (ILLUS., bottom of page).. **250-350**

Trailing Violets Teapot in Dainty Kettle Garlands Shape

Shelley Rosebud Teapot in Dainty Repeat Shape

Her Majesty Teapot in Dainty Shape by Shelley

Shelley China, Dainty Scenic Shape, Her Majesty (tractor) patt., from the Souvenir Ware group, 1920 (ILLUS.).. **50-150**

Popular Shelley Dainty Blue Teapot

Shelley China, Dainty Shape, Dainty Blue patt., the original & most sought-after Shelley design, 1896-1966+ (ILLUS.)... **500-600**

Shelley China, Dainty Shape, undecorated, ca. 1912-25, overall 7 1/8" l., 4" h. (ILLUS., below left).......................

Undecorated Dainty Shape Teapot

Dorothy Teapot with Tea Tile

Shelley Draped Rosebud Teapot & Other Pieces in Ely Shape

Shelley China, Dorothy Shape, patt. No. 8063, w/matching tea tile w/earlier Wileman backstamp, teapot overall 9 5/8" l., 6 1/4" h., the set (ILLUS., right, bottom previous page) **200-500**

Shelley China, Draped Rosebud patt. No. 13510, Repeat litho style, Ely shape from the Best Ware group, 1944, teapot only (ILLUS. w/other pieces, top of page) **150-250**

Shelley China, Early Gainsborough Shape, Versailles patt. No. 11426, Birds style, from the Best Ware group, 1925, teapot only (ILLUS. w/other pieces, bottom of page) **250-350**

Shelley China, Ely Shape, Rose Pansy-Forget-Me-Not Chintz gold banding, rare, ca. 1935-1965 (ILLUS., next column) **600-900**

Rare Ely Shape Shelley Teapot

Versailles Teapot & Other Pieces in Early Gainsborough Shape

Shelley Loganberry Teapot & Hot Water Jug in Eve Shape

*Art Deco Eve Shape Teapot
with Laburnum Pattern*

Shelley China, Eve Shape, Art Deco design, Laburnum patt., 1933-1944 (ILLUS.).. **600-900**

Art Deco Eve Bellflower and Leaves Teapot

Shelley China, Eve Shape, Bellflower and Leaves patt. No. 12559, from the Best Ware group, 1936 (ILLUS.)................... **300-400**

Shelley China, Eve Shape, hot water pot, Loganberry, Green patt. No. 12435, Fruit style, Best Ware group, 1935 (ILLUS. left with Eve Loganberry teapot & tea tile).. **350-450**

Shelley China, Eve Shape, Loganberry Green patt. No. 12435, Fruit style, from the Best Ware group, 1935, add at least $100 for stand, teapot only (ILLUS. right w/stand & hot water jug, top of page).. **350-450**

Shelley Yachts Teapot in Foley Shape

Shelley China, Foley Shape, Yachts patt., Faience style, from the Best Ware group, 1905 (ILLUS.).. **200-300**

Shelley Daffodil Time Teapot

Shelley Blue Duchess Teapot in Gainsborough Shape

Shelley China, Gainsborough Shape, Blue Duchess patt. No. 13403, Elegant style, from the Best Ware group, 1943 (ILLUS.).. **100-200**

Shelley Bluebell Wood Teapot

Shelley China, Globe Shape, Bluebell Wood patt. No. 12108, Scenic style, from the Best Ware group, 1932 (ILLUS.)..... **100-200**

Shelley China, Globe Shape, Daffodil Time patt. No. 13370, Scenic style, from the Best Ware group, 1942 (ILLUS., top of page).. **100-200**

Globe Teapot with Flower Basket

Shelley China, Globe Shape, white ground decorated w/a colorful basket of flowers, undated (ILLUS.)................................... **100-200**

Green Daisy Teapot in Henley Shape

Shelley China, Henley Shape, Chintz Green Daisy patt. No. 13450, from the Best Ware group, 1943 (ILLUS.)........... **200-300**

Marguerite Teapot & Other Pieces in Henley Shape

Shelley China, Henley Shape, Marguerite patt. No. 13688, Chintz style, from the Best Ware group, 1949, teapot only (ILLUS. w/stand & sugar & creamer - add at least $100 for stand & about $150 for sugar & creamer) **150-250**

Art Deco Mode Shape with Blocks Pattern

Shelley China, Mode Shape, Art Deco design, Blocks patt., 1929-1934 (ILLUS.) **600-900**

Mode Art Deco Pot with Pink Florals

Shelley China, Mode Shape, floral decoration w/pink blossoms, light blue trim, factory second, 1929-34, 9 1/8" l., 4 7/8" h. (ILLUS.) **350-500**

New York Shape Floral Decor Teapot

Shelley China, New York Shape, decorated w/delicate bands of colorful flowers, 1890-1905 (ILLUS.) **150-250**

Shelley London Crested Teapot in New York Shape

Shelley China, New York Shape, London patt., Crested style, from the Souvenir Ware group, 1910 (ILLUS.) **50-150**

Shelley Poppies Teapot, Cup & Saucer in Princess Shape

Shelley Teapot in New York Shape

Saltcoats Crest on New York Teapot

New York Teapot with Blue Sprigs

Shelley China, New York Shape, Plain style, white w/green trim on rim, handle, finial & spout, from the Best Ware group, 1940, teapot only (ILLUS. w/stand - add at least $100 for stand) **50-150**

Shelley China, New York Shape, Saltcoats Crested design, 1890-1905, overall 5 3/4" l., 4" h. (ILLUS., top next column) **70-100**

Shelley China, New York Shape, scattered blue floral sprigs, 1890-1905 (ILLUS., next column)... **75-125**

Black Cloisonne Teapot & Other Pieces in Queen Anne Shape

Blue Iris Teapots of Various Sizes in Queen Anne Shape by Shelley

Shelley China, Princess Shape, Poppies, orange patt. No. 12227, Floral style, from the Best Ware group, 1933, teapot only (ILLUS. w/matching cup & saucer, top of previous page) **350-550**

Shelley China, Queen Anne Shape, Black Cloisonne patt. No. 8321, Chintz style, from the Best Ware group, 1910, teapot only (ILLUS. w/stand & other pieces - add at least $100 for stand, bottom of previous page) **500-700**

Shelley China, Queen Anne Shape, Blue Iris patt. No. 11561, Floral style, from the Best Ware group, 1919, various sizes, each (ILLUS. of various sizes, top of page) **300-400**

Queen Anne Teapot with Pattern No. 11495

Shelley China, Queen Anne Shape, Pattern No. 11495, stylized florals in panels, introduced in 1926 (ILLUS.) **250-450**

Shelley Woodland Bluebells Scenic Teapot in Queen Anne Shape

Regent Shape Hot Water & Teapot in the Blackberry Pattern

Shelley China, Queen Anne Shape, Woodland Bluebells patt. No. 12155, Scenic style, from the Best Ware group, 1933 (ILLUS., bottom previous page) **200-300**

Shelley China, Regent Shape, Blackberry patt., hard to find, 1933-1966 (ILLUS. left with hot water pot, top of page)............. **600-900**

Shelley China, Regent Shape, hot water pot, Blackberry patt., 1933-1966 (ILLUS. right with Regent teapot, top of page)... **600-900**

Shelley Floral Phlox Teapot in Regent Shape

Shelley China, Regent Shape, Phlox patt. No. 12190, orange, Floral style, from the Best Ware group, 1933 (ILLUS.)... **100-200**

Specially Made Pot with Tea Tile

Shelley China, Shamrock patt., wide waisted cylindrical shape w/rim spout, angled handle, concave flat cover w/button finial, overall floral sprig decoration, made for Letheby & Christopher, caterers, pot w/ca. 1925 Shelley mark, matching tea tile w/the Late Foley mark, teapot 6 3/8" w., 4 3/4" h., the set (ILLUS.)...................... **200-300**

Tall Teapot Made for Ideal China Co.

Shelley China, tall trumpet shape w/ring handle & finial, made for the Ideal China Co., Canada, registration number 781613, overall 7 1/4" h. (ILLUS.)......... **250-400**

Shelley China, Tulip Shape, Chinese Peony Chintz patt., black background, rare... **600-900**

Shelley Chinese Peony Chintz Teapot with Blue Background

Shelley China, Tulip Shape, Chinese Peony Chintz patt., dark blue background, very rare (ILLUS.) .... **900+**

Front & Back of Tulip Shape Teapot with Pattern 0144

Shelley China, Tulip Shape, Pattern No. 0144, made for the Ideal China Co., Canada, ca. 1938-45, 6 1/4" h. (ILLUS. of both sides) **200-350**

Grouping of Shelley & Wileman Teapots in the Shamrock (No. 8064) Pattern

Shelley China & Wileman & Co., grouping of Shelley & Wileman & Co. teapots in patt. No. 8064, each (ILLUS. left to right: Shelley New York Shape, Shelley tapered teapot on tea tile; Wileman smaller semi-porcelain teapot with pewter-repaired spout; tall Wileman semi-porcelain teapot; larger Wileman semi-porcelain teapot) **200-450**

Thermolite Chapus, paneled conical body w/a neck ring & short cylindrical neck w/conical cover & tapering cylindrical knob, paneled angled spout & angled handle, overall scattered floral sprigs, France, ca. 1940s (ILLUS.) **125**

Colorful Alexandra Shape Teapot

Wileman & Co., Alexandra Shape, patt. No. 3737, introduced in 1887 (ILLUS.) **600-900**
Wileman & Co., Dainty Shape, patt. No. 7447, introduced in 1896, designed by William Morris, shape continued in production until factory closing in 1966 (ILLUS., bottom of page) **300-350**

Thermolite Chapus French Teapot

Dainty Shape Teapot with Pink Roses Pattern No. 7447

Dainty Shape Teapot with Floral Pattern No. 9056

Wileman & Co., Dainty Shape, patt. No. 9056, 1896-1966, 5 1/2" h. (ILLUS.) **300-600**

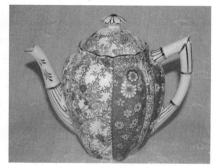

Wileman Jungle Print Tall Teapot

Wileman & Co., Daisy Shape, Jungle Print patt., 1885-1914, 7 1/4" l., 6 1/8" h. (ILLUS., of
both sides).. **400-600**

Empire Shape Teapot with Bold Red & Blue Florals

Wileman & Co., Empire Shape, patt. No. 0888, shape introduced in 1893 (ILLUS.) **600-900**

Wileman Empire Shape Teapot with Leafy Pattern 6531

Empire Shape Pot with Pattern 5044

Wileman & Co., Empire Shape, patt. No.
5044, 1893-1912, overall 9 1/4" l., 5" h.
(ILLUS.).. **300-600**
Wileman & Co., Empire Shape, patt. No.
6531, introduced in 1893 (ILLUS., top of
page).. **400-800**
Wileman & Co., Empire Shape, Spano Lus-
tra patt., 1893-1912, 5" h. (ILLUS., bot-
tom of page)... **300-600**

Colorful Foley Shape Teapot

Wileman & Co., Foley Shape, patt. No.
7019, introduced in 1894 (ILLUS.)........ **600-900**

Empire Shape Spano Lustra Teapot by Wileman

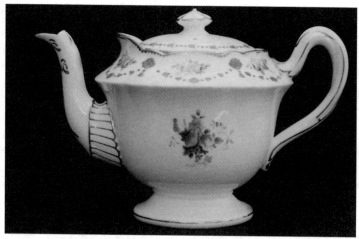

Wileman Gainsborough Teapot with Delicate Florals

Wileman & Co., Gainsborough Shape, un-
numbered floral patt., introduced in 1900
(ILLUS.)... **300-600**
Wileman & Co., hot water pot, tall, lobed cylindrical body, patt. No. 7447 (ILLUS.) .. **100-250**
Wileman & Co., Imperial Shape, first introduced w/an Intarsio patt. in the 1890s,
this example w/a Shelley backstamp,
patt. No. 7666, ca. 1910 (ILLUS., bottom
of page) **1,500-2,000**

Wileman Tall Hot Water Pot

Rare Early Imperial Shape Wileman Teapot

Rare & Unusual Oriental Shape Teapot

Wileman & Co., Oriental Shape, Intarsio decoration, patt. No. 3081, short production period, 1899 (ILLUS.).............. **1,200-1,500**

Tall Wileman Pot in Shamrock Pattern

Wileman & Co., semi-porcelain, tall slightly tapering cylindrical form w/tall serpentine spout, C-form handle & domed cover w/large pointed finial, overall floral spring patt., 8" h. (ILLUS.) **300-450**

Wileman Semi-Porcelain Teapot

Wileman & Co., semi-porcelain, wide half-round body w/wide shoulder to flat mouth, serpentine spout, angled handle, Shamrock patt. No. 8064, 7 3/8" l., 4 1/8" h. (ILLUS.) **200-400**

Fine Wileman Shell Shape Teapot

Wileman & Co., Shell Shape, patt. No. 5137, introduced in 1891 (ILLUS.)........ **500-600**

One Side of the Kilkenny Crest Teapot

Wileman & Co., Victoria Shape, Kilkenny Commemorative decoration, pink floral vine on one side, Kilkenny crest on the other side, 1885-1925, overall 5 7/8" l., 3 7/8" h. (ILLUS.) **75-125**

Grafton China Blue Willow Teapot

Willow Ware, Blue Willow, ovoid body tapering to flaring neck, angled handle, serpentine spout, domed cover w/knob finial, embellished w/silver line decoration, marked "Grafton China," A.B. Jones & Sons, England, ca. 1930s (ILLUS.)....... **125-150**

"Auld Lang Syne" Blue Willow Teapot

Willow Ware, Blue Willow, six-paneled squatty bulbous body on short feet, flat hexagonal neck & cover topped w/figural gold lion finial, gold beaded C-form handle, serpentine spout, embellished w/gold line decoration on feet, spout & lid, the sides of the neck reading "We'll tak a cup o' kindness yet, for days o' auld lang syne" in blue, made for Tiffany & Co., New York by Copeland China, England, ca. 1870s (ILLUS., above) **200**

Willow Ware, Blue Willow, squatty bulbous body tapering to flaring asymmetrical neck, slightly domed cover w/trefoil finial, C-scroll handle, slightly serpentine spout, dark blue handle, spout & finial, Mintons, England, ca. 1900 (ILLUS., bottom of page) **175-200**

Mintons Blue Willow Teapot

Royal Worcester Blue Willow Teapot

Willow Ware, Blue Willow, squatty ovoid body tapering in at shoulder to gently peaked cover w/knob finial, straight spout, C-scroll handle, Royal Worcester porcelain, England, ca. 1920s (ILLUS.)... **150-175**

cover w/petaled finial, straight ribbed spout, overhead metal kettle handles w/porcelain grip, impressed "Copeland," England, 1880 (ILLUS.) **250-300**

Unmarked Porcelain Teapot

Unknown maker, lobed, slightly waisted cylindrical shape w/tapering shoulder & flaring ruffled neck, C-scroll handle, serpentine spout, domed lobed lid w/cut-out finial, the white body w/gold acorn design & green shading, gold highlights on rim, spout, handle & finial, embossing on shoulder & lid, probably Germany, late 19th c., 6" h. (ILLUS.) **125**

Red Willow Mandarin Pattern Teapot

Willow Ware, Red Willow, Mandarin patt., ribbed cylindrical body on short foot, tapering in at shoulder to slightly domed

Porcelain - 1950-2000

Modern French Porcelain Teapot

French porcelain, squatty bulbous pot w/serpentine spout, C-scroll handle & overhanging domed cover w/pointed knob finial, together w/tea strainer insert & drip coffee biggin insert, marked "Porcelaine a feu - France - APILCO," the set (ILLUS.).. 80

Modern Chinese Porcelain Teapot

Chinese porcelain, Ming Lotus patt., traditional squared upright Chinese teapot form w/large domed cover & overhead bail handle, each side decorated w/a landscape of flowers & birds, mark of the Toyo China Company, China, 1981 (ILLUS.).. $20

Coalport China, Canton patt., Kingsware line, footed squatty bulbous gently lobed body w/a wide mouth, domed cover w/arched loop finial, angled spout, C-scroll handle, part of the Wedgwood Group, England (ILLUS., bottom of page) 90

Extra Large Modern Phoenix Teapot

Japanese porcelain, Modern Phoenix (T-Bird) patt., extra large upright squared body w/curved shoulders to a squared domed cover w/ovoid finial, angular spout & squared loop handle, original

Coalport China Canton Pattern Teapot

sticker but unmarked, made by Taka-hashi of Japan, post-1970, 9" l., 7 1/4" h. (ILLUS.).. **25-35**

Unusual Modern Phoenix Pattern Teapot

Japanese porcelain, Modern Phoenix (T-Bird) patt., square body w/angled shoulders, square cover w/ovoid finial, angled upright handle, tall upright square porcelain handle, unmarked but by Takahashi of Japan, post-1970, 6 1/4" l., 8" h. (ILLUS.).. **45**

Modern Phoenix Rectangular Teapot

Japanese porcelain, Modern Phoenix (T-Bird) patt., upright rectangular body w/short angled spout, C-scroll handle, low domed cover w/flower bud finial, un-marked but produced by Takahashi of Japan, post-1970, 8 1/2" l., 5" h. (ILLUS.) **35**

Modern Phoenix (T-Bird) Teapot

Japanese porcelain, Modern Phoenix (T-Bird) patt., upright square body w/angled spout, flat cover w/loop handle, swing bail bamboo handle, marked w/a small square & seven Japanese characters, post-1970, 6" l., 6 3/4" h. (ILLUS.) **30**

Large Modern Phoenix Bird Teapot

Japanese porcelain, Phoenix Bird patt., bulbous nearly spherical body w/a flat rim, upright serpentine spout, woven wicker swing bail handle, w/original liner, extra large size, marked "Made in Japan" in a black square, post-1970, 8" l., 5 5/8" h. (ILLUS.) **45**

Lefton China, Dresden shape, Elegant Rose patt., No. 2032.................................. **55-65**

Lefton China, figural Miss Priss, No. 1516... **150-200**

Lefton Rose Chintz Teapot

Lefton China, footed squatty bulbous lobed body w/serpentine spout, ring handle & cover finial, Rose Chintz patt., ca. 1970s (ILLUS.).. **35**

Small Lefton China Teapot

Lefton China, individual size, Rose Chintz patt., ca. 1960s (ILLUS.) **20**

Lenox China, Christmas Tree patt., figural decorated tree, modern (ILLUS.) **75**

Sunday Brunch Lenox China Teapot

Lenox China, Butler's Pantry Series, Sunday Brunch design, tapering cylindrical ruffled form, undecorated, modern (ILLUS.) **45**

Newer Lenox Garden Party Teapot

Lenox China, Garden Party patt., Butler's Pantry series, modern (ILLUS.) **45**

New Lenox China Pumpkin Teapot

Lenox China, pumpkin-shaped, molded scrolling leaf panels alternating w/plain panels, vine finial, produced in 2004 (ILLUS.) **75**

Lenox Teapot in Butler's Pantry Series

Lenox China, Butler's Pantry Series, tapering cylindrical form w/molded V-shaped panels, undecorated, modern (ILLUS.) **45**

Lenox Summer Enchantment Teapot

Lenox China, Summer Enchantment patt., footed squatty spherical body w/serpentine spout, C-form handle & domed cover w/figural butterfly finial, colorful butterfly & vine decoration, modern (ILLUS.) **75**

Modern Lenox Christmas Tree Teapot

1980s Royal Albert China Teapot

Royal Albert China (Thomas C. Wild & Sons), Moonlight Rose patt., footed bulbous lobed tapering body w/domed cover & pointed finial, ribbed serpentine spout, fancy C-scroll handle, part of the Royal Doulton Group, ca. 1987 (ILLUS.) **125**

Royal Albert Old Country Roses III Teapot

Royal Albert China (Thomas C. Wild & Sons), Old Country Roses III patt., bulbous spherical body w/short spout & C-form handle, domed cover w/knob finial, part of the Royal Doulton Group, manufactured in Indonesia (ILLUS.) **195**

Royal Albert China Teapot with Roses

Royal Albert China (Thomas C. Wild & Sons), Old Country Roses patt., double-gourd stacked style body w/two fancy C-scroll handles, domed cover w/button finial, part of the Royal Doulton Group, manufactured in China (ILLUS.) **65**

1960s Royal Albert China Teapot

Quality Royal Crown Derby Modern Teapot

Shelley Capper's Strawberry Teapot in Dainty Big Floral Shape

Royal Albert China (Thomas C. Wild & Sons), Old Country Roses patt., footed, bulbous lobed tapering body w/domed cover & pointed finial, ribbed serpentine spout, fancy C-scroll handle, part of the Royal Doulton Group, ca. 1962 (ILLUS., previous page) **125**

Royal Crown Derby, Old Avesbury (gold Avesbury) patt., oblong cylindrical body w/narrow angled shoulder, domed cover w/flower finial, straight spout, angled scrolled handle, part of Royal Doulton Tableware, Ltd., England (ILLUS., bottom previous page) **1,350**

Shelley China, Carlisle Shape, Floral Rataud's Orchid patt. No. 2408, from the Best Ware group, 1960 (ILLUS., right)... **100-200**

Shelley China, Dainty Big Floral Shape, Capper's Strawberry patt. No. 2396, from the Seconds group, 1959 (ILLUS., top of page)... **200-300**

Shelley Rataud's Orchid Teapot in Carlisle Shape

Shelley China, Dainty Shape, Thistle patt. No. 13829, from the Best Ware group, 1955 (ILLUS., bottom of page)............. **200-300**

Shelley Thistle Teapot in Dainty Shape

Shelley Chintz Blue Daisy Teapot & Other Pieces in Mayfair Shape

Gainsborough Drifting Leaves Teapot

Shelley China, Gainsborough Shape, Drifting Leaves patt. No. 13848, from the Contemporary group, 1957 (ILLUS.)....... **80-150**

Shelley China, Mayfair Shape, Chintz Blue Daisy patt. No. 14268, from the Best Ware group, 1964 (ILLUS. w/stand & sugar & creamer - add at least $100 for stand & about $150 for sugar & creamer, top of page)........................... **150-250**

English Tuscan Bone China Teapot

Tuscan Bone China, upright diamond-shaped body w/integral handle, inset flat cover, Oriental-style bird & tree decoration, R.H. & S.L. Plant, England (ILLUS.) **75**

Miniature Blue Willow Teapot

Willow Ware, Blue Willow, miniature, lobed ovoid body, domed inset cover w/finial, C-scroll handle, serpentine spout, gold line decoration on handle, spout, rim & finial, Windsor China, England, 3 3/4" h. (ILLUS.).. **15-20**

New Hand-painted Teapot

Zrike porcelain, nearly spherical body w/short cylindrical neck, domed cover w/knob finial, serpentine spout & C-form handle, "In The Garden" h.p. decoration by Michael Sparks, teapot made in China, new (ILLUS.)... **40**

Pottery & Earthenware - 1750-1850

Unusual Early Castleford Teapot

Castleford Pottery, creamy white deep oval paneled body w/an angled shoulder to the molded chainlink neck, serpentine spout & angled scroll handle, low domed cover w/blossom finial, the body divided into various panels outlined in black & molded w/various designs, the largest side panel featuring the Great Seal of the United States, further black outlining, Castleford, England, late 18th - early 19th c., 11" l. (ILLUS.) **$1,035**

Amerillia Flow Blue Teapot

Flow Blue china, Amerillia patt., ribbed oval body style, Podmore, Walker & Co., England, ca. 1834-59 (ILLUS.) **650**

Amoy Octagon Shape Flow Blue Teapot

Flow Blue china, Amoy patt., Octagon body shape, Davenport, England, ca. 1850 (ILLUS.) **650**

Flow Blue china, Amoy patt., Squat Sixteen Panel Fluted body shape, Davenport, England, ca. 1850 (ILLUS., bottom of page) **950**

Flow Blue china, Arabesque patt., Long Octagon body shape, T. J. & J. Mayer, England, ca. 1845 (ILLUS., top next page) **650**

Amoy Squatty Paneled Shape Teapot by Davenport

Arabesque Pattern Teapot with Long Octagon Body Shape

Cashmere Pattern Morley Teapots in Two Sizes

Flow Blue china, Aster & Grapeshot patt., brush-stroke Six-sided Gothic shape, Joseph Clementson, England, ca. 1840, 9" h. **725**

Flow Blue china, Cashmere patt., Broad Shoulder body shape, Francis Morley, England, ca. 1850, each (ILLUS. of two size variations) **950**

Classic Gothic Cashmere Pattern Flow Blue Teapots

Flow Blue china, Cashmere patt., Classic Gothic body shape, Francis Morley, England, ca. 1850, each (ILLUS. of two size variations)... **950**

Split Primary Body Shape Cashmere Teapots

Flow Blue china, Cashmere patt., Split Panel Primary body shape, Francis Morley, England, ca. 1850, each (ILLUS. of two size variations)................................... **1,200**

Flow Blue china, Cashmere patt., Straight Line Primary shape, Francis Morley, ca. 1850 .... **1,200**

Chapoo Teapot in Variant Body Shape

Flow Blue china, Chapoo patt., Double Line Primary body shape, John Wedge Wood (aka Wedg.wood), England, ca. 1850 (ILLUS.)... **550**

Chen-Si Flow Blue Teapot by Meir

Flow Blue china, Chen-Si patt., Eight Sided Primary Belted body shape, John Meir, England, ca. 1835 (ILLUS.)......................... **650**

Tall Chapoo Pattern Flow Blue Teapot

Flow Blue china, Chapoo patt., Tall No Line Primary body shape, John Wedge Wood (aka Wedg.wood), England, ca. 1850 (ILLUS.)... **1,200**

1840s Chinese Pattern Teapot

Flow Blue china, Chinese patt., Sixteen Panel Fluted body shape, T. Dimmock, England, ca. 1845 (ILLUS.)......................... **800**

Clementson Chusan Pattern Flow Blue Teapot

Euphrates Pattern Flow Blue Teapot

Flow Blue china, Chusan patt., Long Hexa-
gon body shape, J. Clementson,
England, ca. 1840 (ILLUS.)......................... **650**
Flow Blue china, Cleopatra patt., Edward
Walley, England, ca. 1845, 9" h. **725**
Flow Blue china, Euphrates patt., Sixteen
Panel Ridged body shape, W. Ridgway,
England, ca. 1840 (ILLUS., right)................ **500**
Flow Blue china, Flensburg patt., Six Sid-
ed Primary body shape, James Edwards,
England, ca. 1847 (ILLUS, bottom of
page.) **450**

*Flensburg Pat-
tern Flow Blue
Teapot by
Edwards*

Flow Blue china, gaudy floral unknown patt., Tall Eighteen Panel Fluted body shape, B. & B., England, ca. 1830 (ILLUS.).. **750**

Mellor & Venables Floral Gaudy Teapot

Flow Blue china, Floral Gaudy patt., free-hand, Vertical Panel Gothic body shape, Mellor & Venables, England, ca. 1849 (ILLUS.).. **650**

Gaudy Flow Blue Teapot

Flow Blue china, Gaudy patt., Classic Gothic shape, Mellor, Venables & Co., England, ca. 1840s (ILLUS.)................ **750-850**

Formosa Pattern Flow Blue Teapot

Flow Blue china, Formosa patt., Flat Panel Primary body shape, W. Ridgway, England, ca. 1840s (ILLUS.)........................ **600**

Gaudy Grape Flow Blue Teapot

Flow Blue china, Grape patt., free-hand Gaudy Ironstone, Ten Panel Primary shape, unknown maker, England, ca. 1840 (ILLUS.).. **650**

Tall Gaudy Floral Flow Blue Teapot

Heath's Flower Flow Blue Teapot

Meigh Hong Kong Pattern Teapot in the Long Octagon Shape

Flow Blue china, Heath's Flower patt., free-hand, Full Panel Gothic body shape, T. Heath, England, ca. 1850 (ILLUS.).............. **650**

Gothic Decagon Heath's Flower Teapot

Flow Blue china, Heath's Flower patt., free-hand, Gothic Decagon body shape, T. Heath, England, ca. 1850 (ILLUS.).............. **650**

Heath's Flower Six Sided Gothic Teapot

Flow Blue china, Heath's Flower patt., free-hand, Six Sided Gothic (Lantern) body shape, T. Heath, England, ca. 1850 (ILLUS.)... **650**

Flow Blue china, Hong Kong patt., Long Octagon body shape, Charles Meigh, England, ca. 1840 (ILLUS., top of page)...... **850**

Hong Kong Flow Blue Teapot by Meigh

Flow Blue china, Hong Kong patt., Ridged Square body shape, Charles Meigh, England, ca. 1840 (ILLUS.)......................... **750**

Flow Blue china, Hong Kong patt., Twelve Panel Fluted body shape, Charles Meigh, England, ca. 1840 (ILLUS., bottom of page) **950**

Hong Kong Teapot in Vertical Panel Gothic Shape

Flow Blue china, Hong Kong patt., Vertical Panel Gothic body shape, Charles Meigh, England, ca. 1840 (ILLUS.).............. **750**

Fluted Hong Kong Pattern Teapot by Meigh

1840s Indian Jar Pattern Flow Blue Teapot

Flow Blue china, Indian Jar patt., Twelve Panel Ridged body shape, J. & T. Furnival, England, ca. 1843 (ILLUS.) **650**

Indian Flow Blue Pattern Teapot

Flow Blue china, Indian patt., Inverted Diamond body shape, F. & R. Pratt, England, ca. 1850 (ILLUS.).......................... **650**

Early Mayer Oregon Pattern Teapot

Flow Blue china, Oregon patt., Classic Gothic body shape, T. J. & J. Mayer, England, ca. 1845 (ILLUS.).......................... **650**

Early Peking Pattern Flow Blue Teapot

Flow Blue china, Peking patt., Six Sided Primary Belted body shape, unknown maker, England, ca. 1845 (ILLUS.)............. **600**

Flow Blue china, Pelew patt., Grape Octagon body shape, E. Challinor, England, ca. 1840, each (ILLUS. in two size variations, bottom of page).................. **650**

Tall Pastoral Pattern Flow Blue Teapot

Flow Blue china, Pastoral patt., Tall Primary Single Line body shape, J. & T. Furnival, England, ca. 1843 (ILLUS.) **1,200**

Two Pelew Pattern Teapots in the Grape Octagon Shape

Pelew Pattern Teapot in Long Decagon Body Shape

Flow Blue china, Pelew patt., Long Decagon body shape, E. Challinor, England, ca. 1840 (ILLUS.)
.... **1,400**

Early Penang Flow Blue Pattern Teapot - 2 column

Flow Blue china, Penang patt., Twelve Panel Fluted shape, W. Ridgway, England, ca. 1840 (ILLUS.)
.... **750**

Scinde Regular & Child's Size Flow Blue Teapots

Flow Blue china, Scinde patt., child's size, Double Line Primary body shape, J. & G. Alcock, England, ca. 1840 (ILLUS. above left with adult size teapot).......................... **1,200**

Flow Blue china, Scinde patt., Double Line Primary body shape, J. & G. Alcock, England, ca. 1840 (ILLUS. above right with child's teapot, top of page).................... **600**

Flow Blue china, Scinde patt., Eight Panel Pumpkin shape body, J. & G. Alcock, England, ca. 1840 (ILLUS., at right)............. **650**

Flow Blue china, Snowflake patt., Plain Round body shape, unknown maker, England, also found in purple or a combination of blue & purple, ca. 1840, each (ILLUS. of two sizes, bottom of page) **750**

Scinde Pumpkin-shape Teapot

Two Sizes of Flow Blue Snowflake Pattern Teapots

Strawberry Pattern Flow Blue Teapot

Flow Blue china, Strawberry patt., free-hand, Cockscomb Handle body shape, J. Furnival & Co., England, ca. 1850, also found in flow mulberry (ILLUS.).................. **950**

Temple Pattern Flow Blue Teapot

Flow Blue china, Temple patt., Oval body shape, Podmore, Walker, England, ca. 1849 (ILLUS.)... **800**

Temple Pattern Teapot in Varied Shape

Flow Blue china, Temple patt., Twelve Panel Bulbous body shape, Podmore, Walker, England, ca. 1849 (ILLUS.) **750**

Tonquin Pattern Flow Blue Teapot

Flow Blue china, Tonquin patt., Full Panel Gothic body shape, W. Adams, England, ca. 1845 (ILLUS.)......................... **650**
Flow Mulberry china, Athens patt., Full-Paneled Gothic shape, Wm. Adams & Son, ca. 1849.. **300**

Athens Mulberry Teapot by Meigh

Flow Mulberry china, Athens patt., Verti-cal-Paneled Gothic shape, C. Meigh, England, ca. 1845 (ILLUS.)......................... **450**

Bluebell & Leaf Brush Stroke Teapot

Flow Mulberry china, Bluebell & Leaf brush stroke patt., Full-Paneled Gothic shape, unknown maker, England, ca. 1850 (ILLUS.)... **550**

Bochara Flow Mulberry Teapot

Flow Mulberry china, Bochara patt., Pedestaled Gothic shape, James Edwards, England, ca. 1850 (ILLUS.)........................ **325**

Corean Teapot with Cockscomb Handle

Flow Mulberry china, Corean patt., Cockscomb handle, Podmore, Walker & Co., England, ca. 1850 (ILLUS.)......................... **695**

Corean Pattern Gothic Teapot

Flow Mulberry china, Corean patt., Full-Paneled Gothic shape, Podmore, Walker, England, ca. 1850 (ILLUS.) **350**

Cotton Plant Mulberry Teapot

Flow Mulberry china, Cotton Plant patt., cockscomb handle, trimmed in polychrome, J. Furnival, England, ca. 1850 (ILLUS.)... **650**

Dora Baltic Shape Teapot

Flow Mulberry china, Dora patt., Baltic shape, E. Challinor, England, ca. 1850 (ILLUS.)... **500**

Flora Pattern Gothic Shape Teapot

Flow Mulberry china, Flora patt., Classic Gothic shape, T. Walker, England, ca. 1847 (ILLUS.)... **325**
Flow Mulberry china, Flower Vase patt., w/polychrome, Prize Bloom shape, T.J. & J. Mayer, England, ca. 1850 .... **560**
Flow Mulberry china, Jeddo patt., Full-Paneled Gothic shape, Wm. Adams, England, ca. 1849 .... **300**

Lady Peel Mulberry Teapot

Flow Mulberry china, Lady Peel patt., Primary shape, F. Morley, England, ca. 1850 (ILLUS.)... **450**

Lasso Pattern Mulberry Teapot

Flow Mulberry china, Lasso patt., Full-Paneled Gothic shape, W. Bourne, England, ca. 1850 (ILLUS.)........................ **450**
Flow Mulberry china, Marble patt., child's, Vertical Paneled Gothic shape, Mellor Venables, England, ca. 1845 .... **350**

Marble Pattern Gothic Shape Teapot

Flow Mulberry china, Marble patt., Vertical
Paneled Gothic shape, Mellor Venables,
England, ca. 1845 (ILLUS.) **350-400**

Pelew Pumpkin-shaped Teapot

Flow Mulberry china, Pelew patt., pumpkin
shape, Edward Challinor, England, ca.
1850 (ILLUS.) **350**
Flow Mulberry china, Peruvian patt., 16-
Paneled shape, John Wedge Wood,
England, ca. 1850 .... **400**
Flow Mulberry china, Phantasia patt.,
w/polychrome, cockscomb handle, J.
Furnival, England, ca. 1850 .... **700**

Primary Shape Scinde Teapot

Flow Mulberry china, Scinde patt., Primary
shape, T. Walker, England, ca. 1847
(ILLUS.) **450**
Flow Mulberry china, Shapoo patt., Prima-
ry shape, T. & R. Boote, England, ca.
1850 .... **450**
Flow Mulberry china, Washington Vase
patt., Classic Gothic shape, Podmore,
Walker, & Co., England, ca. 1850, each
(ILLUS. of two sizes, bottom of page) ... **350-450**

Washington Vase Teapots in Two Similar Sizes

Pink Historical Staffordshire Teapot

Historical Staffordshire, Fulton's Steamboat on the Hudson - Ship Cadmus, the squatty bulbous body w/a serpentine spout & C-scroll handle, white ground transfer-printed in rusty pink w/a scene on each side, the low domed cover & button finial w/further transfer scenes, pink lustre band trim on the rim, handle & spout, Staffordshire, England, ca. 1830-50, restoration to the base, end of spout & cover, 6" h. (ILLUS.) **303**

Small Early Leeds Creamware Teapot

Leeds creamware, spherical body w/fitted cover w/blossom finial, entwined strap handle & serpentine spout, translucent ochre lead glaze decorated w/an overall black sponged decoration, Leeds, England, ca. 1780, restored spout, handle & cover rim, 3 1/2" h. (ILLUS.) **460**

Spatterware, Peafowl patt., footed squatty bulbous body tapering to a flaring rolled neck, long shaped spout & C-scroll handle, low domed cover w/button finial, a light green spatter band around the shoulder above a large h.p. blue, yellow, red & black peafowl, England, ca. 1830, 6" h. (lid slightly undersized & different green, small flake on inner flange) **1,840**

Spatterware, Rainbow patt., flat-bottomed slightly tapering bulbous body w/an incurved shoulder tapering to a flat rim, long shaped spout & C-scroll handle, low domed cover w/button finial, decorated w/green spatter around the shoulder & vertical alternating stripes of red & green spatter around the body, England, ca. 1830, 7" h. (repaired spout & cover, additional flaking on cover) **633**

Rare Yellow Spatterware Teapot

Spatterware, Thistle patt., a flared base tapering to a wide bulbous ovoid body tapering to a cylindrical neck w/flat rim, serpentine spout & C-form handle, low domed cover w/button finial, bright yellow spatter ground centered by a large red & green thistle design, end of spout damaged, English-made, ca. 1830, 7" h. (ILLUS.).. **4,140**

Spatterware, Thumbprint patt., footed wide paneled body w/a squatty bulbous lower section below sides tapering to a flared rim, shaped spout & pointed scroll handle, domed cover w/pagoda finial, dark blue spatter background w/large black spatter overall thumbprints, England, ca. 1825-30, 7 1/2" h. (light overall stains w/a repaired spout & cover)................................ **690**

Staffordshire creamware, lead-glazed, spherical body molded overall w/fruiting vines under a mottled brown & grey glaze, long angular spout & twisted branch loop handle, fitted cover w/arched twig handle, England, late 18th c., 3 3/4" h. (shallow rim chips on cover & pot, tip of spout restored) **2,585**

Early Teapot with Mottled Glaze

Staffordshire creamware, spherical body molded overall w/fruiting vines, a crab-stock spout & handle, cover w/arched twig handle, lead-glazed overall in mottled dark brown & grey, England, late 18th c., shallow rim chips on cover & body, spout tip restored, 3 3/4" h. (ILLUS.).. **2,585**

Small Early Staffordshire Teapot

Staffordshire creamware, squatty spherical body raised on four lion mask & paw feet, low domed cover w/button finial, molded crabstock handle & spout, lead-glazed overall in mottled dark brown, England, ca. 1775, repair to one foot & spout, damage to finial & inner cover collar, 4" h. (ILLUS.) 374

Rare Early Staffordshire Paneled Teapot

Staffordshire creamware, the hexagonal body molded in each panel w/Chinese figures, low domed cover w/pointed knob finial, leaf-molded green spout & handle, the body lead-glazed in mottled dark & light brown, England, ca. 1765, restoration to top rim, slight nick at foot rim, 5" h. (ILLUS.)... 5,463

Staffordshire pottery, black-glazed, modeled as a waisted cylindrical tree stump w/a branch-form handle & shaped spout, flat cover w/arched twig handle, the sides molded in relief as fruiting grapevines, England, early 19th c., 4 3/4" h. (slight nicks on cover & spout, chips on interior rim of pot).. 1,978

Staffordshire pottery, black-glazed, spherical body raised on three small molded paw feet, a short small cylindrical neck w/domed cover w/a figural bird finial, a shaped crabstock spout & loop handle, England, ca. 1775, 5 1/4" h. (restored finial, chips to cover rim, feet & edge of spout) 1,645

Staffordshire pottery, black-glazed, squatty bulbous body raised on three short molded paw feet, crabstock loop handle & shaped spout, the sides molded w/vines of berries & leaves, England, ca. 1770, 4 3/4" h. (chips on cover, pot collar, tip of spout & feet)...................................... 999

Staffordshire pottery, black-glazed, upright paneled oval shape w/a tapering shoulder & flat rim, long shaped spout & shaped C-scroll handle, flattened domed hinged cover w/foliate border & multi-

knob finial, the sides molded in relief w/classical figures within urn-framed columns, England, early 19th c., 6 1/2" h. (hairline in handle, restored chip on spout)... 382

Staffordshire Transfer Wares, dark blue central transfer of a man fishing w/a manor house in background, surrounded by floral rosette design, molded flower finial, ca. 1830, 7 1/2" h. 468

Cinquefoil Panelled Grape Teapot

Tea Leaf China variant, Cinquefoil patt., Panelled Grape shape, J. Furnival (ILLUS.).. 275

Tea Leaf China variant, Morning Glory patt., Portland shape, Elsmore & Forster..... 200

Tea Leaf China variant, Pomegranate patt., Niagara shape, E. Walley (professional lid edge repair)................................... 200

Reverse Teaberry Portland Teapot

Tea Leaf China variant, Reverse Teaberry patt., Portland shape, Elsmore & Forster (ILLUS.)... 375

Tea Leaf China variant, Teaberry patt., New York shape, Clementson (small inside rim chip).. **225**

Wedgwood Decorated Basalt Teapot

Wedgwood, Black Basalt Ware, balusterform body tapering to a flat rim w/low domed cover & button knob, serpentine spout & C-form handle, the black ground h.p. overall w/large blossoms & leaves in shades of brick red, white & green, Josiah Wedgwood, late 18th - early 19th c., 6 3/4" h. (ILLUS.)..................... **1,495**

Wedgwood, Black Basalt Ware, wide baluster-form body w/flat rim & low domed cover w/knob finial, shaped spout & C-scroll handle, black ground applied w/tall deep red Rosso Antico acanthus leaves & bellflowers around the sides, radiating applied leaves around the cover, impressed mark of Josiah Wedgwood, England, early 19th c., 7 1/4" h. (rim nick)........ **743**

Wedgwood, Caneware, footed wide squatty body w/a low domed cover w/button finial, short gently arched spout & arched C-scroll handle, smear-glazed & applied around the middle w/a wide band of tight scrolls & leaftips in green, radiating spearpoints applied around cover, impressed mark of Josiah Wedgwood, England, 19th c., 4" h. (faint spider crack in base)... **2,432**

Wedgwood, "Rosso Antico" Ware, squatty rounded shape w/nearly straight spout, flaring flanged front top rim & high angled handle, dark red ground applied w/Oriental-style white prunus blossoms & branches in relief, impressed mark of Josiah Wedgwood, England, early 19th c., 8 5/8" l. (nick to edge of spout) **1,175**

Wedgwood, "Rosso Antico" Ware, squatty rounded shape w/short slightly curved spout & high squared handle, dark red ground applied w/black bands of stylized Egyptian motifs & hieroglyphs, the slightly domed cover w/radiating fluting & a figural crocodile finial, impressed mark for Josiah Wedgwood, England, early 19th c., 4 1/2" h. (nicks to cover rim, restoration to finial, spout lip & handle, cover slightly misfit)... **881**

White ironstone china, Full Panel Gothic shape, by Jacob Furnival, England, ca. 1840s (ILLUS., top next column).......... **325-350**

Early Full Panel Gothic Shape Teapot

Early Gothic White Ironstone Teapot

White ironstone china, Gothic shape, by T. & R. Boote, England, ca. 1847 (ILLUS.)... **300-325**

Inverted Diamond Ironstone Teapot

White ironstone china, Inverted Diamond shape, by T. J. & J. Mayer, England, ca. 1840s (ILLUS.)..................................... **250-300**

Edwards Pedestaled Gothic Teapot

White ironstone china, Pedestaled Gothic shape, by James Edwards, England, ca. 1845 (ILLUS.)....................................... **300-325**

Ironstone Single Line Primary Teapot

White ironstone china, Single Line Primary shape, by E. Challinor, T. J. & J. Mayer & others, England, ca. 1845 (ILLUS.) ... **225-250**

Chinoiserie Teapot with Swan Finial

Willow Ware, Blue Willow, Chinoiserie style, diamond shaped body w/beveled corners on molded base, tapering slightly to scalloped neck, slightly domed cover tapering slightly to figural swan finial, C-form handle w/thumbrest, straight spout, unmarked, England, ca. 1800 (ILLUS.)...... **350-375**

Unmarked Chinoiserie Teapot

Willow Ware, Blue Willow, Chinoiserie style, ovoid body w/overall narrow ribbing, a short neck & domed ribbed cover tapering to the flat top w/pointed finial, C-scroll handle, slightly serpentine spout, embellished w/gold decoration on rim, spout & finial, unmarked, England, ca. 1800 (ILLUS.)....................................... **250-275**

Unmarked Blue Willow Teapot

Willow Ware, Blue Willow, low ribbed cylindrical body on short foot, tapering shoulder, short cylindrical neck w/scalloped edge, ribbed, slightly domed cover w/flower-form finial, D-form handle, serpentine spout, unmarked, England, ca. 1820 (ILLUS.)....................................... **250-275**

Miles Mason Blue Willow Teapot

Willow Ware, Blue Willow, squatty ovoid body tapering in at shoulder to short neck, C-scroll handle, slightly serpentine spout, tapering cover w/disk finial, embellished w/silver line decoration & band of silver grapevine decoration at shoulder & on cover, Miles Mason, England, ca. 1807-13 (ILLUS.) **300-350**

Yellow-Glazed Earthenware, ovoid body w/flared rim, black transfer of a woman playing piano or harpsichord accompanied by two children playing triangle & tambourine, black stripes, 5 1/8" h. (short rim hairline & lid repairs) **495**

Pottery & Earthenware - 1850-1950

Abingdon Pottery Daisy Pattern Teapot

Abingdon Pottery, Daisy patt., white body w/blue daisy-shaped cover, also found w/a yellow daisy cover, each (ILLUS. of teapot with blue cover) **$65**

Alcock, Lindley & Bloore Teapot

Alcock, Lindley & Bloore, Ltd., squatty bulbous body w/inset domed cover w/knob finial, angled serpentine spout, C-form handle, dark brown w/pale yellow upper band trimmed w/pale blue stripes, England, ca. 1920-40 (ILLUS.) **35**

Alliance Vitrified China Company Teapot

Alliance Vitrified China Co., footed squared body w/shoulder centering a short wide neck & domed cover w/pointed knob finial, serpentine spout, angled handle, printed w/a color floral bouquet, Alliance, Ohio, ca. 1929 (ILLUS.) **45**

Amphora Teapot with Mackintosh Rose

Amphora-Teplitz, bulbous nearly spherical body tapering to a low angled neck, a short angled shoulder spout & a triple-loop handle down the side, the side centered by a large almond-shaped reserve in dark blue decorated w/the Mackintosh Rose design flanked by a wide dark blue medial band w/small pink blossoms on stems, the upper & lower band in white w/mottled blue & scattered small yellow flowerheads, the band & scattered flowerheads continuing around the sides, impressed "Austria - Amphora" in ovals w/a crown, impressed "3964,44," also w/a decorator's mark, ca. 1900-15, 6 1/4" h. (ILLUS.) **450**

Boldly Striped Amphora Teapot

Amphora-Teplitz, bulbous ovoid body tapering to a small angled rim, short shoulder spout & triple loop side handle, boldly painted w/alternating stripes of graduating overlapping blue circles & white stripes w/bands of brown scrolls centered by small dark blue diamonds, black rim, spout & handle, impressed "Austria - Amphora" in ovals w/crown & "Imperial Amphora" in a circle, impressed numbers "3975,46 - G," 1900-15, 6" h. (ILLUS.) **250**

Colorful Amphora Florina Series Teapot

Amphora-Teplitz, Florina Series, spherical body w/a short shoulder spout & simple C-form handle, painted w/a bold design of geometric stylized flowers & leaves w/lenticular frits on both the front & back, in shades of dark rose pink, dark blue & black on a mottled mustard yellow ground, impressed on base "Imperial Amphora" in a circle & "Austria - Amphora" in ovals w/crown & impressed numbers "122212,64," 1900-15, 5 1/2" h. (ILLUS.).. **695**

Amphora King Tut Series Teapot

Amphora-Teplitz, King Tut Series, a footed tall ovoid body tapering to a flat mouth, an arched handle from rim of mouth to shoulder & short angled shoulder spout w/an arched strap to the rim, the sides in lavender blue molded & decorated in the center w/a large winged globe in cobalt blue, green & yellow enclosed by two undulating long blue snakes, other Egyptian symbols scattered around the sides & in rim & base bands, the back further decorated w/a portrait of a bearded Egyptian w/a braided tail at the top of his head & more symbols, marked on base "Made in Czecho-Slovakia - Amphora" in double ovals, impressed numbers "12203," a Roman numeral "I" & an "M" in under-

glaze black & a "J" in underglaze blue, ca. 1918-1939, 8 1/2" h. (ILLUS.) **195**

Amphora King Tut Teapot with Lady

Amphora-Teplitz, King Tut Series, flared foot & ovoid body tapering to a flat mouth, C-form handle from rim to shoulder, angled short shoulder spout w/arched brace to rim, incised & decorated on one side w/standing woman wearing a long blue robe w/a diadem on her head, holding a long staff in one arm & a small jug in the other hand, against a pebbled rose red ground w/stylized blue flowerheads, white & blue zigzag foot band, the reverse side decorated w/squares in a rectangle w/a larger flower matching the two on the other side, marked "Made in Czech-Slovakia - Amphora" in double inked ovals, impressed numbers "12315 - 5" & "1661" painted in underglaze, ca. 1918-39, 8 1/4" h. (ILLUS.) **195**

Amphora Russian Folk Art Teapot

Amphora-Teplitz, Russian Folk Art Series, tall ovoid form w/flared foot & flat rim, arched C-form handle from rim to shoulder, short angled shoulder spout w/an arched brace to the rim, decorated on center front w/a large stylized bust portrait of a Russian cleric w/black beard & brown & blue hat, the portrait enclosed by a ring of blue stars & blue dots w/other bands of dots & teardrops about the top & base, all against a tan ground, the reverse w/a design of multiple triangles enclosed w/a ring of stars, impressed "Austria - Amphora" in ovals & "11892,47 - G" plus a crown, ca. 1907-08, 8 1/4" h. (ILLUS.)... **295**

Blue & Cream Amphora Teapot

Amphora-Teplitz, wide squatty bulbous body tapering sharply to a small cylindrical neck bulbed at the top w/an arched handle from the back of the neck to the shoulder & a double-arch bracket from

the neck to the tip of the long angled straight spout, the center of the side w/a large almond-shaped reserve w/a dark blue ground decorated w/three stylized Macintosh Roses & flanked by a dark blue band continuing up the spout that is decorated w/a dark blue band decorated w/small yellow flower clusters, neck in blue w/matching florals, blue handle & brackets, the background of the body in creamy mottled white ground decorated w/scattered small yellow blossoms, similar to designs by Paul Dachsel, ca. 1906-07, impressed "Austria" & "Amphora" in ovals & a crown, impressed numbers "3974," overall 8" h. (ILLUS.) **695**

Banko Ware Figural Bird Teapot

Banko Ware, figural, model of a peacock, the cover in the top of the back, brightly enameled, beige clay, impressed "Made in Japan" mark, ca. 1920, 6 1/2" l., 4 1/2" h. (ILLUS.) **200**

Colorful Elephant & Rider Banko Teapot

Banko Ware, figural, model of an elephant w/a seated rider atop the cover, grey clay w/brightly enameled blanket on the back, unmarked, Japan, pictured in a dated 1916 Vantine's catalog, 6" l., 6" h. (ILLUS.).. **200**

Banko Teapot with Cranes & Flowers

Banko Teapot with Grapes & Birds

Rare Banko Cottage-shaped Teapot

Banko Ware, figural, modeled as a thatched roof cottage, top of roof forming the cover, applied in relief w/flowers, trimmed w/bright enamels on the grey clay ground, fine woven brass wire bail handle, two impressed signatures on the base, Japan, ca. 1900, 5 1/2" l., 3 1/2" h. (ILLUS.).. **400**

Banko Ware, grayware, squatty bulbous body w/short spout, low domed cover w/twisted applied handle w/further handles flanking the wide mouth, decorated overall w/hand-applied grapes & leaves & brightly enameled w/birds & flowers, impressed artist's signature, Japan, ca. 1900, 5" l., 3 1/2" h. (ILLUS.) **150**

Banko "1000 Treasures" Teapot

Banko Ware, grayware, squatty bulbous body applied w/brightly enameled "1000 Treasures" design in high relief, twisted brown & grey clay rope w/bows applied around the rim & flaring crimped neck, inset cover w/knob finial, includes Banko tea infuser inside, marked w/impressed round Banko signature, Japan, ca. 1900, 4 1/2" l., 4" h. (ILLUS.) **135**

Banko Ware, grayware, squatty bulbous body enameled w/flying cranes & flowers, twisted brown & grey clay applied handle & rope around the crimped flaring neck, inset cover w/knob finial, unsigned, Japan, ca. 1900, 4 1/2" l., 3" h. (ILLUS., top next column).. **50**

Large "Marquetry" Banko Teapot

Banko Ware, marquetry-style, tapestry finish, large spherical body w/a wide flat mouth, woven bamboo swing bail handle, the shoulder trimmed w/large applied green enameled leaves, the body composed of small squares of multicolored clay pressed together to form a checkerboard design, the clays being tinted, not painted on the surface, apparently unmarked, Japan, ca. 1900, 6" l., 5" h. (ILLUS.).. **140**

Small Banko "Marquetry" Teapot

Banko Ware, marquetry-style, tapestry finish, squatty bulbous body w/a wide flared mouth w/an applied tan rope tied in bows under the handle holds, fine braided wire bail handle, the body composed of small squares of multicolored clay pressed together to form a checkerboard design, the clays being tinted, not painted on the surface, Japan, ca. 1900, 4" l., 3" h. (ILLUS.).. **100**

Miniature Swirled Clay Banko Teapot

Banko Ware, miniature, brown & tan swirled clay, hand-formed squatty bulbous body w/an applied rope & bows below the crimped flaring rim, inset cover w/knob finial, enameled floral decoration on the sides, original woven rattan bail handle, Japan, ca. 1900, 3 1/2" l., 2 1/2" h. (ILLUS.) **60**

Banko Teapot with Swirled Clays

Banko Ware, swirled blue & grey clay, tapestry finish, nearly spherical body w/a wide flat mouth, inset domed cover w/applied twig & flower finial, the sides applied w/enameled flowers & branches, wrapped rattan bail handle, marked "Made in Japan," ca. 1920s, 4 1/2" l., 3 1/2" h. (ILLUS.) **60**
Bauer Pottery, Ring-Ware patt., yellow, 2-cup size.. **125**
Bauer Pottery, Ring-Ware patt., yellow, 6-cup size... **100-150**
Bauer Pottery, Ring-Ware patt., orangish red, 2-cup size **125**

Beswick Ware Sairey Gamp Teapot

Beswick Ware, figural Sairey Gamp model, designed by Mr. Watkin, introduced in 1939 (ILLUS.)... **300**
Blue Ridge Dinnerwares, Ball shape, Bluebelle Bouquet patt. **225**

Blue Ridge Adoration Pattern Teapot

Blue Ridge Pottery, Ball shape, Adoration patt., 6 3/4" h. (ILLUS.) **145**

Blue Ridge Cherry Pattern Teapot

Blue Ridge Pottery, Colonial shape, Cherry patt., 8 3/4" h. (ILLUS.) **165**

Blue & White Pottery Teapot

Blue & White Pottery, Swirl patt., spherical body w/row of relief-molded knobs around the shoulder, inset cover w/knob finial, swan's-neck spout, shoulder loop brackets for wire bail handle w/turned wood grip, blue 6" d., 6" h. (ILLUS.) .... **800+**

Floral-decorated American Ironstone Teapot

Brunt (Wm.) & Son, tall ovoid ironstone body w/serpentine spout, C-form handle & domed cover w/arched finial, decorated w/delicate printed florals, East Liverpool, Ohio, 1878-92 (ILLUS.) **65**
Buffalo Pottery, tea ball-type w/built-in tea ball, Argyle patt., blue & white, 1914 .... **300**
Buffalo Pottery, Blue Willow patt. (1905-1916), square, 2 pts., 5 1/2 oz. **350**
Buffalo Pottery, Blue Willow patt. (1905-1916), individual size, 12 oz. **300**

Burford Brothers Decorated Teapot

Burford Brothers, bulbous ovoid ironstone body w/a wide cylindrical neck, embossed w/a long trailing floral vine, domed cover w/arched finial, upright spout, C-form handle, decorated w/gold lustre bands, East Liverpool, Ohio, ca. 1890s (ILLUS.)... **70**

Carr China Company Decorated Teapot

Carr China Company, slightly tapering cylindrical body w/flat rim, thick short spout, angled handle, printed band of scrolls & flowers around the rim, Grafton, West Virginia, 1916-1952 (ILLUS.) **25**

Cartwright Teapot with Pansies

Cartwright Brothers, footed bulbous nearly spherical body w/molded rim w/shoulder rings for wire bail handle w/wooden grip, domed cover w/button final, upright spout, decorated w/large pansies & leaves, East Liverpool, Ohio, late 19th - early 20th c. (ILLUS.) **45**

Moss Rose Teapot by Cartwright Bros.

Cartwright Brothers, Moss Rose patt., footed ovoid body w/domed cover & bar finial, East Liverpool, Ohio, late 19th c. (ILLUS.).. **30**
Catalina Island Pottery, rope edge................. **265**

Cliftwood Art Potteries Pink Teapot

Cliftwood Art Potteries, footed urn-shaped fluted body w/a tapering ringed neck &

flattened cover w/large disk finial, serpentine spout, C-scroll handle, Matte Old Rose glaze, Cliftwood Art Potteries, Morton, Illinois, 1920-40, 8-cup size (ILLUS.) . **40-50**

Cliftwood Art Potteries Green Teapot

Cliftwood Art Potteries, footed urn-shaped fluted body w/a tapering ringed neck & flattened cover w/large disk finial, serpentine spout, C-scroll handle, yellowware w/glossy thin Apple Green glaze, Cliftwood Art Potteries, Morton, Illinois, 1920-40, 8-cup size (ILLUS.).................... **40-50**

Cliftwood Teapot and Trivet

Cliftwood Art Potteries, nearly spherical teapot w/inset cover w/arched handle, serpentine spout, C-form handle, overall dark bluish mulberry drip glaze, on a matching round three-toed trivet, Cliftwood Art Potteries, Morton, Illinois, 1920-40, 8-cup size, 2 pcs. (ILLUS.)................ **80-100**
Coors Pottery, Rosebud patt., orange, 2-cup.. **275**
Coors Pottery, thermo-porcelain, Open Window decal, 5-cup.................................... **175**
Coors Pottery, Rosebud patt., blue, 6-cup...... **225**

Colorful Czechoslovakian Pottery Teapot

Czechoslovakian pottery, nearly spherical body w/low domed cover & large knob finial, ring handle & angled spout, Art Deco design w/brightly enameled fruits & leaves on a mottled grey & white background, marked "Made in Czechoslovakia," ca. 1930, 10 1/2" l., 6 1/2" h. (ILLUS., bottom previous page)... **50**

Doulton-Lambeth Faience Teapot

Colorful Czech Carnival Pattern Teapot

Czechoslovakian pottery, spherical body, Carnival patt., overall colorful confetti design, early 1930s (ILLUS.)............................. **40**

Doulton & Company catalog page - Color illustrations of a variety of earthenware teapots made in the Burslem factory in the 1880s and 1890s (ILLUS., on page 101)..

Doulton-Lambeth Ware, faience, rounded cylindrical body w/long serpentine spout, C-scroll handle & metal rim & hinged cover, stylized floral decoration, ca. 1900 (ILLUS., next column).................................... **1,000**

Doulton-Lambeth Ware, figural, crouching camel w/a heavy load, the Arab driver pulling from behind & forming the handle, ruby glaze, designed by the Moore Brothers, apparently made by Doulton, ca. 1877 (ILLUS., bottom of page)................. **5,000**

Rare Doulton Marqueterie Ware Teapot

Doulton-Lambeth Ware, Marqueterie Ware, diamond lattice & swirl overall design, ca. 1890 (ILLUS.)....................... **4,000**

Early Rare Figural Cameo Teapot

DOULTON & CO.   54

Pekin, a 2584   Bail, b 838   Ceylon, b 837

Ceylon, a 2957   Pekin, a 6617   Tonquin, a 7324

Ceylon, a 710   Pekin, a 6387   Fluted, a 7322

Pekin, a 6902   Marquis, a 7132   Fluted, a 7484

Ball, Ivory,   Marquis, White,   Pekin, a 7459
Dark Blue, Nipon   Emerald Narcissus and Border

Variety of earthenware teapots made in the Burslem factory in the 1880s and 1890s

Rare Doulton-Lambeth Marqueterie Teapot with Scene

Doulton-Lambeth Ware, Marqueterie Ware, low rectangular shape w/straight spout & angled loop handle, large design reserve w/scene of a child against a swirled background, painted by Ada Dennis, ca. 1893 (ILLUS.) **5,000**

Early Doulton-Lambeth Stoneware Teapot with Swimming Fish Design

Doulton-Lambeth Ware, stoneware, molded swimming fish decoration around the body, ca. 1895 (ILLUS.) **2,000**

Doulton-Lambeth Ware, stoneware, overall bold foliate decoration, ca. 1890 (ILLUS., next column) **1,500**

Doulton-Lambeth Ware, stoneware, spherical body molded in relief w/a serpentine dragon design, ca. 1895 (ILLUS., top next page) **1,000**

Doulton-Lambeth Stoneware Teapot

Doulton-Lambeth Dragon Design Teapot

Doulton-Lambeth Teapot with Scene

Doulton-Lambeth Ware, stoneware, tapering cylindrical body w/flaring rim, angled spout, large rectangular panel w/scene of Bladud, the founder of the City of Bath, made for R.S. Carey, Bath, ca. 1894 (ILLUS.) **750**

American Dresden Pottery Works Teapot

Dresden Pottery Works (Potter's Co-Operative), tapering cylindrical body w/ribbed panels, long spout, double-C-scroll handle, domed cover w/loop finial, printed w/delicate floral vines & gold trim, East Liverpool, Ohio, ca. 1900 (ILLUS.) **45**

Ellgreave Teapot with Wild Roses

Ellgreave Pottery Co., footed squatty bulbous body w/a wide flat rim, domed cover w/knob finial, curved spout & C-scroll handle, decorated w/large wild rose blossoms & leaves, England (ILLUS.) **40**

Ellgreave Pottery Teapot with Bird Decor

Ellgreave Pottery Co., footed wide squatty body tapering sharply to a slightly lobed rim & domed cover w/loop finial, serpentine spout & C-scroll handle, decorated w/an exotic bird in a flowering tree, England (ILLUS., previous page) **40**

World War II Fund-raising Teapot

English earthenware, footed cylindrical body w/a rounded shoulder to a low flat rim, black background h.p. w/a pale blue ribbon & bow & pastel colored flowers, cover marked "For England and Democracy," the bottom stamped "Escorted to the United States by the Royal Navy," made in England & sold in the U.S. to help raise money for the war effort, ca. 1940 (ILLUS.).................................. **45**

English Phoenix Bird Pattern Teapot

English earthenware, Phoenix Bird patt., bulbous tapering paneled body w/a flared rim, pointed angled handle, long serpentine spout, pyramidal cover w/square pointed finial, marked w/a crown above "Myott Son & Co. - England - Satsuma," ca. 1930s, 8 3/8" l., 5 3/4" h. (ILLUS.).. **65**

"Roman Chariot" Teapot

English earthenware, "Roman Chariot" patt., squatty ovoid body w/almost flat shoulder, short neck, slightly tapered lid w/knob finial, angled handle, serpentine spout, black body decorated w/horizontal bands of dots & geometric designs in beige, red, white & black, marked "K&B England," ca. 1930s, 5" h. (ILLUS.) **35**

Etruria Pottery Moss Rose Teapot

Etruria Pottery Co. (Ott & Brewer), Moss Rose patt., squatty bulbous lightly ribbed tapering ironstone body w/serpentine spout & pointed C-scroll handle, domed cover w/arched finial, Trenton, New Jersey, ca. 1880s (ILLUS.) **65**

Fiesta Teapot in Cobalt Blue

Fiesta Ware, spherical body on tapering foot, domed lid w/finial, C-form handle, short spout, horizontal ribbing on shoulder, cobalt blue, marked "HLG USA," Homer Laughlin China Company, 7" h. (ILLUS.).. **125**

Fiesta Ware, cobalt blue, medium size (6 cup), Homer Laughlin China Co.................. **225**

Fiesta Ware, forest green, medium size (6 cup), Homer Laughlin China Co.................. **325**

Fiesta Ware, grey, medium size (6 cup), Homer Laughlin China Co............................ **325**

Fiesta Ware, ivory, medium size (6 cup), Homer Laughlin China Co............................ **225**

Fiesta Ware, light green, medium size (6 cup), Homer Laughlin China Co............ **150-175**

Fiesta Ware, red, medium size (6 cup), Homer Laughlin China Co............................ **225**

Fiesta Ware, turquoise, medium size (6 cup), Homer Laughlin China Co.................. **165**

Fiesta Ware, yellow, medium size (6 cup), Homer Laughlin China Co.................. **155-160**

New Wharf Pottery Lancaster Pattern Teapot

Fiesta Ware, cobalt blue, large size (8 cup),
Homer Laughlin China Co............................ **250**
Fiesta Ware, ivory, large size (8 cup), Hom-
er Laughlin China Co. **250**
Fiesta Ware, light green, large size (8 cup),
Homer Laughlin China Co............................ **210**
Fiesta Ware, medium green, medium size,
1950s, Homer Laughlin China Co. .... **1,200+**
Fiesta Ware, red, large size (8 cup), Homer
Laughlin China Co....................................... **250**
Fiesta Ware, turquoise, large size (8 cup),
Homer Laughlin China Co............................ **250**
Fiesta Ware, yellow, large size (8 cup),
Homer Laughlin China Co............................ **210**
Flow Blue china, Argyle patt., Myott, Son &
Co., England, ca. 1898, 6" h. **300**
Flow Blue china, Baltic patt., W.H. Grindley
& Company, England, ca. 1891,
5 1/2" h... **575**
Flow Blue china, Belmont patt., Alfred
Meakin, England, ca. 1891, 8 1/2" handle
to spout, 6" h. **300**
Flow Blue china, Bryonia patt., Paul Utzsh-
neider & Co., German, ca. 1891 .... **400**
Flow Blue china, Coburg patt., John Ed-
wards, England, ca. 1860......................... **1,025**
Flow Blue china, Countess patt., W.H.
Grindley & Co., England, ca. 1891,
6 1/2" h.. **375**
Flow Blue china, Fairy Villas I patt., William
Adams & Sons, England, ca. 1891,
6 1/2" h.. **650**
Flow Blue china, Lancaster patt., squatty
bulbous unnamed body shape, New
Wharf Pottery, England, ca. 1891
(ILLUS., top of page)................................... **500**

Manhattan Pattern Teapot by Alcock

Flow Blue china, Manhattan patt., footed
deeply waisted ruffled unnamed body
shape, Henry Alcock, England, ca. 1900
(ILLUS.)... **450**

Manhattan Flow Blue Teapot

Flow Blue china, Manhattan patt., unnamed body shape, Henry Alcock,

Non Pareil Flow Blue Teapot

England, ca. 1900 (ILLUS., previous page) **450**

Marcheil Neil Flow Blue Teapot

Flow Blue china, Marcheil Neil patt., deeply waisted & lobed unnamed body shape, W.H. Grindley, England, ca. 1895 (ILLUS.) **450**

Flow Blue china, Mentone patt., embossed squatty bulbous body, Johnson Bros., England, ca. 1900 (ILLUS., next column) **150**

Flow Blue china, Non Pareil patt., oblong boat-shaped body, Burgess & Leigh, England, ca. 1891 (ILLUS., top of page) **650**

Mentone Flow Blue Teapot

Flow Blue Osborne Teapot

Flow Blue china, Osborne patt., Ridgways, England, ca. 1905, 10" w. from spout to handle, 7 1/2" h. (ILLUS.) **400**

Quartered Rose and Ring 'O Hearts Blue-trimmed Teapots

Flow Blue china, Quartered Rose body shape w/blue sprigs, copper lustre bands & red & blue pinstripes, J. Furnival, England, ca. 1853 (ILLUS. left with Ring 'O Hearts teapot) **350**

Flow Blue china, Ring 'O Hearts body shape w/blue sprigs, copper lustre bands & red & blue pinstripes, Livesley & Powell, England, ca. 1857 (ILLUS. right with Quartered Rose teapot) **350**

Squatty Shanghai Pattern Flow Blue Teapot

Flow Blue china, Shanghai patt., footed wide squat body, W.H. Grindley, ca. 1891 (ILLUS.) **450**

Alcock Touraine Pattern Flow Blue Teapot

Shanghai Flow Blue Demitasse Teapot

Flow Blue china, Shanghai patt., tall ovoid demitasse pot, W.H. Grindley, ca. 1891 (ILLUS.).. **450**

Flow Blue china, Touraine patt., fluted urn-form unnamed body shape, Henry Alcock, England, ca. 1898 (ILLUS., top of page)... **750**

Flow Blue china, Touraine patt., fluted urn-form unnamed body shape, modern reproduction by the Stanley Potteries, England.. **75**

Vermont Pattern Flow Blue Teapot

Flow Blue china, Vermont patt., ribbed pear-shaped unnamed body, Burgess and Leigh, England, ca. 1895 (ILLUS.)........ **450**

Flow Blue china, Willow patt., oval tankard shape, Keeling & Co., England, ca. 1886 (ILLUS., top next page).............................. **450**

Franciscan Ware, Apple patt., 6 3/4" h. **125**

Franciscan Ware, Arden patt. **95**

Franciscan Ware, Desert Rose patt., 6 1/2" h.. **95**

Franciscan Ware, individual size, Desert Rose patt., 6 1/4" h. **295**

Franciscan Ware, Ivy patt., green rim band, 5 1/2" h... **225**

Keeling & Co. Willow Pattern Teapot

Frankoma Wagon Wheel Pattern Teapot

Frankoma Pottery, Wagon Wheel patt., Desert Gold glaze, Sapulpa, Oklahoma, ca. 1942 (ILLUS.)......................... **25**
Frankoma Pottery, Wagon Wheel patt., Model No. 94j, Desert Gold glaze, Ada clay, 2 cup.. **40**

Dark Green & Gold Fraunfelter Teapot

Fraunfelter China Company, flared base & flaring ovoid body & rounded shoulder tapering to a flat rim, serpentine gold spout & C-form handle, pyramidal cover w/gold button finial, deep green background w/a printed gold band of swags & heart-shaped loops around the shoulder, Model No. 370, marked on the unglazed base, Fraunfelter China Company, Zanesville, Ohio, ca. 1930s, 6 1/2" h. (ILLUS.)... **145**

Fraunfelter China Company Teapot

Fraunfelter China Company, footed wide cylindrical body w/curved shoulder to the metal rim & hinged domed metal cover, C-scroll handle & serpentine spout, stylized exotic bird & scrolls design in black, red & blue, decorated by the Royal Rochester Company, ca. 1930s (ILLUS.).......... **70-75**

W.S. George China Company Teapot

George (W.S.) China Company, squatty bulbous body w/large C-form handle & short spout, disk cover w/disk finial, pale blue glaze, late 1930s - early 1940s (ILLUS.)... **35-40**

American French China Company Teapot

French China Company, footed wide ribbed baluster-form earthenware body w/ruffled rim, domed cover w/loop finial, serpentine spout & fancy C-scroll handle, printed w/a delicate flower cluster, East Liverpool, Ohio, ca. 1900 (ILLUS.)................ **75**

Bolero Pattern W.S. George Teapot

George (W.S.) Pottery Co., Bolero patt., footed spherical ribbed body w/conforming cover w/pointed finial, angled short spout & C-form handle, decorated w/a printed scene of a quaint cottage in trees, ca. 1930 (ILLUS.)............................... **30**

Colorful Tall French Faience Teapot

French faience, a tall tapering octagonal body raised on small paw feet, C-scroll handle & tall angular spout, domed octagonal cover w/a figural reclining dog finial, decorated in bright colors of dark blue, rust red, yellow, green & light blue in a Dutch Delft-influenced design of stylized flowers & lattice panels, a central reserve w/a stylized basket of flowers above a ring w/a French fleur-de-lis, unknown maker, 11" h. (ILLUS.)..................... **300**

W.S. George Teapot with Windmill Scene

George (W.S.) Pottery Co., squatty bulbous body w/a short angled shoulder spout, C-form handle & cover w/a wide disk finial, decorated w/a printed scene of a Dutch windmill, East Palestine, Ohio, early 20th c. (ILLUS.)..................................... **25**

Chrome-cased German Vitreous China Teapot

Schramberger Majolica Teapot

German earthenware, bulbous body w/conical cover & black knob finial, black serpentine spout & C-form handle, the body brightly painted w/large deep red, dark blue & gold flowers & green leaves, Schramberger Majolica Factory, Wurttemberg, Germany, ca. 1920s (ILLUS.) **50**

German earthenware, vitreous china body, Art Deco style, spherical w/large D-form handle & tall serpentine spout, enclosed in a removable chrome case w/hinged cover lined in felt & on wooden ball feet, china body marked "Bauscher Weiden - Bauscher Ivory - Bauscher China, Germany," chrome marked "Germany - Quality Ware - The Keephot - Patents: USA 1932 No. 1,878,996 - Canada 1932 No. 328,014 - Germany D.R.P. - Other Patents Pending, U.S.A. and other countries," 1930s (ILLUS., top of page) **125**

Gibson & Sons, Clifton patt., footed squatty spherical body w/serpentine spout, C-scroll handle, inset cover w/knob finial, decorated w/a delicate lacy white design around the top half, England, early 20th c. (ILLUS., next column.)............................... **35**

Gibson & Sons Decorated Teapot

Gonder Pottery, coiled beehive, Mold No. 662, 5 3/4" h.. **75-100**

Gonder Pottery, rectangular, La Gonda patt., Mold No. 396, 6 1/4" h. **50-75**

Gonder La Gonda Pattern Teapot

Gonder Pottery, upright rectangular form, LaGonda patt., creamy yellow glaze, Mold 914 (ILLUS.).................................... **50-75**

Gonder Pottery, vertical ridges, Mold No. P-424, 6 7/16" h. **75-100**

Gonder Pottery, Mold No. P-31, 6 1/2" h. **15-25**

Grimwades Royal Winton Pink & White Teapot

Grimwades, Ltd., Royal Winton line, footed spherical body w/molded scroll handle & cover w/molded finial, pink ground printed overall w/white florals, ca. 1930s (ILLUS.)... **90**

Hall Adele Shape Teapot

Hall China, Adele shape, Art Deco style, Olive Green (ILLUS.).................................... **200**
Hall China, Airflow shape, Chinese Red.......... **130**
Hall China, Airflow shape, Cobalt Blue w/gold trim, 6-cup.. **100**
Hall China, Aladdin shape, Canary Yellow w/gold trim, w/infuser **65**

Hall China, Aladdin shape, Cobalt Blue w/gold trim, 6-cup... **125**
Hall China, Aladdin shape, Crocus patt........ **1,950**
Hall China, Aladdin shape, oval opening, w/infuser, Cobalt Blue w/gold trim............... **110**
Hall China, Aladdin shape, round opening, Cadet Blue w/gold trim.................................. **75**
Hall China, Aladdin shape, round opening for cover & insert, Gold Swag decoration (ILLUS., bottom of page).......................... **70-75**

Hall Aladdin Marine Blue Teapot

Hall China, Aladdin shape, round opening w/insert, Marine Blue (ILLUS.)................. **65-75**

Hall Aladdin Maroon Teapot

Hall China, Aladdin shape, round opening w/insert, Maroon (ILLUS.) **65-75**

Hall Gold Swag Aladdin Shape Teapot

Aladdin Shape Teapot with Serenade Pattern

Hall China, Aladdin shape, w/infuser, Serenade patt. (ILLUS., top of page)................... **350**
Hall China, Albany shape, Emerald Green w/"Gold Special" decoration........................... **60**
Hall China, Albany shape, Mahogany w/gold trim, 6-cup... **75**

Hall China, Basket shape, Cadet Blue w/platinum decoration................................ **150**

Hall Automobile Shape Teapot

Hall China, Automobile shape, Chinese Red (ILLUS.)... **800**
Hall China, Automobile shape, Turquoise w/platinum trim.. **750**
Hall China, Baltimore shape, Ivory Gold Label line.. **125**

Basket Shape Chinese Red Teapot

Hall China, Basket shape, Chinese Red (ILLUS.)... **300**
Hall China, Basket shape, Warm Yellow......... **175**
Hall China, Basketball shape, Cobalt Blue...... **600**
Hall China, Basketball shape, Emerald Green w/gold decoration............................. **650**

Birch Shape Victorian Line Teapot

Bellevue Shape Orange Poppy Teapot

Hall China, Bellevue shape, Orange Poppy patt. (ILLUS.) **1,800**

Hall China, Birch shape, Victorian line, Blue w/gold decoration (ILLUS., bottom previous page) **175**

Birdcage Teapot with "Gold Special" Decoration

Hall China, Birdcage shape, Canary Yellow w/"Gold Special" decoration (ILLUS.) **500**

Hall China, Birdcage shape, Maroon **350**

Hall China, Birdcage shape, Maroon w/"Gold Special" decoration, 6-cup **400**

Hall China, Boston shape, Canary Yellow, 2-cup **45**

Hall China, Boston shape, Chinese Red **150**

Hall China, Boston shape, Cobalt Blue w/gold Trailing Aster design, 6-cup **150**

Hall China, Boston shape, Crocus patt. **225**

Hall China, Bowknot shape, Victorian line, Pink **50**

Hall Bowling Ball Teapot

Hall China, Bowling Ball shape, Turquoise (ILLUS.) **500**

Hall China, Cleveland shape, Turquoise w/gold decoration **75**

Hall China, Cleveland shape, Warm Yellow **60**

Hall China, Connie shape, Victorian line, Green, 6-cup **45**

Hall China, Cozy Hot Pot, Ivory w/embossed copper-colored metal cover, Forman Family Products, 6-cup **40**

Hall China, Cube shape, Emerald Green **100**

Hall China, Cube shape, Turquoise, 2-cup **140**

Hall China, Donut shape, Chinese Red **500**

Rare Orange Poppy Pattern Donut Shape Teapot

Hall China, Donut shape, Orange Poppy patt. (ILLUS.) **450**

Hall Cameo Rose Pattern Teapot on E-Shape Dinnerware Body

Hall China, E-Shape Dinnerware, Cameo Rose patt. (ILLUS., top of page) 75
Hall China, Flare-Ware line, Gold Lace design... 60

Hall China, French shape, "No-blue," Chinese Red body w/white cover, 2-cup........... 125

French Shape Red & White Teapot

Hall China, French shape, "No-blue," Chinese Red w/white cover (ILLUS.) 140
Hall China, French shape, Old Rose w/gold French Flower decoration, 6-cup 50

Football Commemorative Teapot

Hall China, Football shape, commemorative, "Hall 200 Haul, East Liverpool, Ohio" Ivory (ILLUS.) 125
Hall China, Football shape, Maroon 600

Hall Globe No-Drip Pink Teapot

Hall China, Globe No-Drip patt., dark pink w/standard gold decoration (ILLUS.).............. 90
Hall China, French shape, Maroon w/gold decoration, 6-cup 45

Hall White French Shape 1-Cup Teapot

Hall China, French shape, white, 1-cup size (ILLUS.)... 50
Hall China, Globe shape, No-Drip, Addison Grey w/Standard Gold decoration, 6-cup....... 65
Hall China, Hollywood shape, Indian Red 150
Hall China, Hook Cover shape, Cadet Blue w/gold decoration... 50

Hall Jewel Tea Autumn Leaf Aladdin Teapot

Hook Cover Chinese Red Teapot

Hall China, Hook Cover shape, Chinese
Red (ILLUS.) **250**
Hall China, Illinois shape, Canary Yellow **200**

Mustard Yellow Lipton Tea Shape Teapot

Hall China, Lipton Tea shape, Mustard Yel-
low (ILLUS.) **40**

*Illinois Teapot with Maroon &
Gold Decoration*

Hall China, Illinois shape, Maroon w/gold
decoration (ILLUS.) **225**
Hall China, Illinois shape, Stock Brown
w/gold decoration **140**
Hall China, Indiana shape, Warm Yellow
w/gold decoration, 6-cup **450**
Hall China, Jewel Tea Autumn Leaf patt.,
Aladdin shape, round opening for domed
cover (ILLUS., top of page) **75-85**
Hall China, Kansas shape, Ivory w/gold
decoration **400**
Hall China, Lipton Tea shape, Light Yellow **60**
Hall China, Lipton Tea shape, Maroon **45**

Los Angeles Teapot in Cobalt

Hall China, Los Angeles shape, Cobalt Blue
w/Standard Gold trim (ILLUS.) **75**
Hall China, Los Angeles shape, Emerald
Green w/gold decoration, 6-cup **85**
Hall China, Manhattan shape, side handle,
Chinese Red, 8-cup **500**
Hall China, Manhattan shape, side handle,
Cobalt Blue, 2-cup **95**
Hall China, McCormick shape, Turquoise **50**
Hall China, Medallion shape, Crocus patt. **85**
Hall China, Medallion shape, Silhouette
patt. **70**
Hall China, Melody shape, Chinese Red **305**
Hall China, Melody shape, Orange Poppy
patt. **370**

Miniature Hall China Aladdin Teapot

Hall China, miniature, Aladdin shape, light
blue glaze, unmarked, overall 7" l., 5" h.
(ILLUS.).. 15

Moderne Teapot in Marine Blue

Hall China, Moderne shape, Marine Blue
(ILLUS.)... 85

Morning Set Blue Garden Teapot

Hall China, Morning Set shape, Blue Gar-
den patt. (ILLUS.).. 350
Hall China, musical-type, Cadet Blue, 6-cup 200
Hall China, Nautilus shape, Turquoise
w/gold decoration...................................... 225
Hall China, New York shape, Crocus patt. 200
Hall China, New York shape, Red Poppy
patt. 125-150
Hall China, New York shape, Wild Poppy
patt., 4-cup 320-355
Hall China, Ohio shape, Pink w/Gold Dot
decoration (ILLUS., top next column)........... 250
Hall China, Ohio shape, Stock Brown
w/gold decoration....................................... 200
Hall China, Parade shape, Black...................... 65
Hall China, Parade shape, Warm Yellow
w/gold decoration... 75
Hall China, Philadelphia shape, Blue
w/Hearth Scene decoration.......................... 150

Ohio Teapot with Gold Dot Decoration

Chinese Red Philadelphia Teapot

Hall China, Philadelphia shape, Chinese
Red (ILLUS.).. 250
Hall China, Plume shape, Victorian line,
Pink... 40

Radiance Teapot with Acacia Pattern

Hall China, Radiance shape, Acacia patt.
(ILLUS.).. 225
Hall China, Rhythm shape, Canary Yellow
w/gold decoration, 6-cup............................. 150
Hall China, Rhythm shape, Chinese Red........ 350
Hall China, Rhythm shape, Cobalt Blue 180
Hall China, Rutherford shape, ribbed, Chi-
nese Red (ILLUS., next page) 250
Hall China, Sani-Grid (Pert) shape, Chi-
nese Red, 4-cup.. 80
Hall China, Sani-Grid (Pert) shape, Chi-
nese Red, 6-cup.. 75
Hall China, Star shape, Cobalt Blue............... 145
Hall China, Star shape, Cobalt Blue w/Stan-
dard Gold decoration 125

Star Shape Teapot with Gold Stars

Rutherford Ribbed Chinese Red Teapot

Hall China, Star shape, Turquoise w/gold
decoration (ILLUS., top of page) **100-125**
Hall China, Streamline shape, Chinese Red **150**
Hall China, Streamline shape, Fantasy patt.
(ILLUS., bottom of page) **400**
Hall China, Streamline shape, Orange Pop-
py patt. **350**

Hall Sundial - Blue Blossom Teapot

Hall China, Sundial shape, Blue Blossom
patt. (ILLUS.) **300**

Streamline Teapot with Fantasy Pattern

Hall China, Sundial shape, Canary Yellow
w/gold decoration, 6-cup 85
Hall China, Sundial shape, Ivory w/gold
decoration 95
Hall China, Surfside shape, Cadet Blue 175
Hall China, Surfside shape, Canary Yellow 185
Hall China, Surfside shape, Emerald Green
w/gold decoration, 6-cup 200
Hall China, T-Ball Bacharach shape, Black
w/gold label on base, 6-cup 195
Hall China, Tea-for-Four shape, Stock
Green 125

Tea-for-Two Teapot in Pink & Gold

Hall China, Tea-for-Two shape, Pink w/gold
decoration (ILLUS.) 150
Hall China, Tea-for-Two shape, Stock
Brown w/gold decoration 100
Hall China, Thorley series, Apple shape,
Black w/gold decoration 95
Hall China, Thorley series, Grape shape,
Ivory w/Special Gold & rhinestone deco-
ration 295
Hall China, Thorley series, Starlight shape,
Pink w/gold & rhinestone decoration 125
Hall China, Thorley series, Windcrest
shape, Lemon Yellow w/gold decoration 95
Hall China, Tip-Pot Twinspout shape, For-
man Family, Inc., Emerald Green 95
Hall China, Windshield shape, Gamebird
patt. 250
Hall China, Windshield shape, Ivory Gold
Label line 50
Hall China, Windshield shape, Turquoise
w/gold decoration 68

Harker Anna Pattern Teapot

Harker Pottery, Anna patt., bulbous Art
Deco footed body shape, angled handle,
short serpentine spout, line decoration
around rim & lid, floral decoration on
body in shades of blue, violet & rose
w/green leaves, no backstamp, 1930s
(ILLUS.)... 20

Blue Dainty Flower Teapot by Harker

Harker Pottery, Blue Dainty Flower patt.,
Zephyr shape, cylindrical body tapering
in at shoulder, angled handle, serpentine
spout, stepped base, light blue w/cream-
colored stylized floral design on body,
cream finial on lid & line decoration on
rim, part of Cameoware line, ca. 1935
(ILLUS.)... 35

Buckeye Pattern Teapot by Harker

Harker Pottery, Buckeye patt., Zephyr
shape, cylindrical body tapering in at
shoulder, angled handle, serpentine
spout, stepped base, white body decorated w/silver line decoration on rim, lid &
finial & image of large red flower amid
smaller red, green & white flowers &
green leaves, originally called English
Ivy, ca. 1939 (ILLUS.) 25

Emmy Pattern Teapot by Harker

Harker Pottery, Emmy patt., Zephyr shape,
footed squatty ovoid body w/tapering
shoulder, angled handle, short spout, the
body w/vertical embossed chevron lines,
line decoration on lid & finial, the body
decorated w/flowers in deep orange/red,
purple/blue & yellow w/delicate green
leaves, part of the G.C. line, ca. 1940
(ILLUS.)... 15

Harker Gadroon Shape Teapot

Harker Pottery, Gadroon shape, 1940s (ILLUS., top of page) **50**

Harker Honeymoon Cottage Teapot

Harker Pottery, Honeymoon Cottage patt., footed cylindrical body w/slightly tapering shoulder, C-form handle, slightly serpentine spout, the body & lid decorated w/a cottage at the end of a lane bordered w/flowers, all in bright primary colors on white ground, red line decoration on rim, lid & finial, ca. 1930 (ILLUS.)......................... **50**

Rare Lisa Teapot in Gargoyle Shape

Harker Pottery, Lisa patt., Gargoyle or Regal shape, tall rectangular body tapering out to shoulder, then in to rim, long serpentine spout, C-form handle, all ribbed, the handle w/applied thumbrest, the

slightly domed lid w/cut-out applied finial, upper body decorated w/flowers in vibrant blue & violet w/green leaves, teapot rare in this shape, ca. 1930 (ILLUS.) **65**

Harker Pottery, Mallow patt., BakeRite, HotOven ware.. **45**

Harker Pottery, Modern Age/Modern Tulip patt., BakeRite, HotOven ware **20-30**

Harker Pottery Modern Tulip Teapot

Harker Pottery, Modern Tulip patt., zephyr shape, cylindrical ovoid shape tapering in at shoulder, angled handle, slightly serpentine spout, stepped base, gold line decoration on rim, lid & finial, body decorated w/stylized tulip in autumn shades, similar to Jewel Tea Autumn Leaf, ca. 1940 (ILLUS.)... **30**

Petit Point Pattern Teapot by Harker

Harker Pottery, Petit Point patt., Zephyr shape, cylindrical body tapering in at shoulder, angled handle, serpentine spout, stepped base, horizontal band of decoration just below shoulder filled w/petit point-like rendering of flowers in soft shades of pink, blue, yellow & green, line decoration on rim, lid & spout, ca. 1940 (ILLUS.)... 50

Pink Dainty Flower Teapot

Harker Pottery, Pink Dainty Flower patt., cylindrical body tapering in at shoulder, angled handle, serpentine spout, stepped base, pink w/cream-colored stylized floral design on body, cream finial on lid & line decoration on rim, part of Cameoware line, ca. 1935 (ILLUS.)...................... 40

Harker Teapot in Pink Luster

Harker Pottery, Pink Luster patt., spherical body w/C-form handle & short serpentine spout, metallic lustre glaze in pink w/black highlights on rim, finial & lid, ca. 1900 (ILLUS.)... 40

Harker Red Apple Pattern Teapot

Harker Pottery, Red Apple patt., Zephyr shape, cylindrical body, angled handle, serpentine spout, stepped base, a horizontal band of decoration just below shoulder consisting of red apples & yellow pears w/green leaves & blue shading, red highlights on rim, lid, finial & spout, oven-to-table ware, ca. 1930 (ILLUS.)... 45

Tulip Bouquet Teapot by Harker

Harker Pottery, Tulip Bouquet patt., Royal Gadroon shape, squatty lobed bulbous body w/piecrust rim, short foot, ribbed C-scroll handle & slightly serpentine spout, the conforming lid w/applied scroll loop handle, the body, spout & lid decorated w/small flowers in shades of turquoise, pink, blue, purple & orange w/green leaves on white ground, ca. 1940 (ILLUS.)... 20

Vintage Pattern Teapot on Royal Gadroon Shape

Harker Pottery, Vintage patt., Royal Gadroon shape, squatty lobed bulbous body w/piecrust rim, short foot, ribbed C-scroll handle & slightly serpentine spout, the conforming lid w/applied scroll loop handle, the body & lid decorated w/horizontal bands of entwined grapevines w/purple fruit, the finial, spout & handle accented w/green line decoration, ca. 1940 (ILLUS.)... 25

Vintage Pattern Teapot on Zephyr Shape

Harker Pottery, Vintage patt., Zephyr shape, cylindrical body tapering in at shoulder, stepped base, angled handle, slightly serpentine spout, the body decorated w/horizontal band of entwined grapevines w/purple fruit, the rim & finial accented w/green line decoration, ca. 1935 (ILLUS.)... 40

Early Homer Laughlin Shakespeare Shape Teapot

White Rose Pattern Teapot by Harker

Harker Pottery, White Rose patt., cylindrical body tapering in at shoulder, angled handle, serpentine spout, stepped base, blue w/cream-colored stylized floral design on body, cream finial & line decoration on rim, part of Cameoware line made for Montgomery Ward, ca. 1935 (ILLUS.) **45**

Homer Laughlin China Co., Shakespeare shape, floral decoration, East Liverpool, Ohio, 1897-1900 (ILLUS., top of page) **150**
Hull Pottery, Bow-Knot patt., turquoise & blue, B-20-6", 6" h. **450-650**
Hull Pottery, Little Red Riding Hood patt. **400**
Hull Pottery, Water Lily patt.,
    No. L18-6" **250-300**
Hull Pottery, Dogwood patt., No. 507,
    5 1/2" h. **280**
Hull Pottery, Wildflower patt., No. 72,
    8" h. **850-1,200**

Hull Magnolia Gloss Teapot

Hull Pottery, Magnolia Gloss patt., H-20-6 1/2", 1947-48 (ILLUS.). **65**

Laughlin Eggshell Georgian Teapot

Homer Laughlin China Co., Eggshell line, Georgian patt., Newell, West Virginia, Plant #5, ca. 1941 (ILLUS.) **50**

Japanese Aladdin-style Musical Teapot

Kingwood Weeping Gold Decorated Teapot

Japanese earthenware, Aladdin-style, music box insert in the bottom, yellow glaze w/gilt trim, marked "Japan," ca. 1930s, overall 10" l., 7" h. (ILLUS.) **25**

Japanese Earthenware Dark Green Teapot

Japanese earthenware, cylindrical body w/angled shoulder to a small domed cover w/knob finial, short spout & squared handle, overall dark mottled green Rockingham-style glaze, marked "NE-NO

Heatproof Teapot #2 Japan," made to use on a sterno can (ILLUS.) **15**
Jewel Tea Autumn Leaf china, Newport shape w/gold trim, 1978 version **125**

Jewel Tea Autumn Leaf Teapot

Jewel Tea Autumn Leaf china, Newport shape w/gold trim (ILLUS.) **150**
Kingwood Ceramics, squatty bulbous body w/serpentine spout, C-form handle & flattened cover w/arched finial, overall Weeping Gold decoration, East Palestine, Ohio, ca. 1939-49 (ILLUS., top of page) **60**

Knowles Teapot with Floral Decoration

Early Knowles, Taylor, Knowles Teapot

Knowles China Co. (E.M.), footed wide inverted bell-form body w/an angled shoulder, short spout & fancy loop handle, figure-8 shaped cover finial, floral bouquet decoration, ca. 1922 (ILLUS., bottom previous page) **40**

E.M. Knowles Roma Pattern Teapot

Knowles China Co. (E.M.), Roma patt., Newell, West Virginia, ca. 1929 (ILLUS.) **40**

Knowles, Taylor & Knowles Co., footed wide squatty bulbous body w/a narrow shoulder & short cylindrical neck, large C-form handle & short spout, East Liverpool, Ohio, 1905-29 (ILLUS., top of page) **50**

Knowles, Taylor, Knowles Animals Teapot

Knowles, Taylor & Knowles Co., low wide squatty bulbous body w/low domed cover

& knob finial, cute animal decoration, East Liverpool, Ohio, ca. 1905 (ILLUS.) **50**

Plain White Knowles, Taylor, Knowles Teapot

Knowles, Taylor & Knowles Co., plain white ovoid body tapering to a flared rim, domed cover w/double-loop finial, serpentine spout & C-form handle, East Liverpool, Ohio, ca. 1880 (ILLUS.) **65**

Early K.T. & K. Floral Teapot

Knowles, Taylor & Knowles Co., wide scroll-molded cylindrical base below the wide squatty bulbous body tapering to a wide cylindrical neck, short spout, C-scroll handle, domed cover w/loop finial, decorated w/delicate flowers, East Liverpool, Ohio, ca. 1902 (ILLUS.) **45**

Holdcroft Figural Chinaman Teapot

Majolica, Chinaman patt., figural, model of a large brown melon w/green stem spout & handle, the figure of a Chinese man climbing on the side, wearing a dark blue robe, cream-colored pants & black shoes, Holdcroft, England, third quarter 19th c., 9 1/2" l., 7" h. (ILLUS.) **4,400**

Majolica, Chinaman patt., modeled as a rotund seated Chinese man holding a large brown dramatic mask to one side, the mask issuing a green & yellow spout, a rope handle at his other side, his head forming the cover, shown wearing a pale blue jacket w/small red, green & white blossoms & dark green pants & brown shoes, Model No. 1838, Mintons, England, date code for 1874, 8 1/4" h. (ILLUS. far right with two other majolica teapots, page 127) **4,465**

1930s Leigh China Floral Teapot

Leigh China Company, earthenware, footed squatty bulbous body w/flattened cover & lobed finial, squared handle & short serpentine spout, decorated w/bands of stylized blue, red & yellow blossoms on leafy branches, Alliance, Ohio, ca. early 1930s (ILLUS.) **65-70**

Majolica, Bird & Bird's Nest patt., figural, England, late 19th c., professional spout tip repair, 9" l. **1,176**

Etruscan large shell and seaweed teapot with crooked spout, good color, $500+
(Courtesy of Strawser Auction Group)

Etruscan Cauliflower Pattern Teapot

Majolica, Etruscan line, Cauliflower patt., the body molded as a head of cauliflower in creamy white & dark green, green spout & handle, marked on bottom, Griffin, Smith & Hill, Phoenixville, Pennsylvania, late 19th c., minor roughness on interior rim, interior rim chip on cover, 5 1/2" h. (ILLUS.) **374**

American Shell & Seaweed Teapot

Majolica, Etruscan line, Shell & Seaweed patt., spherical body molded as large shells trimmed w/seaweed, mottled green coral-form handle & spout, mottled pink, brown & green cover w/shell finial, Griffin, Smith & Hill, Phoenixville, Pennsylvania, late 19th c., 10" l., 6 1/2" h. (ILLUS.)... **525-575**

Majolica, Fan & Scroll with Insect patt., pebbled background, Fielding & Co., England, late 19th c., minor spout nick, 7" l. **252**

Majolica, Flowering Branch patt., flat-sided moon-shaped body w/concave base, the sides in cobalt blue molded w/a large brown branch w/green leaves & white & pink blossoms, rectangular domed cover w/blossom finial, brown branch spout & handle, probably England, late 19th c., 7" h. (ILLUS. bottom left with three other teapots, page 130) **812**

Majolica, Gondolier patt., the body modeled as an elongated Chinese gondola-style sailing ship w/tall upturned stern & bow, the bow forming the spout, the body of the pot composed of the molded brown cargo, white sail & triangular panels of light blue sky between the rigging ropes, a rigging rope connecting the top of the sail w/the top of the stern, the figure of a bent-over Chinese man forming the finial on the cover, Model No. 3520/30, George Jones, England, diamond registry date of 1876, 12 1/2" h. (ILLUS. center top with two other majolica teapots, page 128) **32,900**

English Japonisme Majolica Teapot

Majolica, Japonisme style, a flattened demi-lune form in turquoise blue, the flat cover w/a small squared finial, straight angled spout & simple C-form handle, the shoulder molded w/a stylized fret design, the sides molded w/an Oriental figure preparing tea in a garden & a large stylized blossom on a leafy stem, England, possibly by Joseph Holdcroft or Samuel Lear, ca. 1880, 9 3/4" l. (ILLUS.) **2,271**

Figural Lemon Mintons Teapot

Majolica, Lemon patt., model of a large yellow lemon w/molded green leaves around the sides & forming the base, green stem spout & handle, cover modeled as an inverted mushroom, Mintons, England, date code for 1873, Shape No. 643, 7" l., 4 1/2" h. (ILLUS.) **8,800**

Majolica, Mintons Fish patt., figural, limited edition produced by Royal Doulton, 20th c. **616**

Majolica, Monkey & Coconut patt., the body modeled as a large mustard yellow coconut w/the figure of a seated brown monkey at one end grasping the nut, wearing a black jacket w/dark red blossoms & green leaves, the grey head w/pale green knob finial forming the cover, molded green leaves below the curved brown bamboo-form spout, the tail of the monkey forming the handle, Mintons, England, third quarter 19th c., minor hairline in spout, 8 1/2" h. (ILLUS., top next page)... **6,440**

Mintons Monkey & Coconut Figural Teapot

Three Rare Victorian Figural Majolica Teapots

Majolica, Monkey & Coconut patt., the bulbous body modeled as a seated grey monkey wearing a dark blue outfit w/large pink polka dots, its arms & legs wrapped around a large mustard yellow coconut w/green leaves, the stem forming the spout, the monkey's head & shoulders forming the cover w/a blue knob finial, Model No. 1844, Mintons, England, date letter for 1874, 9" h. (ILLUS. far left with two other majolica teapots, bottom previous page) **8,225**

Monkey on Coconut Figural Teapot

Majolica, Monkey on Coconut patt., modeled as a large cobalt blue coconut w/green leaves & a dark grey figure of a monkey seated at the top end above the brown branch handle, brown branch spout, small cover w/figural pink bud &

green leaves, J. Roth, England, late 19th c., 10" l., 7 1/4" h. (ILLUS.) **3,696**

Rare Mintons Majolica Teapot

Majolica, oblong sad iron-shaped body w/a short spout, high arched fixed handle, the cobalt blue body molded w/a band decorated w/alternating grey mouse & pink blossom, the top of the handle molded w/the figure of a curled up white cat looking down at a grey mouse & carrot forming the finial of the flat cover, Mintons, England, possibly designed by Christopher Dresser, Model No. 622, date letter for 1876, 7 1/2" h. (ILLUS.) **47,000**

Very Rare Holdcroft Putto in Rowboat Teapot

George Jones Figural Rooster Majolica Teapot

Majolica, Putto Rowing Boat patt., wide low squatty rounded body on three scroll feet, the body in cobalt blue w/a straight brown spout & C-form brown handle, the top modeled w/the figure of a winged putto seated in a model of a tan rowboat w/pale green interior & green oars, Holdcroft, England, third quarter 19th c., very rare, professional repair to arm of figure, 8" l., 6" h. (ILLUS., bottom previous page)...... **15,680**

Majolica, Ribbon, Bow, Daisy & Wheat patt., fine details, Fielding & Co., England, late 19th c., 6" h. **392**

Majolica, Rooster patt., model of a large, colorful, realistic rooster in shades of brown, yellow & green, red comb & wattle, oval base, George Jones, England, third quarter 19th c., 11" l. (ILLUS., top of page).. **7,700**

Majolica, Shell, Seaweed & Waves teakettle, wide squatty angled body molded w/pink & green seashells & seaweed on a cobalt blue ground, low domed cover w/shell finial, dark blue spout, overhead green ropetwist handle, England, late 19th c., professional rim repair on cover, 8" h. (ILLUS. top left with three other teapots, bottom of page).............................. **1,344**

Four Nice Majolica Teapots

Extremely Rare Figural Spikey Fish Mintons Teapot

Majolica, Spikey Fish patt., the body modeled as a large grey & green bulbous fish raised on green waves, a large branch of brown seaweed w/a shell thumbrest forming the handle, angled brown straight spout emerging from the mouth, the small cover w/an arched spiky fin handle, Mintons, third quarter 19th c., extremely rare, professional repair to spout, base rim & rim of cover, 9 1/2" l., 7" h. (ILLUS.).. **29,120**

Majolica, Stork & Water Lily patt., upright rectangular body, molded brown corner & edge bands framing cobalt blue panels, all on small brown tab feet, each side w/a grey stork among green water lilies, stepped rectangular cover w/band of green leaves & a brown twig finial, long angled brown branch spout & squared branch handle, probably England, late 19th c., professional repair to spout & cover finial, 6 1/2" h. (ILLUS. bottom right with three other teapots, previous page) **280**

Majolica, Vulture & Snake patt., an elaborately modeled design w/a large standing vulture w/a yellow & black body & pink neck & head grasping the head & body of a large writhing green snake, both on a rockwork base, Model No. 1851, designed by H.H. Crealock, Mintons, England, dated ca. 1872, 8 3/8" h. (ILLUS.)... **89,625**

Majolica, Wild Rose & Trellis patt., spherical body composed of alternating cobalt blue bands & yellow bands of basketweave w/wild rose leafy vine, blue spout w/molded leafy vine, angled brown twig handle, domed cover w/basketweave & leaves w/arched twig finial, probably England, late 19th c., crazing, hairline, 7" h. (ILLUS. top right with three other teapots, previous page) **448**

McCoy Pottery Shaded Brown Teapot

McCoy Pottery, spherical body w/molded rings around the bottom, short spout, squared handle, low domed cover w/pointed loop finial, shaded brown glaze, ca. 1948 (ILLUS.) **25**

Extraordinary Mintons Majolica Teapot

Early American Ironstone Teapot

McNichol, Burton & Co., simple baluster-shaped white ironstone body w/serpentine spout, C-form handle & domed cover w/bar finial, East Liverpool, Ohio, 1870-1892 (ILLUS.).. **65**

Morton Pottery Advertising Teapot

Morton Pottery Company, globe-shaped w/serpentine spout, C-form handle, low domed cover w/knob finial, the side impressed w/a rectangular panel advertising "Krug's Market - Meats & Groceries," overall mottled brown & green Woodland glaze on a yellowware body, Morton Pottery Company, Morton, Illinois, ca. 1930s (ILLUS.).. **95-125**

Morton Teapot with Woodland Glaze

Morton Pottery Company, spherical body w/serpentine spout, C-form handle, low domed cover w/knob finial, yellowware w/overall dark brown & green sponged Woodland glaze, Morton Pottery Compa-

ny, Morton, Illinois, early 20th c. (ILLUS.).. **75-100**

Small "Tea Time" Morton Teapot

Morton Pottery Company, squatty bulbous body embossed w/a clock face under "Tea Time" on each side, short spout, C-form handle, disk cover w/button finial, forest green glaze, 4-cup size, Morton Pottery Company, Morton, Illinois, 4 3/4" h. (ILLUS.) **30-40**

Pilgrim Blue Morton Twin Tea Set

Morton Pottery Company, twin tea set, an upright rectangular cov. hot water & cov. teapot w/curved front & back edges & angled handle, on a fitted conforming tray base, dark Pilgrim Blue glaze in blue & green sponging, each pot 2-cup size, Morton Pottery Company, Morton, Illinois, early 20th c., the set (ILLUS.)....... **150-175**

Ovoid Morton Rockingham Teapot

Morton Pottery Works, bulbous ovoid pineapple-shaped body tapering to a small mouth, tall serpentine spout, C-scroll handle, small domed cover w/button finial, overall dark brown Rockingham glaze, Morton Pottery Works (Rapp Bros.), Morton, Illinois, 1877-1917, 8-cup size (ILLUS.) **80-90**

10   Rockingham Ware

EMMET TEA POTS. Per Doz.

36s	$2.65
30s	3.00
24s	3.50

PINEAPPLE TEA POTS.

42s	2	pints	$2.40
36s	2½	pints	2.65
30s	3¼	pints	3.00
24s	4	pints	3 50
18s	5¼	pints	4.25
12s	7	pints	5.50

Emmet and Pineapple Shape Morton Pottery Works Teapots in Catalog

Morton Pottery Works, Emmet patt. teapot, footed spherical body, brown Rockingham glaze, Model 36s, Morton Pottery Works (Rapp Bros.), Morton, Illinois, 1877-1917, 5-cup size (ILLUS. at top in catalog page) 45-50

Morton Pottery Works, Emmet patt. teapot, footed spherical body, brown Rockingham glaze, Model 30s, Morton Pottery Works (Rapp Bros.), Morton, Illinois, 1877-1917, 7-cup size (ILLUS. at top in catalog page) 55-60

Morton Pottery Works, Emmet patt. teapot, footed spherical body, brown Rockingham glaze, Model 24s, Morton Pottery Works (Rapp Bros.), Morton, Illinois, 1877-1917, 8-cup size (ILLUS. at top in catalog page) 65-75

Morton Pottery Works Pear-shaped Pot

Morton Pottery Works, individual size, pear-shaped body w/upright spout & C-scroll handle, small domed cover w/large knob finial, overall medium brown Rockingham glaze, Morton Pottery Works (Rapp Bros.), Morton, Illinois, 1877-1917, 1 1/2 cup size (ILLUS.).............................. **40-50**

Acorn-shaped Morton Pottery Teapot

Morton Pottery Works, inverted acorn shape, serpentine spout, branch handle, small domed cover w/knob finial, overall dark brown Rockingham glaze, Morton Pottery Works (Rapp Bros.), 1877-1917, 3 3/4 cup size (ILLUS.).............................. **80-90**

Morton Pottery Works Miniature Pot

Morton Pottery Works, miniature, squatty flat-bottomed shape w/flared neck & fitted cover w/knob finial, paneled spout & angled handle, overall brown Rockingham glaze, Morton Pottery Works (Rapp Bros.), Morton, Illinois, 1877-1917, 1 3/4 oz. (ILLUS.)... **75-100**

Morton Pottery Works, ovoid pineapple-shaped body, light brown Rockingham glaze, Model 42s, Morton Pottery Works (Rapp Bros.), Morton, Illinois, 1877-1917, 2-cup size (ILLUS., top of column)............ **80-90**

Ovoid Pineapple-shaped Morton Teapot

Morton Pottery Works, Pineapple patt. teapot, footed ovoid body, brown Rockingham glaze, Model 42s, Morton Pottery Works (Rapp Bros.), Morton, Illinois, 1877-1917, 4-cup size (ILLUS. at bottom on catalog page, page 132)....................... **30-40**

Morton Pottery Works, Pineapple patt. teapot, footed ovoid body, brown Rockingham glaze, Model 36s, Morton Pottery Works (Rapp Bros.), Morton, Illinois, 1877-1917, 5-cup size (ILLUS. at bottom on catalog page, page 132)...................... **40-50**

Morton Pottery Works, Pineapple patt. teapot, footed ovoid body, brown Rockingham glaze, Model 30s, Morton Pottery Works (Rapp Bros.), Morton, Illinois, 1877-1917, 7-cup size (ILLUS. at bottom on catalog page, page 132)...................... **50-60**

Morton Pottery Works, Pineapple patt. teapot, footed ovoid body, brown Rockingham glaze, Model 24s, Morton Pottery Works (Rapp Bros.), Morton, Illinois, 1877-1917, 8-cup size (ILLUS. at bottom on catalog page, page 132)...................... **60-70**

Morton Pottery Works, Pineapple patt. teapot, footed ovoid body, brown Rockingham glaze, Model 18s, Morton Pottery Works (Rapp Bros.), Morton, Illinois, 1877-1917, 10-cup size (ILLUS. at bottom on catalog page, page 132)............... **70-80**

Morton Pottery Works, Pineapple patt. teapot, footed ovoid body, brown Rockingham glaze, Model 12s, Morton Pottery Works (Rapp Bros.), Morton, Illinois, 1877-1917, 14-cup size (ILLUS. at bottom on catalog page, page 133)............... **80-90**

Squatty Morton Pottery Works Teapot

Morton Pottery Works, squatty bulbous body w/a low cylindrical neck, low domed cover w/button finial, serpentine spout, C-scroll handle, overall dark brown Rockingham glaze, Morton Pottery Works (Rapp Bros.), Morton, Illinois, 1877-1917, 6-cup size (ILLUS.) **50-60**

Morton Rebecca at the Well Teapots

Morton Pottery Works, Rebecca at the
Well patt., tapering cylindrical body
w/domed cover, serpentine spout, C-
scroll handle, dark brown Rockingham
glaze, Morton Pottery Works (Rapp
Bros.), Morton, Illinois, 1877-1917, 7 pt.
size (ILLUS. left with other Rebecca at
the Well teapot, top of page)................ **175-200**

Morton Pottery Works, Rebecca at the
Well patt., tapering cylindrical body
w/domed cover, serpentine spout, C-
scroll handle, light brown Rockingham
glaze, Morton Pottery Works (Rapp
Bros.), Morton, Illinois, 1877-1917, 8 1/2
pt. size (ILLUS. right with other Rebecca
at the Well teapot, top of page)............. **150-175**

Myott, Son & Company Floral Teapot

Myott, Son & Company, bulbous inverted
pear-shaped body, serpentine spout & C-
scroll handle, low cover w/scroll loop finial, decorated around the shoulder w/flo-
ral sprays & latticework, England, ca.
1930 (ILLUS.)... **45**

American Moss Rose Pattern Teapot

Moss Rose pattern china, spherical body
w/C-scroll handle, serpentine spout &
ringed & domed metal cover, produced
by Knowles, Taylor, Knowles Pottery,
East Liverpool, Ohio, late 19th - early
20th c. (ILLUS.).................................... **100-125**

Occupied Japan Earthenware Teapot

Occupied Japan earthenware, squatty
bulbous body w/serpentine spout & angled handle, Hadson Company mark,
1945-52 (ILLUS.) **25**

Extremely Rare George Ohr Pottery Teapot

Ohio Porcelain Co. Round Teapot

Ohio Porcelain Co., footed spherical body w/short spout, squared handle & dome cover w/squared loop finial, blind incised "OPCo.," Zanesville, Ohio, 1940-50 (ILLUS.)... **15**

Small George Ohr Pottery Teapot

Ohr (George) Pottery, a cylindrical slightly waisted body w/a flattened shoulder centering a short cylindrical neck, serpentine spout & long C-form handle, small inset cover w/large mushroom knop, covered overall in a green speckled glossy glaze, stamped "GEO. E. OHR/BILOXI, MISS.," minor restoration to spout, rim & cover, 6 1/2" l., 4 1/4" h. (ILLUS.) **5,581**

Ohr (George) Pottery, a large size pot w/a footring supporting the wide squatty bulbous body tapering to a cupped neck w/inset flat cover, long serpentine spout & simple C-form handle, covered in a spectacular white, red & pink glaze sponged on an amber ground, stamped "G.E. OHR/ Biloxi, Miss.," late 19th - early 20th c., 12 1/2" l., 5 1/2" h. (ILLUS., top of page)... **55,813**

American Moss Rose Pattern Teapot

Operative Pottery, Moss Rose patt., footed ovoid body w/molded ribbing around the base, flared neck & domed cover w/pointed button finial, tall spout & angled molded handle, unlisted maker, probably East Liverpool, Ohio, ca. 1890s (ILLUS.).............. **50**

Ott & Brewer Ironstone Teapot

Ott & Brewer, bulbous tapering ovoid ironstone body w/a flared rim, domed cover w/bar handle, serpentine spout, C-scroll handle, decorated w/a long delicate flowering vine design, Trenton, New Jersey, ca. 1870-80 (ILLUS.) **75**

Pioneer Pottery Pearl China Teapot

Pioneer Pottery, wide squatty bulbous body w/a small cover & flaring finial, angled spout & C-form handle, decorated w/a fine sprig design, stamped "Pearl China," East Liverpool, Ohio, ca. 1930s (ILLUS.) **35**

Porcelier Pottery Molded Teapot

Porcelier Pottery, domed molded rockwork design w/a molded figure of a girl & flowers, Greensberg, Pennsylvania, 1931-54 (ILLUS.) **45**

Potter's Co-Operative "Perfect" Teapot

Potter's Co-Operative, footed body w/wide squatty base tapering up the ribbed sides to a flat rim, domed cover w/scroll finial, tall serpentine spout, fancy C-scroll handle, delicate printed floral decoration, East Liverpool, Ohio, base stamped "Perfect" in a rust-colored cartouche, ca. 1900 (ILLUS.) **60**

Potter's Co-Operative Ovoid Teapot

Potter's Co-Operative, footed bulbous ovoid body w/a wide flat rim, domed cover w/arched finial, long serpentine spout & C-scroll handle, molded details, East Liverpool, Ohio, ca. 1880s (ILLUS.) **70**
Purinton Pottery, Peasant Garden patt., domed lid, 6-cup size **325-350**

Quimper Modern Movement Pattern Teapot & Creamer

Fine Decor Riche Decorated Teapot

Quimper Pottery, Decor Riche patt., a swirled & waisted Rococo Louis XV-style body w/a low domed cover w/dark blue ring finial, a long serpentine spout & an ornate dark blue C-scroll handle, w/large scene of dancing peasants in a landscape & dark blue & mustard yellow trim, marked "HenRiot Quimper 126," mint, 9 1/4" h. (ILLUS.) 350

Detailed HB Quimper Pattern Teapot

Quimper Pottery, HB Quimper patt., simple ovoid body w/a squared angled spout & squared angled handle, low domed cover w/a pointed finial, decorated w/a colorful scene of a French peasant in a landscape, naive flowers, leaves, ermine tails

& lattice around the top, signed only "HB 7/4" on the bottom, mint, 9" h. (ILLUS.) **350**

Quimper Pottery, teapot & matching creamer, Modern Movement patt., the tall tapering paneled teapot w/a long upright spout, angled handle, the domed pan-eled cover w/a tall ovoid finial, creamer in a similar shape, each h.p. w/bold shades of orange, dark blue, black & green on a white ground, panels w/figures, lattice or stylized flower burst designs, mark of HB, Quimper, France, near mint, teapot 9 3/4" h., 2 pcs. (ILLUS., top of page).......... **275**

Unusual Quimper Drip-type Teapot

Quimper Pottery, two-part drip-type, color-ful Rouen-inspired decoration, the cylin-drical top section w/angled handle & low domed cover w/button finial & a sieve bottom painted w/a scene of a Breton peasant playing a musical instrument in a landscape, a fancy border in dark blue w/gold & green scrolls, florals & leaves, this section for holding the loose tea to which hot water is added, the lower squatty bulbous pot w/a long serpentine spout & C-form handle decorated around the upper half w/a matching band of dark blue, gold & green, marked "HB Quimper 8/274," mint, overall 9 1/2" h. (ILLUS.)......... **425**

"Fruits de la Mer" Pattern Teapot

Quimper Pottery, "Fruits de la Mer" patt., black glaze ground w/conch shells & seaweed decoration, by Guy Trevoux, Henriot Quimper, 9 1/2" h., mint (ILLUS.)............ **250**

Redware Teapot Glazed in Drippy Blue

Redware pottery, wide slightly waisted cylindrical body w/a thin shoulder & low flat neck, serpentine spout & C-scroll handle, inset cover w/button finial, ivory-colored base clay covered in a mottled runny dark blue, the base & interior glazed in dark reddish brown, 19th c., minor glaze flakes on spout, 5 1/2" h. (ILLUS.) **138**

Rockingham Rebecca at the Well Teapot

Rockingham-glazed pottery, footed ovoid body w/swan's-neck spout & C-form handle, domed cover w/bud-form finial, mottled brown glaze w/relief-molded scene of Rebecca at the well, early 20th c., Ohio, 8 1/2" h. (ILLUS.)................................ **200**

Standard Glaze Rookwood Teapot

Rookwood Pottery, footed wide squatty bulbous body w/a short angled spout, flat rim w/low domed cover sprig finial, an arched real bamboo swing bail handle, Standard Glaze, decorated w/dark golden yellow leafy & flowering branches on a shaded brown to dark green to mustard yellow ground, Shape No. 404W, 1894, Josephine Zettel, 7" l., 4" h. (ILLUS.)........... **881**

Unusual Rookwood Turkish Teapot

Rookwood Pottery, tall Turkish-style pot, a narrow footring supporting the bulbous ovoid lower body tapering sharply to a tall cylindrical neck w/a domed cap cover & gold button finial, tall slender serpentine spout joined to the neck w/a delicate S-scroll bracket, long arched handle from the top of the neck to the shoulder, creamy ground h.p. on one side w/a scene of a blue frog seated on shore & holding a fishing pole, the reverse decorated w/a scene of sandcrabs, in shades of dark blue, tan & dark blue w/ornate

Doulton Self-Pouring Kingsware Patent Teapot

gold trim, dull semi-matte glaze, mark attributed to M.L. Nichols, dated 1883, 11" h. (ILLUS., previous page) **1,725**

Roseville Pottery, Peony patt., gold ground **200-250**

Roseville Pottery, Snowberry patt., shaded green ground, No. 1TP **200-250**

Roseville Pottery, Bushberry patt., blue ground, No. 2 .... **250-350**

Roseville Pottery, Bushberry patt., russet ground, No. 2 .... **150-250**

Roseville Pottery, Peony patt., green ground, No. 3 .... **150-225**

Roseville Pottery, Magnolia patt., green ground, No. 4 .... **350-400**

Roseville Pottery, Magnolia patt., tan ground, No. 4 .... **250-350**

Roseville Pottery, Clematis patt., green ground, No. 5 .... **150-200**

Roseville Pottery, Freesia patt., blue ground, No. 6 .... **200-250**

Roseville Pottery, Freesia patt., green ground, No. 6 .... **150-250**

Roseville Pottery, Freesia patt., terra cotta ground, No. 6 .... **150-250**

Roseville Pottery, Zephyr Lily patt., blue ground, No. 7T **250-350**

Roseville Pottery, Zephyr Lily patt., green ground, No. 7T **100-200**

Roseville Pottery, Zephyr Lily patt., terra cotta ground, No. 7T **200-250**

Roseville Pottery, Wincraft patt., brown & yellow ground, No. 271-P **100-150**

Royal Doulton China, Kingsware line, self-pouring style, relief-molded half-length portraits on side, J.J. Royle's Patent design, ca. 1900 (ILLUS., top of page) **2,000**

Royal Doulton China, Morrisian Ware, footed wide urn-shaped body w/a squared handle & serpentine spout, design of a dancing lady, ca. 1900 (ILLUS., bottom of page) **1,000**

Royal Doulton Morrisian Ware Teapot

Extremely Rare Royal Doulton Stoneware Toby Teapot

Royal Doulton China, stoneware, figural Toby shape, designed by Harry Simeon, ca. 1925, extremely rare (ILLUS., top of page)................................ **7,500**

Royal Doulton Ware, Cadogan-style pot, decorated in the Crows patt., ca. 1907 (ILLUS., right)... **2,000**

Royal Doulton Ware, figural Old Charley model, designed by Charles Noke, introduced in 1939 (ILLUS., bottom of page)... **2,000**

Royal Doulton Cadogan Teapot

Early Royal Doulton Old Charley Teapot

Early Royal Doulton Sairey Gamp Teapot

Royal Doulton Ware, figural Sairey Gamp model, designed by Charles Noke, introduced in 1939 (ILLUS.)... **2,000**

Early Royal Doulton Tony Weller Teapot

Royal Doulton Ware, figural Tony Weller model, designed by Charles Noke, introduced in 1939 (ILLUS.)... **2,000**

Royal Doulton Teapot with Band of Polar Bears

Royal Doulton Ware, footed very wide squatty low body tapering to a flat rim & conical cover w/disk finial, short angled spout & loop handle, overall crackled background w/a center band of walking polar bears, ca. 1920s (ILLUS., above) **90**

Royal Doulton Ware, footed wide squatty bulbous body w/a wide flat neck & inset cover w/button finial, serpentine spout & C-form handle, decorated w/floral clusters, England, early 20th c. (ILLUS., right) **90**

Early Royal Doulton Floral Teapot

Royal Doulton Ware, Kingsware line, Dame patt. w/motto around base, introduced in 1901 (ILLUS., bottom of page) ... **1,000**

Early Royal Doulton Kingsware Dame Pattern Teapot

Royal Doulton Old Leeds Spray Pattern Teapot

Royal Doulton Kingsware Witch Teapot

Royal Doulton Ware, Kingsware line, Witch
patt., introduced in 1902 (ILLUS.) **500**

Royal Doulton Ware, Nightwatchman
scene... **125**

Royal Doulton Ware, Old Leeds Spray
patt., squatty octagonal body, angled

spout & squared handle, England, ca.
1912 (ILLUS., top of page)......................... **100**

Doulton Coaching Days Series Teapot

Royal Doulton Ware, Series Ware, color
scene from the Coaching Days Series,
introduced in 1905 (ILLUS.)........................ **500**

Royal Doulton Dickensware Series Teapot

Rare Royal Doulton Gnomes Series Teapot

Royal Doulton Ware, Series Ware, color scene from the Dickensware Series, introduced in 1908 (ILLUS., bottom previous page) **600**

Royal Doulton Ware, Series Ware, color scene from the Gnomes Series, introduced in 1927 (ILLUS., top of page) **2,000**

Royal Doulton Ware, Series Ware, color scene from the Night Watchman Series, introduced in 1909 (ILLUS., right) **500**

Royal Doulton Ware, Series Ware, color scene of a young woman standing alone in a landscape, from the Shakespeare Series, introduced in 1912 (ILLUS., bottom of page) **600**

Teapot from Night Watchman Series

A Royal Doulton Teapot from the Shakespeare Series

Shakespeare Series Teapot with Rosalind

Royal Doulton Ware, Series Ware, color scene of Rosalind from the Shakespeare Series, introduced in 1912 (ILLUS.) **500**

Teapot from Royal Doulton Open Door Series

Royal Doulton Ware, Series Ware, elderly woman seated by the fire, from the Open Doors Series, introduced in 1914 (ILLUS.) **650**

Landscape Scene on a Royal Doulton Woodland Series Teapot

Sketches from Teniers Series Teapot

Jock of the Bushveld Series Teapot

Royal Doulton Ware, Series Ware, from the Jock of the Bushveld Series, introduced in 1911 (ILLUS.) **1,250**

Royal Doulton Ware, Series Ware, landscape scene from the Sketches from Teniers Series, introduced in 1905 (ILLUS.) .. **1,000**

Royal Doulton Ware, Series Ware, landscape w/trees & cottage from the Woodland Series, introduced in 1908 (ILLUS., top of page) **600**

Royal Doulton Athens Series Teapot

Royal Doulton Gondoliers Series Teapot

Royal Doulton Ware, Series Ware, low wide body decorated w/Grecian figures, from the Athens Series, introduced in 1910 (ILLUS., bottom previous page) **600**

Royal Doulton Ware, Series Ware, Queen Elizabeth at Moreton Hall series **125**

Royal Doulton Ware, Series Ware, scene from the Gondoliers Series, introduced in 1908 (ILLUS., top of page) **600**

Royal Doulton Ware, Series Ware, scene from the Hunting Series, introduced in 1947 (ILLUS.) **600**

Sir Roger de Coverley Series Teapot

Royal Doulton Ware, Series Ware, scene from the Sir Roger de Coverley Series, introduced in 1911 (ILLUS.) **600**

Hunting Series Ware Teapot

Dutch Landscape from Royal Doulton Dutch Series

Hamlet Teapot from the Shakespeare Series

Royal Doulton Ware, Series Ware, scene of a Dutch family from the Dutch Series, introduced in 1904 (ILLUS., bottom previous page) **500**

Royal Doulton Ware, Series Ware, scene of Hamlet from the Shakespeare Series, introduced in 1912 (ILLUS., top of page) **500**

Royal Doulton Ware, Series Ware, scene of Old Mother Hubbard from the Nursery Rhymes Series, designed by William Savage Cooper, introduced in 1903 (ILLUS., bottom of page)............................. **650**

Old Mother Hubbard Teapot from Nursery Rhymes Series

Shakespeare Series Teapot with Scene of Romeo

Royal Doulton Ware, Series Ware, scene of Romeo from the Shakespeare Series, introduced in 1912 (ILLUS.)... **500**

Teapot from Royal Doulton Coaching Days Series

Royal Doulton Ware, Series Ware, squatty shape, color scene from the Coaching Days Series, introduced in 1905 (ILLUS.) **500**

Doulton Titanian Ware Bird of Paradise Teapot

Royal Doulton Ware, Titanian Ware, Bird
  of Paradise patt., introduced in 1919
  (ILLUS.).. **800**
Russel Wright Designs, American Modern
  line, white glaze, Steubenville Pottery
  Co. (ILLUS., right) **110-135**
Russel Wright Designs, Casual China, Re-
  styled teapot, Cantaloupe glaze, Iroquois
  China Co., mid-1950s (ILLUS., bottom of
  page) **600-750**

American Modern White Teapot

Rare Cantaloupe Casual Restyled Teapot

Mustard Gold Casual Restyled Teapot

Russel Wright Designs, Casual China, Restyled teapot, Mustard Gold glaze, Iroquois China Co., mid-1950s (ILLUS.) ... **250-350**

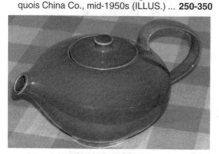

Ripe Apricot Casual Restyled Teapot

Russel Wright Designs, Casual China, Restyled teapot, Ripe Apricot glaze, Iroquois China Co., mid-1950s
(ILLUS.).. **150-175**

Sebring China Co., bulbous ovoid body
molded down the sides w/fanned devices
forming a panel printed w/a large floral
cluster, tall serpentine spout, C-scroll
handle, domed cover w/arched loop finial, East Liverpool, Ohio, ca. 1890s
(ILLUS., next column) **75**

Early Sebring China Company Teapot

Sebring China Hexagonal Teapot

Sebring China Company, individual size,
footed tapering hexagonal body w/an-
gled handle & tall spout, paneled domed
cover w/pointed finial, white w/a stylized
scroll & blossom design in black, pink &
gold, thin blue pinstripes, Sebring,
Ohio, ca. 1930s (ILLUS.) **45-50**

Bellflower Blue-glazed Shawnee Teapot

Clover Blossom Shawnee Teapot

Shawnee Pottery, Bellflower patt., light blue glaze, marked "U.S.A.," 6 3/4" h. (ILLUS., bottom previous page) **30-35**

Shawnee Pottery, Clover Blossom patt., embossed decoration, gold trim, marked "U.S.A.," 6-cup, 6 1/2" h. **425-575**

Shawnee Pottery, Clover Blossom patt., embossed decoration, marked "U.S.A.," 6-cup, 6 1/2" h. (ILLUS., top of page) ... **125-150**

Shawnee Pottery, Cornware, either "Corn King" or "Corn Queen" line, gold trimmed, marked "Shawnee 75," 30 oz., either **275-375**

Shawnee Pottery, Cornware, either "Corn King" or "Corn Queen" line, marked "Shawnee 75," 30 oz., either **75-95**

Conventional Floral Shawnee Teapot

Shawnee Pottery, Conventional patt., h.p. dark red blossom on leafy stem, marked "U.S.A.," 6 1/4" h. (ILLUS.) **25-30**

Shawnee King Corn Teapot

Shawnee Pottery, Cornware line, King Corn patt., 30 oz. (ILLUS.) **85**

White Corn Gold-trimmed Shawnee Teapot

Shawnee Pottery, Cornware line, White Corn patt., gold-trimmed, 30 oz. (ILLUS.)... **275-375**

Shawnee Crisscross Pattern Teapot

Shawnee Pottery, Crisscross patt., marked "U.S.A.," 6" h. (ILLUS.).............................. **25-30**
Shawnee Pottery, Decorative Ribbed patt., marked "U.S.A.," 5" h. **25-30**
Shawnee Pottery, Elite patt., marked "U.S.A.," 6 3/4" h. **45-50**
Shawnee Pottery, Elite patt., w/gold trim & decals, marked "U.S.A.," 6 3/4" h............. **75-85**
Shawnee Pottery, Embossed Rose patt., marked "U.S.A.," 6 1/4" h. **45-55**
Shawnee Pottery, Embossed Rose patt., w/gold trim, marked "U.S.A.," 6 1/4" h....... **65-75**
Shawnee Pottery, Fern or Wheat patt., individual size, yellow glaze, 2-cup................ **45-50**
Shawnee Pottery, Fern or Wheat patt., yellow glaze, 6" h. **30-35**

Gold-trimmed Fern Pattern Teapot

Shawnee Pottery, Fern or Wheat patt., yellow glaze, gold trim & decal, 6" h. (ILLUS.)... **75-95**

Shawnee Figural Cottage Teapot

Shawnee Pottery, figural Cottage, marked "U.S.A. 7," 5 1/2" h. (ILLUS.) **375-450**

Yellow & Blue Shawnee Elephant Teapots

Shawnee Pottery, figural Elephant patt., blue or yellow glaze, marked "U.S.A.," 6 1/2" h., each (ILLUS., top of page)..... **150-200**

Shawnee Pottery, figural Elephant patt., green glaze, marked "U.S.A.," 6 1/2" h. **175-225**

Shawnee Pottery, figural elephant w/burgundy, green & brown h.p. on white ground, marked "U.S.A.," 6 1/2" h. (ILLUS.).. **225-275**

Shawnee Figural Elephant Teapot

Rare Airbrushed Granny Ann Teapot

Two Granny Ann Teapots in Green & Burgundy

Two Granny Ann Teapots with Gold & Floral Decals

Shawnee Pottery, figural Granny Ann, airbrushed decoration w/blue apron & burgundy shawl, marked "Patented Granny Ann U.S.A.," each (ILLUS., center, right previous page) **500-650**

Shawnee Pottery, figural Granny Ann, green apron & shawl w/burgundy & yellow trim, w/gold decal shawl & trim, marked "Patented Granny Ann U.S.A." (ILLUS. right with other Granny Ann teapot, bottom previous page) **375-450**

Shawnee Pottery, figural Granny Ann, green apron & shawl w/burgundy & yellow trim, no gold decal shawl & trim, marked "Patented Granny Ann U.S.A." (ILLUS. left with other Granny Ann teapot, bottom previous page) **150-200**

Shawnee Pottery, figural Granny Ann, in peach w/blue trim or purple w/blue trim, marked "Patented Granny Ann U.S.A.," either **95-125**

Shawnee Pottery, figural Granny Ann, lavender apron w/gold trim & floral decals or peach apron w/blue & red trim w/gold trim & floral decals, marked "Patented Granny Ann U.S.A.," each (ILLUS. of both designs, top of page)............................... **225-275**

Shawnee Pottery, figural Tom the Piper's Son, airbrushed blues & reds w/gold trim, marked "Tom the Piper's Son Patented U.S.A. 44".. **150-175**

Rare Version of Tom the Piper's Son Teapot

Shawnee Pottery, figural Tom the Piper's Son, airbrushed matte reddish orange & greenish yellow w/gold trim, marked "Tom the Piper's Son Patented U.S.A. 44" (ILLUS.) **325-375**

Shawnee Pottery, figural Tom the Piper's Son, white body w/h.p. trim or airbrushed in blues & reds, marked "Tom the Piper's Son patented U.S.A. 44," 7" h., each (ILLUS. of both designs, below)............. **85-125**

Two Versions of the Tom the Piper's Sons Teapot

Gold-trimmed Sunflower Shawnee Teapot

Shawnee Pottery, figural Tom the Piper's Son, white body w/h.p. trim w/patches & gold trim, marked "Tom the Piper's Son patented U.S.A. 44," 7" h. **175-200**

Shawnee Pottery, Flower & Fern patt., 5-cup size, 5 1/4" h. **30-35**

Shawnee Pottery, Flower & Fern patt., gold-trimmed, 5-cup size, 5 1/4" h. **75-85**

Shawnee Pottery, Pennsylvania Dutch patt., marked "U.S.A. 10," 10 oz., two-cup size, also found in 14 oz., 18 oz., 27 oz. & 30 oz. sizes, each (ILLUS. of 10 oz. size) **50-65**

Horizontal Ribbed Shawnee Teapot

Shawnee Pottery, Horizontal Ribbed patt., h.p. floral vine decoration, marked "U.S.A.," 6" h. (ILLUS.)............................. **35-45**

Shawnee Pottery, Horizontal Ribbed patt., w/gold trim & depending on the h.p. decoration, marked "U.S.A.," 6" h. **65-85**

Shawnee Pottery, Laurel Wreath patt., 6 3/4" h. **30-35**

Shawnee Pennsylvania Dutch Teapot

Shawnee Rosette Pattern Teapot

Shawnee Pottery, Rosette patt., yellow glaze, marked "U.S.A.," 6" h. (ILLUS.)...... **20-25**

Shawnee Pottery, Snowflake patt., 5-cup size, 5 1/2" h. **30-35**

Shawnee Pottery, Sunflower patt., gold-trimmed, marked "U.S.A.," 30 oz., 6 1/4" h. (ILLUS., top of page) **125-175**

Shawnee Pottery, Sunflower patt., marked "U.S.A.," 30 oz., 6 1/4" h. **65-85**

Swirl Pattern Teapot by Shawnee

Shawnee Valencia Pattern Teapot

Shawnee Pottery, Swirl patt., turquoise blue glaze, marked "U.S.A.," 6 1/2" h. (ILLUS., previous page) **25-30**

Shawnee Pottery, Valencia patt., dark bluish green glaze, 7 1/2" h. (ILLUS., top of page) **75-100**

Shelley China, Auto Teapot Shape, lithographed Chintz Jacobean patt. No. 7850, from the Best Ware group, 1913 (ILLUS., right)...................................... **130-230**

Shelley China, Character Shape, Lord Chamberlain patt. No. 3356, from the Intarsio group, 1898 (ILLUS., bottom of page) **600-1,000**

Shelley Chintz Jacobean Teapot

Shelley Chamberlain Character Teapot

Basket of Fruit Teapot in Tulip Shape

Shelley China, Tulip Shape, Basket of Fruit patt. No. 8204, Floral style from the Stenciled group, 1918 (ILLUS.) **120-160**

Stanford Pottery Tomato Teapot

Stanford Pottery, bulbous tomato-shaped body, marked "Pantry Parade - Distributed by China and Glass Distributors, Inc., New York, NY," Sebring, Ohio, ca. 1949 (ILLUS.)... **50**

Sterling China Co., footed tapering ovoid shape, decorated w/a picture of a dancing Chinese girl, Chinese line, a Russel Wright design, ca. 1949, Wellsville, Ohio (ILLUS., top next column) **65**

Sterling China Company, octagonal foot below the wide tapering octagonal body w/flared rim & domed octagonal cover w/button finial, long paneled spout & angular handle, American Limoges earthenware body decorated w/a color transfer scene of Dutch children, Wellsville, Ohio, ca. 1900 (ILLUS., next column) **65**

Russel Wright-designed Chinese Teapot

Sterling China Teapot with Dutch Children

Steubenville China, wide low octagonal body w/a wide shoulder sloping to a wide flat rim, flat cover w/flaring finial, short spout & pointed angular handle, Steubenville, Ohio, early 20th c. (ILLUS., bottom of page)... **35**

Long, Low Steubenville China Teapot

Fine Sumida Ware Half-round Teapot

Sumida Ware, long half-round flat-bottomed body w/flattened sides & short shoulder spout, the curved cover w/figural child finial, the sides applied w/scene of a child on a red lacquered chair contemplating a large vase w/plant, flowing flambé glaze, black paint on the bottom, applied blue & white signature for artist Ryosai (1845-1905), Japan, ca. 1895, 7" l., 5" h. (ILLUS.) **495**

Early Taylor, Smith & Lee American-made Teapot

Taylor, Smith & Lee, wide squatty body w/molded details & wide slightly scalloped rim, domed cover w/scroll loop finial, C-scroll handle & serpentine spout, printed floral decoration, East Liverpool, Ohio, 1899-1901 (ILLUS.) **90**

Taylor, Smith & Taylor Paramount Ivory Teapot

Taylor, Smith & Taylor Floral Teapot

Taylor, Smith & Taylor, Paramount Ivory, wide squatty octagonal body w/low flaring rim, angled spout, angled loop handle, inset domed cover w/knob finial, printed floral sprigs in each panel, ca. 1928-45 (ILLUS., bottom previous page) **45**

Rose-embossed Taylor, Smith, Taylor Teapot

Taylor, Smith & Taylor, squatty bulbous lobed body molded around the bottom w/clusters of roses, low ruffled mouth w/short spout, C-form handle, domed lobed cover w/blossom finial, March 1932 (ILLUS.) **85**

Taylor, Smith & Taylor Vistosa Teapot

Taylor, Smith & Taylor, Vistosa shape, squatty bulbous body w/molded lobes & swirled bands, fitted cover w/button finial, floral-embossed C-form handle, transfer-printed florals, ca. 1944 (ILLUS.) **50**

Taylor, Smith & Taylor earthenware, squatty bulbous lobed & swirled body w/matching lobed cover, C-scroll handle w/embossed blossom & short, wide spout, Paramount shape, decorated w/rust red & orange blossoms & green leaves, Chester, West Virginia, late 1930s - mid-1940s (ILLUS., top of page) **30-35**

Bamboo Shape Tea Leaf Teapot

Tea Leaf Ironstone, Bamboo shape, Alfred Meakin, England, 1870s, one of the most common body styles (ILLUS.) **125-165**

Tea Leaf Ironstone, Bordered Fuchsia patt., Anthony Shaw (finial repair) **700**

Tea Leaf Ironstone, Cable patt., Cochrane, England, gold lustre band **50**

Huron Shape Tea Leaf Teapot

Tea Leaf Ironstone, Huron shape, Wm. Adams, England, ca. 1858, early & elusive body style (ILLUS.)............................... **500-650**

Rare Jumbo Shape Tea Leaf Teapot

Tea Leaf Ironstone, Jumbo shape, Henry Alcock, England, ca. 1880s, rare & unusual example, w/elephant heads in finial & on the handle (ILLUS.)....................... **500-650**

Draped Leaf Teapot with Morning Glory

Tea Leaf Ironstone variant, Draped Leaf shape, Morning Glory decoration, W. Baker & Co., England, ca. 1870s-80s (ILLUS.).. **300-400**

New York Shape with Teaberry Design

Tea Leaf Ironstone variant, New York shape, Teaberry decoration, J. Clementson, England, ca. 1858 (ILLUS.)........... **400-500**

Rare Prairie Teapot with Coral Decor

Tea Leaf Ironstone variant, Prairie shape, Coral decorative motif, J. Clementson, England, ca. 1860s, rare motif (ILLUS.).. **650-850**

Thompson Pottery Glenwood Teapot

Thompson Pottery, Glenwood patt., East Liverpool, Ohio, 1916-1938 (ILLUS.) **30**

Smaller "Lakes" Teapot by Watcombe

Torquay Pottery, faience "Lakes" decoration, very wide sharply tapering cylindrical body w/small inset cover w/knob finial, a very popular pattern in England but seldom offered in the U.S., Watcombe Pottery, 6" l., 4" h. (ILLUS.)........................... **165**

Watcombe Faience "Lakes" Teapot

Torquay Pottery, faience "Lakes" decoration, wide tapering cylindrical body w/small inset cover w/knob finial, a very popular pattern in England but seldom offered in the U.S., Watcombe Pottery, 7" l., 4" h. (ILLUS.) **195**

Royal Torquay Rosy Sunset Ships Teapot

Torquay Pottery, faience Rosy Sunset Ships patt., flat-bottomed wide tapering cylindrical body w/angled shoulder & conical cover w/knob finial, decorated w/a scene of sailing ships at sunset, Royal Torquay Pottery, 4 7/8" l., 3 1/2" h. (ILLUS.).. **95**

Rare Aller Vale Miniature Teapot

Torquay Pottery, miniature, colored scrolling B-1 decoration, Aller Vale Pottery, 5 1/4" l., 3 1/2" h. (ILLUS.) **350-400**

Miniature Longpark Crocus Teapot

Torquay Pottery, miniature, Crocus patt., wide low tapering cylindrical body w/wide shoulder tapering to conical cover w/knob finial, straight spout, C-form handle, Longpark Pottery, 4 1/4" l., 2 1/2" h. (ILLUS.)... **250**

Mini Royal Watcombe Sailing Ship Teapot

Torquay Pottery, miniature, Sailing Ship patt., spherical body w/angled spout, C-form handle & inset cover w/knob finial, Royal Watcombe Pottery, 4 7/8" l., 3" h. (ILLUS.).. **180-250**

Miniature Black Cockerel Teapot

Torquay Pottery, Motto Ware, Black Cockerel patt., miniature size, wide squatty bulbous tapering body w/angled spout & C-form handle, conical cover w/button finial, reads "Duee drink a cup a tay," Longpark Pottery, 4 1/2" l., 2 1/2" h. (ILLUS., previous page) **250-295**

Small Blue Spikey Tail Cockerel Teapot

Torquay Pottery, Motto Ware, Blue Spikey Tail Cockerel patt., wide squatty body w/inset domed cover w/knob finial, angled spout & high C-form handle, reads: "Guid morn!," Aller Vale Pottery, small size (ILLUS.) **125**

Blue-Tailed Cockerel Pattern Teapot

Torquay Pottery, Motto Ware, Blue-Tailed Cockerel patt., squatty bulbous tapering body w/wide mouth & inset cover w/button finial, reads: "Ye may get better cheer but no' wi' better heart. Guid morn," Aller Vale Pottery, 7 1/2" l., 4" h. (ILLUS.)..... **150-175**

Longpark Brown Cockerel Motto Ware Teapot

Torquay Pottery, Motto Ware, Brown Cockerel patt., wide squatty bulbous body w/short spout, C-form handle, tapering cover w/pointed finial, motto reads "Dawntee be fraid out now," Longpark Pottery (ILLUS.) **195-225**

Unusual Cat Pattern Aller Vale Teapot

Torquay Pottery, Motto Ware, Cat patt., wide bulbous body w/inset cover w/knob finial, comical stylized cat on a green background, reads "The Midnight Warbler," Aller Vale Pottery, 6 7/8" l., 4 1/8" h. (ILLUS.) **425**

Old English Cock Fight Faience Teapot

Torquay Pottery, Motto Ware, Cock Fight patt., faience, wide flat bottom w/slightly tapering cylindrical sides & narrow angled shoulder, inset cover w/knob finial, reads: "Old English Cock Fight," Watcombe Pottery, 6 1/2" l., 4 1/4" h. (ILLUS.).. **295**

Colored Cockerel Longpark Motto Ware Teapot

Torquay Pottery, Motto Ware, Colored Cockerel patt., footed deep half-round body w/curved shoulder to wide flat rim & inset flat cover w/button finial, C-form handle & upright spout, motto reads "Duee drink a cup a tay," Longpark Pottery (ILLUS.)... **125-150**

Rare Colored Cockerel Christmas Gift Teapot

Rare Large Longpark Motto Ware Teapot with the Colored Cockerel Pattern

Colored Cockerel Longpark Teapot

Torquay Pottery, Motto Ware, Colored Cockerel patt., ovoid body w/long serpentine spout & C-form handle, conical cover w/pointed finial, reads "We'el tak a cup o' kindness fer Auld Lang Syne," Longpark Pottery, 5 1/4" w., 6" h. (ILLUS.).................................... **125-150**

Torquay Pottery, Motto Ware, Colored Cockerel patt., special Christmas gift presentation piece, inscription reads: "To Mother - From Florrie - Xmas 1928 - Tak yourself a nice cup of tay," Longpark Pottery, very rare, 8" l., 5 1/2" h. (ILLUS. of both sides, top of page)............................... **350**

Torquay Pottery, Motto Ware, Colored Cockerel patt., very large & rare design, wide low tapering cylindrical body w/an angled shoulder decorated w/a band of dots, conical cover w/button finial, short spout & large C-scroll handle, long motto reads "May we all in travelling thro this so

called vale of tears - Find ever true and constant friends to share the cup that cheers," some professional restoration, Longpark Pottery, 9" l., 5" h. (ILLUS. of both sides, second from top of page).......... **350**

Rare Watcombe Colored Cockerel Teapot

Torquay Pottery, Motto Ware, Colored Cockerel w/mottled blue wing patt., reads "Cum me artiez an 'ave a cup o tay," Watcombe Pottery, rare, 7 1/2" l., 5" h. (ILLUS.)... **250**

Toy Size Cottage Pattern Teapot

Watcombe Green Motto Ware Teapot

Torquay Pottery, Motto Ware, Cottage patt., toy size, footed spherical body w/an angled spout, C-form handle & small cover w/knob finial, reads "For my dolly," Royal Watcombe Pottery, 4 7/8" l., 3 1/4" h. (ILLUS., previous page).......... **175-200**

Motto Ware Gray Cockerel Teapot

Torquay Pottery, Motto Ware, Gray Cockerel patt., footed spherical body w/a serpentine spout, C-form handle & small cover w/knob finial, reads "Good morning," Watcombe Pottery, 7 7/8" l., 4 3/4" h. (ILLUS.) **275**

Watcombe Faience Cock Fight Teapot

Torquay Pottery, Motto Ware, Old English Cock Fight patt., faience decoration, wide slightly tapering cylindrical body w/serpentine spout & long C-form handle, small inset cover w/knob finial, rim reads "The English Cock," Watcombe Pottery, 6 1/2" l., 4 1/4" h. (ILLUS.) **250-300**

Watcombe Lindisfarne Castle Teapot

Torquay Pottery, Motto Ware, scene of Lindisfarne Castle, miniature, faience decoration, spherical body w/angled spout, C-form handle, small cover w/knob finial, reads "Lindisfarne Castle - Holy Island," Royal Watcombe Pottery, 4 3/4" l., 3" h. (ILLUS.) **180-200**

Torquay Pottery, Motto Ware, wide flat-bottomed tapering cylindrical shape w/angled shoulder to a flat mouth w/a tapering cover w/double-knob finial, straight spout, C-form handle, reads "Du'ee drink a cup ov tay," green glaze, Watcombe Pottery, 6 1/2" w., 3 1/2" h. (ILLUS., top of page)............................ **125-150**

Small Souvenir Sea Gull Pattern Teapot

Torquay Pottery, souvenir ware, Sea Gull patt., miniature, spherical body w/a serpentine spout, C-form handle & small cover w/knob finial, reads "Lands End," Royal Watcombe Pottery, 4 7/8" l., 3" h. (ILLUS.)... **180-200**

Rare Tiny Mini Aller Vale Teapot

Torquay Pottery, tiny miniature size, early Forget-Me-Not h.p. decoration, white clay, Aller Vale Pottery, ca. 1890s, rare (ILLUS.)... **200**

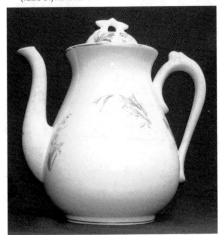

Early Trenton Pottery Teapot

Trenton Pottery, ovoid body tapering to a flaring rim, domed cover w/bar finial, printed leafy sprig decoration, Trenton, New Jersey, ca. 1870 (ILLUS.) **60**
Vernon Kilns Pottery, Moby Dick patt., Rockwell Kent Designs, blue, 6-cup...... **150-175**
Vernon Kilns Pottery, Vernon's 1860 patt........ **75**

Wade Lustre-decorated Teapot

Wade earthenware, squatty bulbous body w/a cream ground h.p. w/large deep red blossoms w/yellow centers, green leaves & light brown brushstrokes, copper lustre-decorated handle, spout & cover, marked "Wadeheath - England," Wade,

Heath & Co., England, ca. 1930s, 9" l., 4 3/4" h. (ILLUS.) **65**

Wade, Heath & Co. Carousel Teapot

Wade, Heath & Co., cylindrical body modeled as a colorful carousel w/pointed cover, Wade, England mark, ca. 1927 (ILLUS.)... **40**

Warwick Portrait Teapot

Warwick China, h.p. portrait, "Gibson Girl" decor, turquoise & pink, matte finish, signed "H. Richard Boehm," marked w/IOGA knight's helmet in green, decor code M5, rare in this color, ca. 1910, 7 1/2" h. (ILLUS.) **425**

Warwick Tudor Rose Pattern Teapot

Warwick China, Tudor Rose patt., Banquet Weight Ware, Wheeling, West Virginia, 1912-35 (ILLUS.) **50**

Josiah Wedgwood Jasper Ware Teapot

Wedgwood (Josiah), Jasper Ware, squatty bulbous form in green w/white relief Classical figures, regular size (ILLUS.) **65**

1940s Wedgwood Queens Ware Pot

Wedgwood Queens Ware, footed squatty bulbous body in creamy white w/a short angled spout, upright squared handle & tapering domed cover w/knob finial, applied light blue grapevine band around shoulder & cover, marked "Wedgwood Embossed Queens Ware of Etruria & Barlaston," Josiah Wedgwood & Sons, England, ca. 1940, 8 3/4" l., 5" h. (ILLUS.).. **70**

Weil Ware Teapot with Bamboo Design

Weil Ware, bulbous body w/a serpentine spout & angled handle, fitted cover w/squared handle, greyish white ground decorated w/yellow bamboo stalks & green leaves, The California Figure Company, Los Angeles, ca. 1930s-40s, 7 1/4" h. (ILLUS.) **75**

Wheeling Potteries, LaBelle China line, bulbous tapering body w/short ruffled neck, serpentine spout, C-scroll handle & low domed cover w/double-loop finial, overall rose vine decoration, Wheeling, West Virginia, ca. 1893 (ILLUS., next column) **45**

Early La Belle China Floral Teapot

American Moss Rose Pattern Teapot

Wheeling Pottery Co., Moss Rose patt., tapering cylindrical ironstone shaped w/flared rim & domed cover w/bar finial, serpentine spout & C-scroll handle, Wheeling, West Virginia, 1880-86 (ILLUS.)... **65**

Alcock's Pear White Ironstone Teapot

White ironstone china, Alcock's Pear shape, by John Alcock, England, ca. 1860 (ILLUS.)....................................... **125-150**

Three Boote's 1851 Shape Pieces

Alternate Panels Ironstone Teapot

Clementson Canada Shape Teapot

White ironstone china, Alternate Panels
shape, unknown potter, England, mid-
19th c. (ILLUS.) **125-150**

White ironstone china, Boote's 1851
shape, adult size, by T. & R. Boote,
England, ca. 1851 (ILLUS. left with other
Boote's 1851 pieces, top of page)......... **300-325**

White ironstone china, Boote's 1851
shape, child's size, by T. & R. Boote,
England, ca. 1851 (ILLUS. center with
other Boote's 1851 pieces, top of
page) **200-250**

White ironstone china, Boote's 1851
shape cov. creamer, a ca. 1960s reproduction by Red Cliff, based on the early
shape (ILLUS. right with other Boote's
1851 pieces, top of page)........................ **35-45**

White ironstone china, Canada shape, by
Clementson Bros., England, ca. 1877
(ILLUS.)... **275-300**

Ceres Shape White Ironstone Teapot

Grape Octagon Teapots in Two Sizes

White ironstone china, Ceres shape, by Elsmore & Forster, England, ca. 1857 (ILLUS., previous page) **250-350**

White ironstone china, Grape Octagon shape, adult size, various makers, ca. 1850s (ILLUS. right with child's teapot, top of page) **150-200**

White ironstone china, Grape Octagon shape, child's size, various makers, ca. 1850s (ILLUS. left with full-sized teapot, top of page) **175-225**

White ironstone china, Hyacinth patt., W. & E. Corn, England, ca. 1870 (ILLUS.) **135**

Edwards Lily of the Valley Teapot

White ironstone china, Lily of the Valley shape, by James Edwards, England, ca. 1860s (ILLUS.) **200-225**

Hyacinth Pattern Teapot by W. & E. Corn

Ironstone Loop & Dot Shape Teapot

White ironstone china, Loop & Dot shape,
by E. & C. Challinor, England, ca. 1865
(ILLUS.)... **190-210**

Plain Seashore White Ironstone Teapot

White ironstone china, Plain Seashore
shape, molded dolphin on handle & finial,
by W. & E. Corn, ca. 1885 (ILLUS.) **125-150**

Plain Shape White Ironstone Teapot

White ironstone china, Plain shape, by W.
& E. Corn, England, ca. 1880s
(ILLUS.)... **75-100**

Portland Shape Ironstone China Teapot

White ironstone china, Portland shape, by
Elsmore & Forster, England, ca. 1860s
(ILLUS.)... **240-260**
White ironstone china, Prairie shape (aka
New Grenade shape), adult size, by T. &
R. Boote, England, ca. 1850s **200-225**

Prairie Shape Ironstone Child's Teapot

White ironstone china, Prairie shape (aka
New Grenade shape), child's size, by T.
& R. Boote, England, ca. 1850s
(ILLUS.)... **175-200**

Prize Bloom White Ironstone Teapot

White **ironstone china,** Prize Bloom shape, by T. J. & J. Mayer, England, ca. 1853 (ILLUS., previous page) **250-300**

Rib & Chain Shape Ironstone Teapot

White ironstone china, Rib & Chain shape, by J.W. Pankhurst, England, ca. 1860s (ILLUS.).. **225-250**

White Ironstone Tulip Shape Teapot

White ironstone china, Tulip shape, by Elsmore & Forster, England, ca. 1855 (ILLUS.).. **200-225**

Blue-trimmed Tulip Shape Teapot

White ironstone china, Tulip shape, trimmed in blue, by Elsmore & Forster, England, ca. 1855 (ILLUS.)................... **290-320**

White Ironstone Tuscan Shape Teapot

White ironstone china, Tuscan shape, by John Edwards, England, ca. 1853 (ILLUS.).. **150-175**

Virginia Shape White Ironstone Teapot

White ironstone china, Virginia shape, by Brougham & Mayer, England, ca. 1855 (ILLUS.).. **200-230**

Western Shape Child's Teapot

White ironstone china, Western shape, child's size, by J.F., ca. 1860 (ILLUS., previous page) **175-200**

Wheat & Clover Ironstone Teapot

White ironstone china, Wheat & Clover shape, by Turner & Tompkinson, England, ca. 1860s (ILLUS.) **220-250**

Tall Williamson Pottery Teapot

Williamson (H.M.) & Sons, tall slightly flaring cylindrical body w/a flattened rim & cover w/pointed finial, serpentine spout & angled side handle, Gainsborough patt., England, ca. 1908 (ILLUS.) **120**

Wedgwood & Co. Blue Willow Teapot

Willow Ware, Blue Willow, footed Gothic Panel Octagon shape, flared neck w/inset domed cover w/pointed finial, C-scroll handle, serpentine spout, Wedgwood & Co., England, ca. 1908+ (ILLUS.) **175-200**

Buffalo Pottery Blue Willow Teapot

Willow Ware, Blue Willow, individual size, spherical body on short foot, short cylindrical neck w/inset slightly domed cover w/button finial, C-form handle, serpentine spout, Buffalo Pottery, Buffalo, New York, 1911 (ILLUS.) **150-175**

Mason's Ironstone Blue Willow Teapot

Willow Ware, Blue Willow, John Turner Willow patt., footed rectangular shape w/incurved corners, tapering shoulder, rectangular beveled cover w/open loop finial, overhead stationary handle, angled

Hammersley & Co. Blue Willow Teapot

spout, Mason's Ironstone, England, ca. 1890+ (ILLUS., previous page) **200-225**

Royal Corona Ware Teapot

Willow Ware, Blue Willow, squatty ovoid body on short foot, flattened dome cover w/button finial, C-form handle, gently serpentine spout, dark blue spout, handle & finial, gold highlights, Royal Corona Ware, S. Hancock & Sons, England, early 20th c. (ILLUS.) **225-250**

Willow Ware, Blue Willow, squatty ovoid body on short foot, incurved neck, C-scroll handle, slightly serpentine spout, inset cover tapering to peaked circular finial, decorated w/bands of gold beading at shoulder & on cover, gold decoration on rim, handle, spout & finial, Hammersley & Co., England, ca. 1912-39 (ILLUS., top of page)............................ **150-175**

Doulton & Co. Blue Willow Teapot

Willow Ware, Blue Willow, squatty ovoid body tapering in at shoulder to short cylindrical neck, slightly tapering inset cover w/disk finial, angled handle, slightly curved spout, shoulder reads "We'll tak a cup o' kindness yet, for days o' auld lang syne," Doulton & Co., England, ca. 1882-91 (ILLUS.).. **200**

Blue Willow Teapot with "Barber Pole" Decoration

Willow Ware, Blue Willow, squatty ovoid body w/short waisted neck, C-scroll handle & serpentine spout, peaked cover w/disk finial, neck w/band of gold vining decoration on dark blue ground, spout & handle w/blue & white "barber pole" stripes, gold line decoration at base, handle, spout, neck, cover & finial, marked "Pattorn" on base, England, 19th c. (ILLUS., top of pager).......................... **250-275**

Gaudy Willow Teapot by Buffalo Pottery

Willow Ware, Gaudy Willow patt., ovoid body on short foot, C-form handle, serpentine spout, slightly domed cover w/flat top & knob finial, rust, green & dark blue design, dark blue handle, spout & finial, gold highlights, marked "First Willow Ware Made in America," Buffalo Pottery, Buffalo, New York, 1905 (ILLUS.)......... **450-500**

Willow Ware, Blue Willow, spherical body on short tapering foot, short neck w/inset cover w/button finial, C-scroll handle, serpentine spout, on matching round trivet, Grimwades, England, early 20th c., teapot 6" h., 2 pcs. (ILLUS., next column) **250-275**

Blue Willow Teapot & Trivet

Blue Willow Teapot with Bamboo Look

Willow Ware, Blue Willow, tapering cylindrical shape slanting in at base, cover w/finial in the form of a curved bamboo shoot, the C-form handle & straight spout decorated in gold to resemble bamboo, gold highlights, marked on base "Semi China," England, early 20th c., 6" h. (ILLUS.)... **250-275**

Wood & Sons Tsing Pattern Teapot

Wood & Sons, Tsing patt., footed squatty bulbous hexagonal body w/flared rim, pointed cover, paneled spout & squared handle, Woods Ware line, England, ca. 1920 (ILLUS.)... **50**

Zeisel (Eva) Designs, footed tapering bulbous body decorated w/colorful polka dots, No. 3356, Pattern 3369, produced by Schramberg Co., Germany, ca. 1930 (ILLUS.).. **1,200**

Gobelin 13 Teapot

Zeisel (Eva) Designs, Schramberg Co., Gobelin 13 patt., Germany, 1930s (ILLUS.)... **900**

Zeisel (Eva) Designs, Town and Country Dinnerware - for Red Wing Potteries, ca. 1947, blue (ILLUS., bottom of page)..... **200-225**

Early Zeisel Teapot by Schramberg

Zeisel Town & Country Teapot in Blue

Modernistic Teapot by an Unknown Maker

Bronze Town and Country Teapot

Zeisel (Eva) Designs, Town and Country Dinnerware - for Red Wing Potteries, ca. 1947, bronze (ILLUS.).................................. **250**

Unknown maker, earthenware, bulbous wide inverted pear-shaped modernistic body w/tapering spout & down-curved pointed handle, wide flat cover w/swirl finial, stylized brown & green sprig decoration, possibly by the Stetson China Company (ILLUS., top of page) **25-30**

Unmarked Earthenware Teapot

Unknown maker, ovoid earthenware w/stationary overhead handle, short curved spout, domed lid w/disk finial, body w/band of embossed scroll decoration, additional floral decoration in blue & yellow, early 20th c., 5" to top of handle (ILLUS.)... **25**

Unmarked Oriental-style Teapot

Unknown maker, earthenware square body w/beveled corners & tapering shoulder, oval lid w/finial, overhead reed bail handle, short serpentine spout, the white ribbed body & lid w/applied maroon flower & log decoration, cobalt blue base, shoulder & end of spout, probably Oriental, early 20th c., 5" sq. (ILLUS.) **30**

Unmarked Teapot Possibly by Brock

Unknown maker, squatty bulbous tapering body in white decorated w/pink, blue & brown floral sprigs & a blue rim band, short spout, domed cover w/button finial, twisted wire swing bail handle, possibly by the Brock China Company (ILLUS.)..... **50-55**

Black Americana

Black Fireman Head Containers

Black Fireman biscuit jar, smiling head w/mustache & red helmet complete w/badge, wire bail handle, Japan (ILLUS. far right w/other Black Fireman pieces, above).................................... **$400-500**

Black Fireman cookie jar, smiling head w/mustache & red helmet complete w/badge, wire bail handle, Japan (ILLUS. second from right w/other Black Fireman pieces).. **500-700**

Black Fireman salt & pepper shakers, smiling head w/mustache & red helmet complete w/badge, wire bail handle, Japan, pr. (ILLUS. far left w/other Black Fireman pieces) **150**

Black Fireman teapot, smiling head w/mustache & red helmet complete w/badge, wire bail handle, Japan (ILLUS. third from left w/other Black Fireman pieces).. **450**

Black Mammy cookie jar, ceramic, figural, full-figure Mammy w/basketweave handle, Weller lookalike, Maruhon Ware, Japan (ILLUS. back row second from right with other Maruhon Ware pieces, below).. **2,500**

Black Mammy pitcher, cov., water, ceramic, Weller lookalike Mammy figure w/her white kerchiefed head forming the cover, wearing white & blue plaid dress w/large blue-dotted white apron, Maruhon Ware, Japan (ILLUS. back row far left with other Maruhon Ware pieces, below) **1,000**

Black Mammy sugar bowl (or jam jar), cov., ceramic, Weller lookalike Mammy figure w/her white kerchiefed head forming the cover, wearing white & blue plaid dress w/large blue-dotted white apron, Maruhon Ware, Japan (ILLUS. front row right with other Maruhon Ware pieces, below) **800**

Grouping of Ceramic Mahuron Ware Kitchen Pieces

Polka Dot Mammy Creamer, Sugar & Teapot

Black Mammy syrup pitcher (or creamer), cov., ceramic, Weller lookalike Mammy figure w/her red kerchiefed head forming the cover, wearing white & red plaid dress w/large red-dotted white apron, Maruhon Ware, Japan (ILLUS. front row left with other Maruhon Ware pieces, previous page) 800

Black Mammy teapot, ceramic, Weller lookalike Mammy figure w/her red kerchiefed head forming the cover, wearing white & red plaid dress w/large red-dotted white apron, Maruhon Ware, Japan (ILLUS. front row far right with other Maruhon Ware pieces, previous page) 1,200

Polka Dot Mammy creamer, ceramic, figural Polka Dot Mammy w/plaid apron, loop handles (ILLUS. front right with sugar bowl & teapot, top of page) 800

Polka Dot Mammy sugar bowl, ceramic, figural Polka Dot Mammy w/plaid apron, loop handle (ILLUS. front left with creamer & teapot, top of page) 1,000

Polka Dot Mammy teapot, ceramic, figural Polka Dot Mammy w/plaid apron, loop handle (ILLUS. back center with creamer & sugar bowl, top of page) 2,000

Colorful Black Mammy Teapot

Black Mammy teapot, ceramic, figural, modeled as black Mammy w/the base formed by her wide green skirt & apron, holding a long red wedge of watermelon at front, yellow blouse & white striped kerchief, bottom marked "USA," overall crazing, 8" l., 8" h. (ILLUS.) 94

Rare Polka Dot Mammy Teapot

Polka Dot Mammy teapot, ceramic, head of Polka Dot Mammy, Japan, ca. 1940s (ILLUS.) 1,000

Pottery & Earthenware - 1950-2000

Royal Canadian Art Pottery Teapot

Canadian pottery, squatty bulbous body w/serpentine spout, C-form handle & inset domed cover w/arched finial, h.p. w/large stylized blossoms, Royal Canadian Art Pottery, Hamilton, Ontario, 1980s (ILLUS.).. **$25**

Colorful Modern Canadian Teapot

Canadian pottery, wide squatty rounded body w/short spout & loop handle, inverted cup forming cover, decorated w/colorful bands, marked "Psyanki (sp?) - Easter Egg Design," Vegreville, Alberta, Canada (ILLUS.).. **25**

Modern Capodimonte Squatty Teapot

Capodimonte earthenware, fancy scroll-footed squatty bulbous body tapering to a domed cover, serpentine ribbed spout & ornate scrolling overhead handle, applied w/large roses & leaves, Naples, Italy, 1990s (ILLUS.) **50**

Tall Modern Capodimonte Teapot

Capodimonte earthenware, tall tapering bulbous body on scroll feet, high domed cover w/pointed finial, tall ribbed serpentine spout & C-scroll handle, overall molded scroll bands & the side applied w/very large rose blossoms, Naples, Italy, 1990s (ILLUS.) **35**

Modern Cauldon Potteries Teapot

Cauldon Potteries, Ltd., spherical body w/serpentine spout & C-form handle, domed cover w/knob finial, h.p. w/large flowers, Ceracraft line, England, 1996 (ILLUS.).. **35**

Modern New Zealand Teapot & Trivet

Crespin Pottery, tapering ovoid body w/angled spout, C-form handle & small cover w/knob finial, h.p. w/a stylized rooster, w/matching round trivet, Havelock North, New Zealand, 1992, the set (ILLUS.)............ **20**

Modern Version of Popular Calico Pattern

Crownford China, Calico patt., bulbous body w/serpentine spout, angled handle & domed cover w/knob finial, overall dark blue w/white blossoms, England, 1990s (ILLUS.)... **35**

Modern Delft Pottery Blue & White Teapot

Delft pottery, squatty bulbous body w/angled spout & C-form handle, small cover w/button finial, overall h.p. stylized blue florals, Delft, Holland, 1992 (ILLUS.).............. **50**

Fitz & Floyd Napoleon Teapot

Fitz and Floyd, figural Napoleon Bonaparte, Emperor of the French, from the Figures from History series, produced in Taiwan, 1994 (ILLUS.) **90**

Franciscan Ware Desert Rose Teapot

Franciscan Ware, Desert Rose patt., Gladding, McBean, Los Angeles, ca. 1960 (ILLUS.)... **100**

Modern French Stoneware Teapot

French stoneware, bulbous squatty body w/short cylindrical neck, domed cover w/knob finial, short spout & C-form handle, h.p. w/stylized flowers, handmade by Keraluc, France, 1994 (ILLUS.) **45**

Gibson & Sons Teapot with Roses

Gibsons, pumpkin-shaped body w/serpentine spout & C-scroll handle, low domed cover w/knob finial, decorated w/scattered roses, made in England mark, ca. 1940s (ILLUS.)... **35**

Hall Aladdin Shape Wildfire Pattern Teapot

Hall China, Aladdin shape, Wildfire patt.,
w/oval infuser, 1950s (ILLUS.)...................... **75**

Hall Reissued Donut Shape Teapot

Hall China, Donut shape, Autumn Leaf
patt., 1993 reissue (ILLUS.)........................ **150**

Reissued Hall Automobile Teapot

Hall China, Automobile shape, Autumn
Leaf patt., reissue for China Specialties
w/commemorative stamp on the bottom,
1993 (ILLUS.).. **175**

Commemorative Hall Donut Teapot

Hall China, Donut shape, part of a limited
edition produced for the East Liverpool
High School Alumni Assoc., No. 2 of 16,
1997 (ILLUS.)... **100**

*Special Birdcage Shape Autumn Leaf
Hall Teapot*

Hall China, Birdcage shape, Jewel Tea Autumn Leaf patt., specially produced for
the Autumn Leaf Club in 1995 (ILLUS.) **150**

*Limited Edition Hook Cover Shape
Cameo Rose Teapot*

Hall China, Hook Cover shape, Cameo
Rose patt., part of a limited edition pro-
duced exclusively for China Specialties,
Strongsville, Ohio, fewer than 500 made
(ILLUS.).. **95**

Aladdin Pattern Teapot in Teal Green

Harker Pottery, Aladdin patt., short squatty bulbous shape w/short neck, loop handle, squatty serpentine spout, short foot, domed lid w/disk handle, in deep teal green w/cream highlights on finial & rim, ca. 1950 (ILLUS.) **20**

Harker's Rebecca at the Well Rockingham Reproduction Teapot

Harker Pottery, Rebecca at the Well patt., cylindrical body tapering in at shoulder,

short foot & neck, domed inset lid w/turned finial, C-scroll handle w/thumbrest, turned serpentine spout, brown body embossed w/scene of Rebecca at the Well, part of Harker's line of Rockingham reproductions, the date of 1840 on bottom referring to the year Harker Pottery opened, ca. 1960 (ILLUS.) **40**

Laughlin Rhythm Shape Floral Teapot

Homer Laughlin China Co., Rhythm shape, decorated w/printed scattered rose blossoms, April 1951, Plant #5, double-stamped "Household Institute - Rhythm HLC D51N4," Newell, West Virginia (ILLUS.) **40**

Homer Laughlin China Company, Debutante shape, Flame Flower patt., wide low modern streamlined body w/long loop handle & short angled shoulder spout, flattened cover w/scroll finial, designed by Don Schreckengost, Newell, West Virginia, 1950s (ILLUS., bottom of page) **50-55**

Homer Laughlin Debutante Teapot in Flame Flower Pattern

1970s Homer Laughlin Teapot

Homer Laughlin China Company, Dover
shape, Bayberry patt., tapering octagonal body w/domed cover, long angled
handle & serpentine spout, Newell, West
Virginia, 1970s (ILLUS.) **35-40**

Hull Pottery, Serenade patt., No. S17,
5" h., 6-cup **135**

Hull Pottery, House 'N Garden line, Mirror
Brown, 6" h.. **25-35**

Hull Pottery, Parchment & Pine patt., No.
S-11, 6" h. **80**

Japanese pottery, footed baluster-form
white body w/ruffled rim, domed cover
w/C-scroll finial, upright spout & C-scroll
handle, the sides molded w/a large turkey below a band of fruits, molded fruits
on spout, marked "Napcoware - Japan"
(ILLUS.).. **20**

Weeping Gold Kingwood Teapot

Kingwood Ceramics Company, Weeping
Gold design, squatty bulbous body w/C-
form handle & serpentine spout, flattened
cover w/arched handle, overall mottled
gold glaze, probably made in the late
1970s or early 1980s, East Palestine,
Ohio (ILLUS.) **45-50**

Japanese Napcoware White Teapot

Modern Korean Pottery Teapot

Reissued Minton Chinaman Figural Teapot

Reissued Minton Cockerel Teapot

Korean pottery, bulbous melon-lobed body w/serpentine spout, C-form handle & low domed cover w/knob finial, h.p. w/stylized flowers, marked "Casualstone - Korea" (ILLUS., previous page) **25**

Majolica, figural Chinaman patt., produced by Minton, based on Victorian original, limited edition of 2,500, introduced in 2000 (ILLUS., bottom previous page) **650**

Majolica, figural Cockerel patt., produced by Minton, based on Victorian original, limited edition of 2,500, introduced in 2000 (ILLUS., top of page) **700**

Reissued Minton Majolica Fish Pattern Teapot

Majolica, figural Fish patt., produced by Minton, based on Victorian original, limited edition of 2,500, introduced in 2000 (ILLUS.) **750**

New Minton Figural Tortoise Teapot

Minton Reissue of Monkey Teapot

Majolica, figural Monkey model, made by Minton, reissue of Victorian original, limited edition of 1,793, introduced in 1993 (ILLUS.)... **850**

New Minton Majolica Mushroom Teapot

Majolica, Mushroom patt., designed by Gordon Brooks, produced by Minton, limited edition of 1,000, introduced in 2002 (ILLUS.)... **750**

Majolica, Tortoise patt., produced by Minton, limited edition of 2,500, introduced in 1999 (ILLUS., top of page)......................... **750**

McNichol Hotel Ware Teapot

McNichol (D.E.) Pottery, ROLOC hotel ware, heavy body, printed w/the Seal of West Virginia, Clarksburg, West Virginia, 1940-60 (ILLUS.) **35**

Modern Meakin Classic White Teapot

Meakin (J. & G.), Classic White design, footed squatty bulbous ribbed body w/flaring ruffled rim, domed cover w/flared finial, ribbed serpentine spout, C-scroll handle, all-white, part of the Wedgwood Group, England, 1962 (ILLUS.) **50**

Modern Jeff Scholes Pottery Teapot

New Zealand pottery, bulbous ovoid body tapering to a flat rim w/domed cover & knob finial, angled spout & C-form handle, hand-made by independent pottery, Jeff Scholes, 1992 (ILLUS.) 50

Yorktown Line Teapot by Pfalzgraff

Pfalzgraff Pottery, Yorktown line, bulbous body tapering in at shoulder, flaring neck, domed lid w/finial, C-form handle, short serpentine spout, body decorated w/simple floral design in cobalt blue, blue line decoration on rim (ILLUS.) 45

Modern Portuguese Molded Teapot

Portuguese earthenware, rounded cylindrical body molded w/spearpoint leaves & sprigs, molded angled spout, C-scroll handle, molded domed cover, Cream Ware II Sparta Group, DECMA Abrigada, Portugal, 1989 (ILLUS.) 45

Modern Portuguese Pottery Teapot

Portuguese pottery, squatty bulbous body w/a short spout & loop handle, small cover w/button finial, h.p. w/a large colorful blossom, marked "Y OAL - Portugal," 1985 (ILLUS.) 20

1960s Price & Kensington Teapot

Price & Kensington Potteries, squatty bulbous footed body w/flaring ruffled rim, serpentine spout, fancy C-scroll handle, low domed cover w/knob final, printed w/scattered colorful flowers, England, 1962+ (ILLUS.) 40

1970s Quimper Pottery Teapot

Quimper pottery, paneled body w/paneled cover & angled handle, h.p. peasant-style decoration, HB Quimper, France, 1975 (ILLUS.) 80

Red Cliff Sydenham Shape White Teapot

Red Cliff Company, all-white Sydenham shape, copy of Victorian ironstone original design, produced by Hall China for Red Cliff, ca. 1960s (ILLUS.) **95**

Red Cliff Grape Leaf Pattern Teapot

Red Cliff Company, all-white tall paneled & tapering body w/domed cover, molded Grape Leaf patt., produced by Hall China for Red Cliff, ca. 1960s (ILLUS.) **150**

Red Wing Pottery Bob White Teapot

Red Wing Pottery, Bob White patt., cream ground h.p. w/stylized quails, ca. 1956, 7 1/2" h. (ILLUS.) **125**
Red Wing Pottery, Bob White patt., teapot & stand, the set **140**
Red Wing Pottery, Village Green line **22**
Roseville Pottery, Raymor patt., Avocado green, No. 174 .... **100-150**
Roseville Pottery, Apple Blossom patt., blue ground, No. 371-P.............................. **300**
Roseville Pottery, Bittersweet patt., yellow ground, No. 871-P....................................... **225**

Beswick Figural Panda Teapot

Royal Doulton Ware, Beswick Ware, figural Panda, introduced in 1989 (ILLUS.)......... **300**

Bunnykins Aussie Explorer Teapot

Royal Doulton Ware, Bunnykins Series, Aussie Explorer patt., designed by Shane Ridge, limited edition of 2,500, introduced in 1996 (ILLUS.)............................... **225**

Two Views of the Bunnykins Geisha Girl Teapot

Royal Doulton Ware, Bunnykins Series, figural Geisha Girl model, designed by Martyn Alcock, limited edition of 2,500, introduced in 1998 (ILLUS. of two views, top of page) **225**

Bunnykins Lord of the Manor Teapot

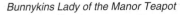

Bunnykins Lady of the Manor Teapot

Royal Doulton Ware, Bunnykins Series, figural Lady of the Manor, designed by Shane Ridge, limited edition of 1,500, introduced in 2003 (ILLUS.) **300**

Royal Doulton Ware, Bunnykins Series, Lord of the Manor patt., designed by Shane Ridge, limited edition of 1,500, introduced in 2003 (ILLUS., top next column) **300**

Royal Doulton Ware, Bunnykins Series, USA President model, designed by Shane Ridge, limited edition of 2,500, introduced in 1995 (ILLUS., next column) **250**

Bunnykins USA President Teapot

Both Sides of the Cowboy & Indian Figural Teapot

Royal Doulton Ware, figural Cowboy and Indian model, designed by Anthony Cartlidge, limited edition of 1,500, introduced in 2002 (ILLUS. of both sides, above) **300**

Modern Long John Silver Doulton Teapot

Royal Doulton Ware, figural Long John Silver w/parrot, 1989 (ILLUS.).......................... **165**

Modern Royal Doulton Falstaff Teapot

Royal Doulton Ware, figural Falstaff model, 1989 (ILLUS.).. **175**

Royal Doulton Ware, figural Norman and Saxon model, designed by Anthony Cartlidge, limited edition of 1,500, introduced in 2003 (ILLUS. of both sides, below) **300**

Two Views of the Norman & Saxon Royal Doulton Teapot

Two Views of the Doulton Pirate and Captain Teapot

Royal Doulton Old Salt Teapot

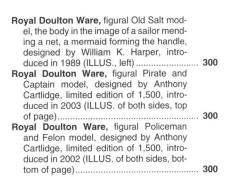

Royal Doulton Ware, figural Old Salt model, the body in the image of a sailor mending a net, a mermaid forming the handle, designed by William K. Harper, introduced in 1989 (ILLUS., left) **300**

Royal Doulton Ware, figural Pirate and Captain model, designed by Anthony Cartlidge, limited edition of 1,500, introduced in 2003 (ILLUS. of both sides, top of page) **300**

Royal Doulton Ware, figural Policeman and Felon model, designed by Anthony Cartlidge, limited edition of 1,500, introduced in 2002 (ILLUS. of both sides, bottom of page) **300**

Both Sides of the Doulton Policeman & Felon Teapot

Front & Back of the Sodden & Sobriety Figural Teapot

Royal Doulton Ware, figural Sodden and Sobriety model, designed by Anthony Cartlidge, limited edition of 1,500, introduced in 2003 (ILLUS. of both sides, above) **300**

Rozart Floral-decorated Teapot

Rozart Pottery, two-cup size, hi-glaze, shaded grey ground h.p. w/large white & pink blossoms & dark green leaves, late 1960s+ (ILLUS.) **175**

Sadler (James) & Sons, bold Art Deco-style shape & decoration marked "Inspired by Clarice Cliff's Art Deco Bizarre

Ware of the 1930s," England, modern (ILLUS., bottom of page).............................. **50**

Shorter & Son Figural King Cole Teapot

Sadler Clarice Cliff-style Art Deco Teapot

Three Sizes of the Uhl Pottery Teapot

Shorter & Son, figural Old King Cole, colorful decoration, Crown Devon group, England, post-1950 (ILLUS., previous page) **40**

LuRay Teapot with Experimental Glaze

Taylor, Smith & Taylor, LuRay shape, experimental "ombre" glaze, ca. 1950s (ILLUS.) **45**

LuRay Shape Teapot with 601 Design

Taylor, Smith & Taylor, LuRay shape w/601 Design, 1950s (ILLUS.) **65**

Uhl Pottery, spherical body w/long serpentine spout, C-form handle, low rim w/inset flattened cover w/knob finial, one of three sizes made, marked w/the circle mark on the bottom & also usually an incised number, made in various colors including white, yellow, brown, at least three shades of blue, a scarce shade of green, dark blue, pink, teal, black or purple are most desirable today, value depends on color, large size, 8-cup (ILLUS. in dark blue at far right with other Uhl teapots, at top of page) **100**

Uhl Pottery, spherical body w/long serpentine spout, C-form handle, low rim w/inset flattened cover w/knob finial, one of three sizes made, marked w/the circle mark on the bottom & also usually an incised number, made in various colors including white, yellow, brown, at least three shades of blue, a scarce shade of green, dark blue, pink, teal, black or purple are most desirable today, value depends on color medium size, 4-cup (ILLUS. in light blue in the center with other Uhl teapots, at top of page) **125**

Uhl Pottery, spherical body w/long serpentine spout, C-form handle, low rim w/inset flattened cover w/knob finial, one of three sizes made, marked w/the circle mark on the bottom & also usually an incised number, made in various colors including white, yellow, brown, at least three shades of blue, a scarce shade of green, dark blue, pink, teal, black or purple are most desirable today, value depends on color, small size, 2-cup (ILLUS. in dark blue at far left with other Uhl teapots, at top of page) **200**

Vernon Kilns Pottery, Santa Barbara patt. (ILLUS., bottom of page) **65-80**

Santa Barbara Pattern Teapot

Watt Pottery Autumn Foliage Teapot

Two Rare Apple Pattern Watt Teapots

Vernon Kilns Pottery, Tam O'Shanter patt. **45-55**

Watt Pottery, Autumn Foliage patt., No. 505, 9" w., 5 3/4" h. (ILLUS., top of page) **650-750**

Watt Pottery, Apple patt., No. 505, 5" h. (ILLUS. on left with other Apple teapot, 2nd from top of page)............................. **2,800+**

Watt Pottery, Apple (three-leaf) patt., No. 112, rare, 6"h. (ILLUS. right with other Apple teapot)............................... **1,200-1,500+**

Wedgwood (Enoch), Old Castle patt., baluster-shaped body w/a bold Imari-style decoration, England, after 1965 (ILLUS.)... **130**

Modern Josiah Wedgwood Teapot

Wedgwood (Josiah), Mandarin patt., Queen's shape, Barleston, England (ILLUS.)... **35**

Enoch Wedgwood Old Castle Teapot

Gold Wheeling Decorating Company Teapot

Wheeling Decorating Company, squatty bulbous body w/serpentine spout & C-form handle, domed cover w/large knob finial, lightly embossed leaves & blossom design under an overall drippy gold glaze, Wheeling, West Virginia, ca. 1950s (ILLUS.).. **25**

Modern Blue & White Arthur Wood Teapot

Wood (Arthur) & Son, upright paneled oblong body w/angled shoulder to low domed cover w/disk finial, serpentine spout, C-form handle, dark blue w/white floral bouquets, England, 1980s (ILLUS.)...... **50**

Dark Pink & Gold Arthur Wood Teapot

Wood (Arthur) & Son, squatty bulbous body tapering to a short flared & ruffled neck, inset cover, serpentine spout, C-scroll handle, dark rose ground h.p. w/large gold blossoms, England, 1970s (ILLUS.)... **30**

Lyric Pattern Teapot by Schmid

Zeisel (Eva) Designs, bird-shaped w/woven wicker bail handle, Lyric patt., produced by Schmid, 1965 (ILLUS.)................. **225**

White & Blue Floral Arthur Wood Teapot

Wood (Arthur) & Son, squatty bulbous body w/a wide flat mouth & inset cover, serpentine spout, C-scroll handle, white upper half, handle & spout, pale blue cover & lower half, decorated w/sprigs of blue & pink flowers & gold trim, England, ca. 1930s (ILLUS.)......................... **30**

Tri-tone Teapot

Zeisel (Eva) Designs, Hall China Company - Kitchenware, 6-cup, Tri-tone, ca. 1954 (ILLUS.)... **85**

White Hallcraft Teapot

Zeisel (Eva) Designs, Hallcraft - Tomorrow's Classic Dinnerware, ca. 1950, 6-cup, White (ILLUS.)...................................... **160**

Blue Roses Teapot

Zeisel (Eva) Designs, Johann Haviland Company, Blue Roses patt., 1950s (ILLUS.).. **65**

Lacey Wings Teapot with Bird Decoration

Zeisel (Eva) Designs, Monmouth Dinnerware, Lacey Wings patt., wire handle w/ceramic grip, Prairie Hen, w/bird decoration, ca. 1952 (ILLUS.) **150**

Pals Teapot

Zeisel (Eva) Designs, Monmouth Dinnerware, Pals patt., in the form of a stylized bird w/"dancing turnips" decoration, ceramic ribbon handle, ca. 1952 (ILLUS.) **375**

Reissue of the Riverside Design Teapot

Zeisel (Eva) Designs, Riverside design reissue, distributed by The Orange Chicken, made by World of Ceramics, 2002 (ILLUS.).. **200**

Schmid Bird-shaped Teapot

Zeisel (Eva) Designs, Schmid Dinnerware, bird-shaped, rattan handle, Lacey Wings, 1950s (ILLUS.)... **50**

Zeisel (Eva) Designs, Watt Pottery, rattan handle, Animal Farm patt., ca. 1954............ **600**

Reissue of early Schramberg Zeisel-designed Teapot

Zeisel (Eva) Designs, wide low cylindrical shape w/polka dot decoration, reissue of a Schramberg 1929 design, Pattern 3366, produced for the Metropolitan Museum of Art, 2000 (ILLUS., above)............... **125**

Zeisel (Eva) Designs, wide squatty bulbous body on small base, woven wicker bail handle, design produced by Klein Reed, 2002 (ILLUS.)... **200**

New Eva Zeisel Design by Klein Reed

PART II - METALWARE TEAPOTS

Brass

Small Marked Brass Teakettle

Teakettle, deep cylindrical sides w/domed top w/low domed cover & knob finial, long angled spout, overhead strap bail swing handle, marked "Toronto Fletcher Co. Ltd.," early 20th c., 6" l., 3 3/8" h. (ILLUS.).. **$30**

Early 19th Century Brass Teakettle

Teakettle, flat-bottomed bulbous body w/a short cylindrical neck, angled snake spout, upright shape strap swing bail handle, ringed domed cover w/knob finial, early 19th c., 9 1/2" h. (ILLUS.) **604**

Brass Teakettle with Glass Handle

Teakettle, wide squatty bulbous body raised on four small knob feet, serpentine spout, fixed upright scrolls in handle joined by a baluster-form blue opaline glass hand grip, probably Europe, late 19th c., 10" l. (ILLUS.).................................... **51**

Copper

Two Early Copper Teakettles

Teakettle, bulbous ovoid body w/a flat bottom, wide short cylindrical neck w/a fitted domed cover w/brass knob finial, angled snake-form spout, overhead swing strap bail handle, possibly European, early 19th c., 10 liter size, body 11 1/2" h., w/handle 15 1/2" h. (ILLUS. left with smaller teakettle)....................................... **1,150**

American Dovetailed Copper Teakettle

Teakettle, flat-bottomed dovetailed body w/a wide base & tapering sides to a short cylindrical neck w/a fitted low domed cover w/baluster-form finial, angular snake spout, overhead brass strap swing bail handle, stamped number "6," American-made, 19th c., overall 13" l. (ILLUS.) **1,208**
Teakettle, flat-bottomed spherical body w/an overall hand-hammered design, flat dished cover w/knob finial, serpentine spout, fixed uprights joined by a turned black wood grip forming the handle, mark of the Gorham Mfg. Co., Providence, Rhode Island, date code for 1883, 7 1/2" h. (ILLUS. left with other Gorham teakettles, top next page)..................... **200-400**

Three Gorham Victorian Teakettles

Tall Oval Copper Teakettle

Teakettle, oval cylindrical body w/deep sides below the wide angled shoulder, ringed domed cover w/mushroom finial, angular snake spout, fixed tall brass curved supports joined by a bar handle, tin-lined, 19th c., 11" h. (ILLUS.) **201**

Revere Ware Copper Teakettle

Teakettle, Revere Ware, domed beehive body w/applied black Bakelite handle and bird whistle spout, marked on bottom "Revere Solid Copper - Rome, N.Y.," 7 1/4 x 7 1/2" (ILLUS.) **100**

Marked Copper Teakettle

Teakettle, wide cylindrical ringed body w/domed shoulder centering a domed cover w/turned finial, marked "Britton" on applied strap swivel handle, knob handle on cover, old solder repairs to handle, spout & base, 9 1/2 x 12 3/4", 12" h. (ILLUS.).. **225**

Teakettle, wide flat bottom & slightly tapering cylindrical sides w/a wide rounded shoulder centering a short neck w/a fitted domed cover w/knob finial, angular snake-form spout, tall fixed brass scrolled uprights joined by a copper bar forming handle, early 19th c., 11" d., 12 1/4" h. (ILLUS. right with 10 liter teakettle, page 198) **805**

Three Graduated Scottish Copper Teakettles

Teakettle on stand, flat-bottomed spherical hand-hammered body applied w/polished silver designs of flowering stalks, butterflies & storks in the Japanesque taste, flat dished cover w/knob finial, serpentine spout, fixed uprights joined by a turned black wood handle, mark of Gorham Mfg. Co., Providence, Rhode Island, date code for 1883, 7 1/2" h. (ILLUS. right with other Gorham teakettles, top previous page) **2,350**

Teakettle on stand, kettle w/wide squatty bulbous hand-hammered body applied w/dark silver figures of butterflies, birds & flowering branches in the Japanesque taste, a short neck w/a fitted domed & ribbed cover w/button finial, serpentine spout, fixed short copper scrolls joined by a high arched wooden handle, raised on a stand w/forked uprights above a platform w/a burner & raised on four canted legs, mark of Gorham Mfg. Co., Providence, Rhode Island, date code for 1883, 11" h. (ILLUS. center with other Gorham teakettles, top previous page) **1,293**

Teakettles, wide slightly flaring cylindrical body w/wide rounded shoulder centering a flat mouth, ringed domed cover w/acorn finial, angled spout, fixed overhead brass handles w/cylindrical copper grip, Scotland, ca. 1900, graduated sizes 11" h., 13" h. & 14" h., the set (ILLUS., top of page) **403**

Copper Teapot on Iron Legs

Teapot, bulbous nearly spherical body w/an angled shoulder to a short cylindrical neck w/a fitted domed cover w/scroll finial, tapering cylindrical side handle fitted w/a baluster-turned black wood handle w/pointed terminal, body raised on three straight riveted wrought-iron legs, probably Europe, 19th c., wear, spout pressed in, 8" h. (ILLUS.) **125**

Graniteware

Scarce Chrysolite Tea Steeper

Tea steeper, Chrysolite & White Swirl (dark green & white) patt., cylindrical w/rim spout & black strap side handle, domed cover w/knob finial, late 19th - early 20th c., 4 1/4" d., 5" h. (ILLUS.) **$450**

Blue & White Tea Steeper with Tin Lid

Tea steeper, Blue & White Swirl patt., cylindrical w/rim spout, strap side handle, domed tin cover w/wooden knob finial, 5" d., 5" h. (ILLUS.) **250**

Large Blue & White Swirl Teakettle

Teakettle, Blue & White Swirl patt., wide flat bottom & domed body w/a domed cover w/knob finial, wire bail swing handle w/turned wood grip, serpentine spout, late 19th - early 20th c., 10" d., 7" h. (ILLUS.) **300**

Miniature Solid Blue Teakettle

Teakettle, Solid Blue, miniature, wide flat bottom & domed body w/domed cover & knob finial, serpentine spout, overhead swing strap handle, late 19th - early 20th c., 3" d., 2 1/2" h. (ILLUS.) **400**

Columbian Graniteware Teakettle

Teakettle, Blue & White Swirl patt., wide flat bottom & domed body w/domed cover & knob finial, wire swing bail handle w/turned wood grip, serpentine spout, Columbian Ware, late 19th - early 20th c., 10 1/2" d., 7" h. (ILLUS.) **650**

Cobalt Blue & White Swirl Teakettle

Teakettle, Cobalt Blue & White Swirl patt., wide flat bottom w/high domed body, domed cover w/knob finial, serpentine spout, coiled iron swing bail handle, late 19th - early 20th c., 7 1/4" d., 7 1/4" h. (ILLUS.).. **800**

Diamond Ware Blue & White Teapot

Teapot, Blue Diamond Ware (Iris Blue & White Swirl patt.), bulbous body tapering to a domed cover w/button finial, serpentine spout, C-form handle, late 19th - early 20th c., 5 1/2" d., 6" h. (ILLUS.)................ **700**

Graniteware Agate Ware Child's Teapot

Teapot, child's, Agate Ware, ovoid body on disk foot, tapering to domed lid w/finial, C-form handle, serpentine spout, decorated w/simple line decoration in blue, 3 1/2" h. (ILLUS.) **35**

Teapot, Grey Mottled patt., spherical w/low domed cover & wooden knob finial, serpentine spout, C-form handle, late 19th - early 20th c., 3 1/2" d., 5" h. (ILLUS. right with other miniature Grey Mottled teapot) **200**

Toy White Agate Ware Teapot

Teapot, toy-sized, Agate Ware, overall white, domed cover, strap handle, long serpentine spout, probably made in Germany or Austria, ca. 1890, 5" l., 3" h. (ILLUS.) **75**

Blue Willow Graniteware Teapot

Teapot, Willow Ware design, Blue Willow, slightly tapering cylindrical shape w/shoulder sloping in to short neck, C-form handle, serpentine spout, slightly domed lid w/finial, dark blue handle, spout, finial & rim, early 20th c. (ILLUS.) **50-75**

Teapot, Grey Mottled patt., spherical w/low domed cover & wooden knob finial, straight spout, C-form handle, late 19th - early 20th c., 3 1/2" d., 5" h. (ILLUS. left

Grey Graniteware Miniature Teapots

with other miniature Grey Mottled teapot)... **200**

Bulbous Solid Blue Teapot

Teapot, Solid Blue, bulbous body w/hinged domed cover w/button finial, serpentine spout, C-form strap handle, late 19th - early 20th c., 4 1/2" d., 5 1/4" h. (ILLUS.)... **80**

Blue Willow Enamel Teapot

Teapot, Willow Ware design, Blue Willow, slightly tapering cylindrical body, short shoulder sloping to lid w/button finial, C-form handle, serpentine spout, unmarked, 7" h. (ILLUS.) **75-85**

Small Grey Mottled Teapot & Strainer

Teapot & tea strainer, Grey Mottled patt., small tapering cylindrical body w/a serpentine spout suspending a wire basket-form strainer, C-form strap handle, domed tin cover w/wooden knob finial, late 19th - early 20th c., 3 1/2" d., 5 3/4" h. (ILLUS.) **275**

Pewter

American, footed tall tapering ovoid body w/a flared rim & hinged domed cover w/wooden wafer finial, double-scroll metal handle w/black paint, touch mark of John Palethorp & John Connell, Philadelphia, ca. 1820-40, 10 3/4" h. (finial glued, minor dents, cover hinge w/some resoldering) **$523**

American, individual size, pear-shaped w/hinged domed cover w/finial post, short shaped spout & scrolled wooden handle, crowned touch mark for S. Ellis, England, 19th c., 5 1/2" h. (some dents, slightly out of shape, repair in base) **605**

Rare Early American Pewter Teapot

American, pear-shaped body w/a hinged domed cover w/turned metal finial, serpentine spout, ornate C-scroll wooden handle, "Lovebird" touch mark, Pennsylvania, ca. 1800, 7" h. (ILLUS.) **8,963**

Sheffield Plate

Early Sheffield Plate Tea Urn

Tea urn, tall urn-form body raised on a slender pedestal above a round domed & ringed base, low domed cover w/an urn-form finial, long arched loop strap side handles, extended spigot near the bottom w/a decorative scroll handle, unmarked, England, ca. 1800, some small dents, 18" h. (ILLUS., at left) **$431**

Silver Plate

American Silver Plate & Sterling Silver Teakettles on Stands

Teakettle on stand, footed paneled bulbous body w/a wide conforming shoulder centering a short rolled neck, hinged pointed & domed cover w/pointed finial, a fixed reeded loop overhead handle, scroll-trimmed serpentine spout, raised on open serpentine side supports on a paneled round base centered by a burner, mark of Reed & Barton, late 19th - early 20th c., overall 13" h. (ILLUS. left with Whiting sterling teakettle on stand, above) **$230**

Fine English Silver Plate Kettle & Stand

Teakettle on stand, Victorian, Orientalist taste, the decagonally paneled body tapering to a short neck w/thin pierced gallery & hinged domed & stepped cover w/spherical finial, a pointed Arabesque arch fixed overhead handle, serpentine spout, the panels engraved as arches enclosing ornate quatrefoils above a chain band, raised on a platform base w/a wide top & thin gallery around a narrower pierced & paneled pedestal enclosing the burner, the wide dished & paneled base w/short columns forming the feet, by Elkington & Company, Birmingham, England, 1854, overall 10 1/2" w., overall 8 1/2" h. (ILLUS.) **1,150**

Attractive Silver Plate Teapot

Teapot, cov., round foot below the wide squatty bulbous body tapering to a short flared neck w/a domed hinged cover, leafy scroll-trimmed spout & C-scroll handle, marked on bottom "Silver on Copper [crown] S [shield]," probably England, late 19th - early 20th c., 8" h. (ILLUS.)......... **100**

English Silver Plate Willow Ware Teapot

Early 20th Century Silver Plated Teapot

Teapot, round flat base below the wide rounded lower body w/a gadrooned medial band below the tall tapering sides w/a flaring rim, hinged domed cover w/knob finial, tall slender serpentine spout, C-scroll handle, trademark w/a lion on either side of a shield above "Silverplated - Est. 1905," early 20th c., 9 1/4" w., 9 3/4" h. (ILLUS.)............................ **65**

Early 20th Century English Silver Plate Teapot with Dated Inscription

Teapot, squatty bulbous boat-shaped body w/widely flaring flanged rim & hinged stepped, domed cover w/wooden disk finial, ribbed serpentine spout, pointed angular handle, the sides w/an ornate engraved floral cartouche enclosing a gift inscription dated 1911, marks for an English silver plate firm, 11 1/2" l., 5 3/8" h. (ILLUS.).. **85**

Teapot, Willow Ware design, flattened bulbous body on four ribbed button feet, flat lid w/ebony finial, straight spout, C-form ebony handle held in place w/two silver plate grips, engraved overall w/geometric designs around center medallion of Willow Ware design, unmarked, England, late 19th c. (ILLUS., top of page)......... **250-275**

Secessionist Silver Plate Pot on Stand

Teapot on stand, the domical plated handhammered copper teapot w/a domed cover & knop finial, serpentine spout, angular loop raffia-wrapped handle, raised on a platform stand w/four flat panel supports on the flaring round base centered by a hinged sterno burner, the teapot & stand decorated w/embossed Germanic Secessionist floral medallions, base stamped "WMF/91," Wurttembergische Metallwarenfabrik, Esslingen, Germany, early 20th c., 11" d., 11 1/2" h. (ILLUS.) **646**

Sterling & Coin Silver - American

Coin, Classical style, a round ringed & domed foot tapering to a short pedestal below the round-bottomed cylindrical body decorated w/a wide band of guilloche enclosing stars & accented w/acanthus leaves on a linework ground, the wide rounded shoulder tapering to a short cylindrical neck w/a hinged domed cover w/a spherical finial, a squared serpentine spout topped w/a patera roundel, a tall upright squared flute-carved fruitwood handle, mark of Chaudron's & Rasch, Philadelphia, ca. 1812, 9" h............ **$1,058**

Extraordinarily Rare Colonial American Teapot

Coin, footed spherical body w/a hinged double-domed cover w/baluster-form finial, octagonally faceted straight spout, C-scroll wooden handle w/octagonally faceted handle joins, base also w/mark of maker Simeon Soumaine, New York, New York, ca. 1730, overall 10 1/4" l. (ILLUS.)... **207,500**

Very Rare Early Philadelphia Silver Teapot

Federal Era American Teapot

Coin, inverted pear-shaped body on a disk foot, domed hinged cover w/pointed finial, serpentine spout w/cast leafy scrolls, C-scroll wooden handle w/scrolled silver terminal & leaf-clad joins, the shoulder engraved w/diaperwork, rocaille scrolls & flowering vines, the edge of the cover engraved w/a scallop band, base engraved w/block initials "H" over "IM," also w/mark of maker John Bayly, Philadelphia, ca. 1765, overall 9 1/4" l. (ILLUS., previous page) **71,700**

Coin, oval upright body w/a flat shoulder centered by a hinged domed cover w/pineapple finial, straight angled spout, C-scroll wooden handle w/silver joins, the sides engraved w/a drapery cartouche enclosing a monogram, mark on base of Daniel Van Voorhis, New York, New York, ca. 1790, 7 1/8" h. (ILLUS., top of page) **4,780**

Coin, teakettle on stand, the bulbous fluted body w/a ring-banded short neck & hinged domed cover w/flower finial, scroll-trimmed serpentine spout, arched scroll swing handle, raised on a burner base w/four ornate scroll legs ending in shell feet & joined by serpentine straps centered by the burner ring, engraved inscription w/later date, mark of Ball, Tompkins & Black, New York City, ca. 1839-51, no burner, overall 15" h., the set (ILLUS., next column) **1,150**

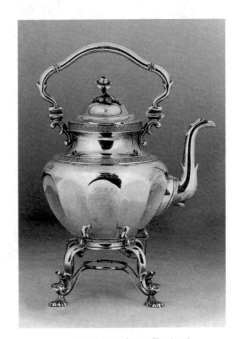

American Coin Silver Teakettle

Victorian Coin Silver Kettle on Stand

Coin, teakettle on stand, the wide squatty inverted pear-shaped body raised on leafy scroll legs, the low domed cover w/a flowerhead finial, ornate scroll-cast spout, scrolled overhead swing bail handle, resting on a round platform base centered by a burner & raised on tall leafy scroll legs w/shell feet, the shoulder engraved w/a monogram & crest, mark of Grosjean & Woodward, New York, New York, retailed by Lincoln & Foss, Boston, ca. 1850, overall 14 1/2" h. (ILLUS.).. **1,434**

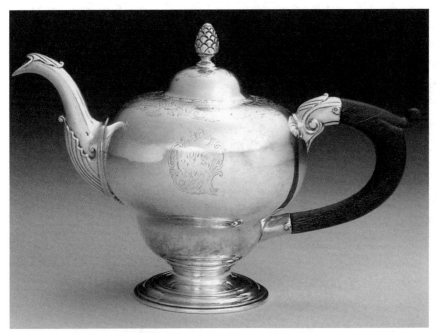

Rare Colonial Rhode Island Teapot

Coin, wide bulbous inverted pear-shaped body on a domed foot, domed hinged cover w/a pinecone finial, serpentine spout w/cast shell & scroll decoration, black wooden C-scroll handle w/scroll-decorated joins, the body engraved w/a rococo cartouche enclosing monogram "HPG," the shoulder engraved w/a strap-work bird & mask border, base w/mark of Samuel Casey, South Kingstown, Rhode Island, ca. 1760, overall 10" l. (ILLUS.)... **47,800**

Sterling, teakettle on stand, Classical deep oblong body w/wide band of fluting around the lower half, the wide tapering shoulder fitted w/a hinged domed & reed-ed cover w/button finial, a fixed arched overhead handle w/ivory insulators, serpentine spout, raised on slender curved upright supports above an oval base centered by a burner, tiny bun feet on base, the pot inscribed on the side "EEH 1899," Whiting Mfg. Co., New York, New York, Pattern No. 5800, ca. 1900, 8 1/2" w., overall 11 1/4" h. (ILLUS. right with Reed & Barton silver plate teakettle on stand, page 202)... **690**

Sterling, teakettle on stand, footed pear-shaped body w/flaring rim & hinged domed cover w/button finial, overhead swing bail handle w/ivory insulators, leaf-capped serpentine spout, raised on open arched scroll supports above a square platform centered by a squatty bulbous burner, stepped base on ball feet, mark of Arthur J. Stone, Gardner, Massachusetts, & craftsman's mark of Arthur L.

Hartwell, ca. 1910, overall 13 1/4" h. (ILLUS., below).. **1,912**

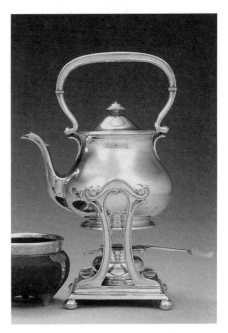

Early 20th Century Kettle on Stand

Tiffany Silver Teakettle on Stand

Sterling, teakettle on stand, rectangular body w/concave corners & rounded bottom, conforming stepped shoulder & hinged domed cover w/disk finial, paneled serpentine spout, swing bail handle at top, raised on paneled arched supports above a conforming platform base centered by a burner, marked "Tiffany & Co. - Makers - Sterling Silver - 18389," 2 3/4 pints, early 20th c. (ILLUS.) **1,430**

Sterling Silver - English & Other

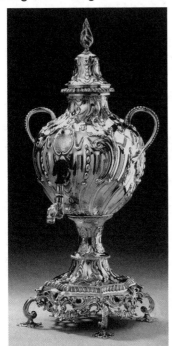

Elaborate George III Silver Tea Urn

Tea urn, George III era, bulbous ovoid body & tall waisted pedestal chased overall w/ornate leafy scrolls & auricular bands, the tapering neck w/a rolled gadrooned rim below the high domed matching cover w/openwork flame finial, small beaded loop shoulder handles, the foliate-clad spigot w/wood tap handle, the flaring base w/a gadrooned band above an elaborate openwork apron composed of ornate scrolls raised on four C-scroll legs w/scalloped feet, one side of body engraved w/armorials, the cover & base engraved w/a crest, marks of Louisa Courtauld, London, England, 1767, overall 22 3/4" h. (ILLUS.) **10,575**

Fine George III Silver Tea Urn

Tea urn, George III era, tall Classical urn-form body decorated w/drapery & floral garlands below a narrow shoulder band & fluted tapering neck w/flared rim floral-chased domed cover w/figural pineapple finial, slender molded arched C-scroll side handles, a reeded spigot w/ivory handle at the base of the body just above the slender flaring fluted pedestal w/a round gadrooned base band above the square base w/swag & rosette decoration & raised on four tiny claw-and-ball feet, some wear to reeding & tube incorrectly engraved "George III, London 1791, Chas. Wright," Charles Wright, London, 1771, 13" w., overall 23" h. (ILLUS.) **6,325**

Simple Elegant George III Tea Urn

English George II Silver Kettle on Stand

Tea urn, George III era, tall Classical urn-form body w/a tall slender tapering cover w/acorn finial, beaded shoulder band, long arched reeded side handles, a projecting spigot near the base w/a dark ivory handle, raised on a slender flaring pedestal on a square foot, interior fitted w/a heating column, cover engraved w/a crest, the body engraved w/a coat-of-arms, mark of John Wakelin & William Tayler, London, England, 1784, overall 20 1/2" h. (ILLUS.) **4,780**

Teakettle on stand, George II era, spherical body w/a flat hinged cover w/wooden knop finial, serpentine spout, overhead swing bail handle w/shaped uprights joined by a baluster-turned black wood grip, the body finely engraved w/a border of brickwork, scrolls, putti & foliate as well as a coat-of-arms, on a round stand raised on three leafy scroll legs w/wooden knob feet joined by shaped braces centered by a deep burner, marks of Peze Pilleau, London, England, 1731, burner dating from 1956, overall 22 1/2" h. (ILLUS.) **3,824**

Rare Ornate George II Kettle & Stand

Teakettle on stand, George II era, spherical body w/hinged cover w/pinecone finial, ornately chased w/panels of rocaille & floral garlands against a matted ground, rocaille-clad handle w/sea-monster spout tip, overhead raffia-wrapped swing bail handle w/ornate caryatid uprights, on a round stand w/a ring of chased flowers & shells above the ornate openwork apron decorated w/scrolls & flowers centered by a shell w/mask, raised on three leafy scroll legs joined by serpentine braces to a central ring w/squatty burner, marks of David Willaume II, London, England, 1739, overall 13 3/4" h. (ILLUS.)............. **20,315**

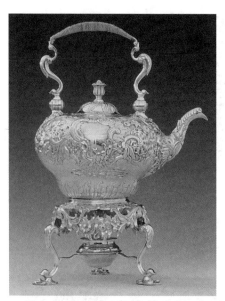

Early Scottish Silver Teakettle & Stand

Teakettle on stand, George II era, wide inverted pear-shaped body chased overall w/ornate flowers, scrolls & quilted shells, the hinged domed cover w/ivory bud finial, overhead bail swing handle w/scrolled supports joined by a wrapped hand grip, on a stand w/ornate openwork leafy scroll & flower apron raised on three leafy scroll legs joined by braces centering a burner, the body also engraved w/a coat-of-arms, mark of James Welsh, Edinburgh, Scotland, 1755, overall 15" h. (ILLUS.)... **10,158**

George IV English Teakettle & Stand

Teakettle on stand, George IV era, squatty bulbous melon-lobed body w/the panels chased w/alternating ornate rococo cartouches & floral bouquets as well as a coat-of-arms & crest, hinged low domed cover w/melon finial, scroll-cast serpentine spout, scrolled & arched overall swing bail handle, raised on a stand w/fluted apron chased w/flowers & raised on leafy scroll legs joined by shaped brackets supporting a central burner, stand also w/engraved crest, mark of William Eaton, London, England, 1821, overall 15" h. (ILLUS.) **1,998**

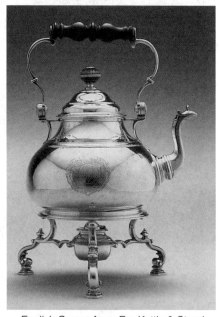

English Queen Anne Era Kettle & Stand

Teakettle on stand, Queen Anne era, wide pear-shaped body tapering to a removable domed cover w/dark ivory knob finial, paneled serpentine spout, overhead swing bail handle w/serpentine supports joined by a baluster-turned wooden grip, the side engraved w/a coat-of-arms, on a round platform raised on three serpentine scroll legs joined by stretchers centering a burner, kettle w/mark of Thomas Parr I, London, England, 1710, burner w/mark of Gabriel Sleath, London, England, 1710, stand apparently not marked, overall 14 3/4" h. (ILLUS.) **11,353**

Teakettle on stand, Victorian, wide bulbous inverted pear-shaped body elaborately chased w/rococo scrolls & floral designs, a serpentine ribbed spout, low domed cover w/chased leaftips & a pointed spiral finial, overhead handle w/ornate scroll uprights joined by a flat strap grip, on a stand w/an ornate openwork flower & scroll apron raised on three leafy-scroll legs joined by braces to a center ring now

English Victorian Silver Kettle & Stand

missing the burner, mark of Charles Stuart Harris, London, England, 1898, 10" w., overall 12 1/2" h. (ILLUS.)............ **2,415**

Fine 18th Century Dutch Silver Teapot

Teapot, Dutch, footed spherical body w/a hinged domed cover cast w/rocaille scrollwork & a wooden knob finial, short arched spout, S-scroll wooden handle, the upper body engraved w/flowers, diaperwork & scrolls, maker's mark indistinct, city mark of Leeuwarden, Holland, ca. 1765, 5" h. (ILLUS.)......................................**2,390**

Teapot, East Indian, inverted melon-form fluted body chased w/large scrolling acanthus leaves, a flaring leaf-cast neck & fluted hinged domed cover w/blossom finial, raised on leafy scroll feet, leaf-cast serpentine spout, ornate leafy C-scroll handle, mark of Hamilton & Co., Calcutta, India, ca. 1850, overall 12" I. (ILLUS. second from left with three other teapots, top page 217) **1,315**

Teapot, English, footed squatty round body w/a wide shoulder & short rolled neck, hinged domed handle, short tree trunk-molded spout applied w/flowering branches continuing on to the body, arched twig-form handle w/ivory insulators, leaf & berry finial on the cover, mark of George R. Elkington, London, England, 1858, finial mark of Robert Garrard, overall 9 1/8" I. **$1,135**

Fine Paul Storr Silver Teapot

Teapot, English, round melon-lobed body resting on leafy feet, the hinged leaf-cast cover w/a removable blossom finial, leaf-trimmed twig handle w/ivory insulators, twig spout w/leaves, the body engraved w/flowers & leaves & a monogram & crest on each side, marked by Paul Storr, London, 1838, 6" h. (ILLUS.) **2,987**

Teapot, English, teapot & stand, pot w/upright serpentine oval shape & straight angled spout, hinged domed cover, C-scroll black wood handle, the body bright-cut w/floral festoons & oval cartouches, one side engraved w/a ship, the conforming stand w/a beaded border & raised on four pad feet, mark of Robert Pinkney & Robert Scott, Newcastle, England, teapot 1783, stand 1784-86, teapot 9 1/2" I., 2 pcs. **2,868**

Early 18th Century Dutch Silver Teapot

Teapot, footed squatty pear-shaped body w/a hinged high domed cover w/wooden knob finial, angled serpentine spout, C-scroll wooden handle, chased overall w/lambrequin, acanthus leaves & shells, engraved inscription on base, mark of Jan Verdoes, Haarlem, Holland, 1736, 6 1/4" h. (ILLUS.) **1,554**

Early English Provincial Silver Teapot

Rare Early Irish Silver Teapot

Teapot, George I era, footed octagonal squatty pear-shaped body w/a domed hinged & paneled cover w/a wood disk finial, paneled scroll-cast serpentine spout, C-scroll wooden handle, one side engraved w/a coat-of-arms, crest & motto, base w/mark of John Hamilton, Dublin, Ireland, 1719-20, 6 1/2" h. (ILLUS.).. **53,775**

Early 18th Century English Teapot

Teapot, George I era, footed spherical body w/small hinged cover w/knop finial, angled faceted straight spout, C-scroll wooden handle, body engraved w/a crest, base engraved w/initials "E.R.," mark of Seth Lofthouse, London, England, 1720, overall 8 1/4" I. (ILLUS.) **4,183**

Teapot, George II era, footed spherical body w/a small flat detachable cover w/reeded border & wooden disk finial, curved spout w/stylized petal join, C-scroll wooden handle, marked "RP," English provincial maker, ca. 1740, overall 8 5/8" I. (ILLUS., top of page) **3,760**

Paul Storr English Silver Teapot

Teapot, George III era, footed wide inverted pear-shaped body w/domed hinged cover w/pointed knob finial, ribbed serpentine spout, C-scroll handle, the body swirl-fluted & decorated w/répoussé & chased rococo floral & scroll designs w/a vacant cartouche, mark of Paul Storr, London, England, 1814, 6 7/8" h. (ILLUS.)... **1,610**

George III Classical Silver Teapot

Group of Four Foreign-made Silver Teapots

Teapot, George III era, oval upright body w/flat shoulder & hinged flat cover w/wooden disk finial, angled straight spout, wooden C-scroll handle, the body engraved around the base & shoulder w/a floral & foliate band, the body engraved w/a coat-of-arms, mark on base of Richard Gardner, London, England, 1774, overall 9" l. (ILLUS., bottom, previous page) 3,585

Teapot, Italian, squatty bulbous body w/a fluted lower half, the upper half ornately embossed w/flowers, scrolls & shells, small fluted cover w/figural fruit finial, short branch-form spout, looped branch-form handle w/ivory insulators, base engraved "Palermo, 23 Febraro 1829. Giovanni Fecarotta fece," overall 9 1/2" l. (ILLUS. far left with three other teapots, top of page) 3,585

Scarce Early English Miniature Teapot

Teapot, miniature, waisted cylindrical body w/flared shoulder & short neck w/fitted domed cover w/knop finial, flat C-scroll handle & angled straight spout, chased w/C-scroll & floral decoration, mark on base of James Goodwin, London, England, 1727, two solder marks on base, 4" h. (ILLUS.) 518

English Teapot by Hester Bateman

Teapot, Neoclassical oval upright body w/flat top & domed hinged cover w/pinecone finial, straight angled spout, C-scroll wooden handle, engraved w/swags of flowers centered by an oval cartouche w/an animal, mark of Hester Bateman, England, 1785, 10" l., 6" h. (ILLUS.) 2,588

Teapot, Portuguese, oblong paneled body & shoulder w/conforming hinged domed cover w/blossom finial, serpentine spout & C-scroll wooden handle, the sides chased w/a large floral medallion, mark of Moitinho de Almeida, Porto, Portugal, ca. 1815, overall 11 3/4" l. (ILLUS. second from right with other three teapots, top of page) 1,000-1,500

Teapot, Spanish Colonial, bulbous nearly spherical body tapering to a domed cover w/a baluster-form finial, serpentine spout, overhead swing strap bail handle, engraved initials on the side, marked on the base w/a later French control mark, late 18th - early 19th c., 6 1/2" h. (ILLUS. far right with other three teapots, above) 1,434

Teapot, Victorian, footed spherical body w/répoussé swirled ribbing below a wide shoulder band of ornate chased flowers & leaves, short cylindrical neck w/ruffled rim, hinged, domed & fluted cover w/squared wooden knob finial, fluted serpentine spout, C-scroll wooden handle, England, worn hallmarks, probably second half 19th c., overall 8" l. (ILLUS., top next page) 288

Fancy Victorian English Silver Teapot

Ornate William IV English Teapot

Teapot, William IV era, fluted squatty bulbous body on four leaf-clad feet, the body chased & applied w/flowers & acanthus leaves, a leaf-clad serpentine spout & leafy scroll handle w/ivory insulators, domed hinged cover w/flowerhead finial, mark of Joseph & Albert Savory, London,

England, 1836, overall 8 1/4" l. (ILLUS.).. **1,912**

English William IV Silver Teapot

Teapot, William IV era, wide inverted pear-shaped body on a disk foot, hinged domed cover w/flame finial, scroll-cast serpentine spout, bifurcated branch handle, the swirling fluted body chased w/panels of rocaille & diaperwork on a matted ground, one side engraved w/a duke's coronet & crest, mark of Paul Storr, London, England, 1832, 7 3/4" h. (ILLUS.)... **2,820**

Teapot & stand, Queen Anne era, wide bulbous pear-shaped body w/a high domed hinged cover w/knob finial, paneled scroll spout, C-scroll wooden handle, one side engraved w/a coat-of-arms, w/a round stand on three scrolled feet & pierced w/vertical flutes & w/a baluster-turned side wood handle, teapot w/mark of Richard Bayley, London, England, 1711, stand w/mark of Lewis Mettayer, London, England, 1706, teapot overall 7 1/4" l., 2 pcs. (ILLUS. of teapot, below)................ **26,290**

Rare Queen Anne English Silver Teapot

Tin & Tole

Toleware Teapot

Tole, oval form w/angled front spout & shaped hinged lid, strap handle, decorative finial, back & front decorated w/two-part rose w/leaves, the lid w/blue/green leaf design, 5 3/4" h. (ILLUS.) **$1,840**

Rare Early American Tole Teapot

Tole, tall oval body w/a slightly domed top fitted w/a hinged strap cover, straight angled spout, C-form strap handle, black ground, decorated on the sides w/a large deep red circle painted w/white leaf sprigs, the circle beneath an arched wreath of red & orange blossoms & shaded green leaves, probably Pennsylvania, ca. 1830, 6" h. (ILLUS.) **5,019**

PART III - MISCELLANEOUS

Glass & Other Materials

Fine Japanese Cloisonné Teapot

Miniature Cloisonné Teapot

Cloisonné, miniature, squatty bulbous body on tiny knob feet, serpentine spout & C-form handle, domed cover w/finial, bright blue ground w/green lappets & red bor-ders decorated w/overall scattered colorful flower blossoms, Japan, late 19th - early 20th c., overall 5" l., 3" h. (ILLUS.)... **$150-300**

Cloisonné, wide half-round body w/flat shoulder & wide cover w/reeded brass knob finial, straight side spout, high metal strap bail handle, overall intricate design of butterflies & flowers, on three small brass feet, Japan, early 20th c., 7" l., overall 7" h. (ILLUS., top of page)............... **400**

Morton Pottery Company salt & pepper shakers, models of tiny white teapots w/h.p. red & blue florals & blue trim, Morton Pottery Company, Morton, Illinois, 1922-76, 2 1/4" h., pr. (ILLUS. right with Morton toy miniature teapot, below).......... **18-24**

Morton Pottery Miniature Toy Teapot & Salt & Pepper Shakers

Two Lovely Fry Foval Glass Teapots

Morton Pottery Company toy, miniature dollhouse-size, ribbed body & angled handle, burgundy glaze, Morton Pottery Company, Morton, Illinois, 1922-76, 2 1/4" h. (ILLUS. left with salt & pepper shakers, bottom previous page).................. **8-12**

Morton Pottery Teapot Wall Pocket

Morton Pottery Company wall pocket, model of a ribbed teapot w/oblong opening at top, white w/h.p. red cherries & green leaves, Morton Pottery Company, Morton, Illinois, 1922-76, 6 1/2 x 8" (ILLUS.)... **25-35**

Central Glass Works, No. 733, Thistle etching No. 310, clear.............................. **220+**

Fry Foval Glass, pearly opalescent body w/applied spout, handle & knob finial, applied sections found in either Jade green or Delft blue, each version (ILLUS. of both, top of page)................................. **250-300**

Pyrex, crystal, w/blue glass handle (ILLUS., below) **50-75**

Pyrex Teapot w/Blue Handle

Tea Sets - 1750-1850

Ceramic

Chinese Export Tea Set for the American Market

Chinese Export Porcelain: cov. teapot, cov. tea caddy, helmet-shaped creamer, cov. cream pot & handleless cup; the oval teapot w/upright sides & a tapering shoulder to the inset cover w/berry finial, the bulbous tapering cream pot w/domed cover, upright flat-sided rectangular tea caddy w/arched shoulder, short neck & domed cap, each piece h.p. on the side in sepia, orange & gold w/a spread-winged American eagle w/shield, made for the American market, late 18th c., teapot 8 1/2" l., the set (ILLUS.).. **$5,175**

Chinese Export Porcelain: tall tapering cov. teapot, short oval cov. teapot, helmet-shaped creamer, cov. sugar bowl, upright rectangular cov. tea caddy, cake plate & two handleless cups & saucers; each piece h.p. w/a sepia & orange spread-winged eagle & shield, gilt trim, late 18th c., tall teapot 10" h., the set (ILLUS., bottom of page).......................... **8,338**

Extensive American-market Chinese Export Tea Set

American-market Chinese Export Tea Set

Chinese Export Porcelain: tall tapering cylindrical cov. teapot, short oval cov. teapot & undertray, upright rectangular cov. tea caddy, serving plate, two large handleless tea cups, one smaller tea cup & saucer; each piece h.p. w/an orange & black spread-winged eagle w/an oval medallion decorated w/the initials "SSD," made for the American market, late 18th - early 19th c., tall teapot 9 1/2" h., the set (ILLUS., top of page)................................ **5,000**

Paris Porcelain: cov. teapot, cov. sugar bowl, creamer & two handled cups & saucers; each w/a squatty bulbous body w/alternating narrow stripes of gold & white, teapot & sugar w/flanged & scalloped rims molded w/shells & inset covers w/acorn finial, the other pieces w/the

same design, France, first half 19th c., teapot 6 1/2" h., the set (ILLUS., below) ... **2,760**

Gold & White Paris Porcelain Tea Set

Early Rockingham Porcelain Tea Set

Early Child's Spatterware Tea Set

Rockingham Porcelain: cov. teapot, cov. sugar bowl, creamer, waste bowl & two cups w/one saucer; teapot & serving pieces w/wide squatty bulbous bodies raised on four tab feet, wide angled shoulders & inset domed covers w/blossom finials, leaf-molded short upturned spout on teapot, arched ornate C-scroll handles, each piece decorated about the shoulder or the interior rim w/a wide scrolled cobalt blue border trimmed w/fancy gilt scrolling, gold line trim, No. 252, England, ca. 1830-43, teapot & handles of sugar discolored, teapot 6 1/2" h., the set (ILLUS., bottom previous page) **259**

Spatterware: child's, cov. teapot, cov. sugar bowl, two handleless cups & saucers; Fort patt., the teapot & sugar w/footed squatty bulbous bodies w/wide tapering paneled shoulders supporting domed covers w/button finials, teapot w/serpentine spout & C-scroll handle, sugar w/rolled tab handles, each piece w/a blue spatter ground centered by a painted fort building in black & brown w/green trees, England, ca. 1830, spout & rim flake on teapot, hairline on base of sugar, one cup w/repaired rim, teapot 4 3/8" h., the set (ILLUS., top of page) **825**

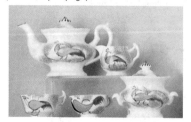

Child's Green Spatterware Tea Set

Spatterware: child's size, two cov. teapots, two cov. sugar bowls, two creamers, four handleless cups & one saucer; Peafowl patt., teapots & sugars w/footed squatty bulbous bodies w/flaring necks & inset domed covers w/pointed knob finials, each piece decorated w/a green spatter center band decorated w/a yellow, red & blue peafowl, similar designs w/slightly varying colors, England, ca. 1830, some damage & repair, teapots 4 1/4" h., the set (ILLUS. of part).................................... **1,610**

Early Spode Porcelain Teawares

Spode Porcelain: cov. teapot & seven handled cups & saucers; the oval pot w/upright sides & a flat shoulder centered by a domed cover w/oval knob finial, serpentine spout & C-form handle, each piece decorated w/a wide orange-painted band trimmed w/stylized white flowerheads & bands of gilt leaves, Pattern No. 878, England, ca. 1820, some gilt wear, two saucers w/hairlines, the set (ILLUS. of part)... **405**

Fine Early Strawberry Pattern Staffordshire Tea Set

Early Staffordshire Teapot from Set

Staffordshire earthenware: cov. teapot, cov. sugar bowl & creamer; each piece w/a black-glazed body trimmed w/gilt fruits, leaves & vines, the teapot w/a squatty spherical molded body raised on three mask & paw feet, a crabstock handle & spout, short cylindrical neck w/a low domed cover w/a figural bird finial, matching forms on other pieces, teapot finial missing head, nick on spout rim of creamer, nicks & chips on sugar bowl & bird cover finial repaired, England, 18th c., teapot 4 7/8" h., 3 pcs. (ILLUS. of teapot) **1,528**

Staffordshire earthenware: two cov. teapots, cov. sugar bowl, creamer, two 7" d. plates & one 9" d. cake plate, nine handleless cups & eleven saucers; h.p. Strawberry patt., the squatty boat-shaped serving pieces w/angled shoul-

ders & inset domed covers, ornate C-scroll handles, all painted w/a design of reddish orange strawberries & green leafy vines, orange banding & some pink lustre trim, England, ca. 1830, teapots 11 1/5" l., the set (ILLUS., top of page) **6,325**

Wedgwood Jasper Diceware Tea Set

Wedgwood Jasper Ware: cov. teapot, cov. sugar bowl & creamer; Diceware patt., each piece w/a black ground w/applied white vinework framing engine-turned dicing w/yellow quatrefoils, Josiah Wedgwood, first half 19th c., footrim chip on teapot ground out, sugar bowl 4" h., teapot 3 7/8" h., the set (ILLUS.) **1,081**

Sterling & Coin Silver - American

Early Classical American Coin Silver Tea Service

Coin: cov. teapot, cov. coffeepot, cov. sugar bowl, creamer & waste bowl; Classical style, each piece raised on a ringed pedestal base supporting the tall bulbous body tapering to a swelled ringed tall shoulder tapering to a ringed neck & domed hinged cover w/flower finial, each piece w/narrow applied bands of acorn, grape & bellflowers, pots w/high arched C-scroll wooden handles & long serpentine leaf-clad spouts, each w/engraved monogram, mark of Curry & Preston, Philadelphia, ca. 1835, coffeepot 9 3/4" h., the set (ILLUS.)........................ **$2,868**

Coin: cov. teapot, cov. sugar bowl & creamer; Classical boat-shaped style, round stepped pedestal base supporting bulbous oblong lower body below a wide curved shoulder band w/leafy vine motif below the curved & rounded shoulder & domed hinged cover w/pineapple finial, high arched fancy C-scroll handles, tall serpentine spout on teapot, each piece w/engraved monogram on the side, mark of Peter Chitry, New York, New York, ca. 1830, teapot 9 3/4" h., the set (ILLUS. of teapot & sugar bowl, bottom of page) **1,195**

Coin: cov. teapot, cov. sugar bowl, creamer & waste bowl; Classical style, each piece of rectangular shape w/a partly fluted body on a conforming base, the finial, rim & base w/a band of embossed shells, a medial body w/bright-cut scrolled floral & foliate designs, acorn designs above the fluting, angular handles, the teapot w/ivory handle insulators, each piece marked by William Thomson, New York, New York, 1815-34, teapot 7 3/4" l., 4 1/2" h., the set (minor imperfections) **39,950**

American Classical Coin Silver Tea Set

Federal Era American Classical Tea Set

Coin: cov. teapot, cov. sugar urn & creamer; Classical style, the oval teapot w/flat sides & a concave shoulder band w/a hinged tapering domed cover w/urn finial, tall helmet-shaped creamer & sugar urn w/tall waisted cover w/urn finial, both on a square foot, each w/bright-cut floral swags centering a cartouche w/drapery mantling, monogram in the cartouche, beaded borders, straight spout on teapot & C-scroll black wood handle, mark of William G. Forbes, New York, New York, ca. 1790, teapot 12 1/2" l., the set (ILLUS.) **13,145**

Fine New York Federal Era Tea Set

Coin: cov. teapot, cov. sugar urn & creamer; each of Classical form, the teapot oval w/beaded border at foot & rim & the hinged cover w/urn finial, straight spout, wooden loop handle, the creamer & sugar of vase form on a square base, each engraved w/a monogram within a mantle, teapot 12 3/4" l., John Vernon, New York, New York, ca. 1792, the set (ILLUS.) **8,365**

Tea Sets - 1850-1950

Ceramic

Lovely Egg-shaped Tea Set with Vines of Pink Roses

American Painted Porcelain: cov. teapot, cov. sugar bowl & creamer; each w/an upright egg-form body raised on four gilt scroll feet, gold loop handles, each h.p. w/a continuous design of leafy vines & pink roses, delicate gold trim bands, made for iced tea, blanks marked "Favorite, Bavaria," early 20th c., the set (ILLUS.) **$200-300**

American Painted Willets Belleek Tea Set

American Painted Porcelain: cov. teapot, cov. sugar bowl & creamer; footed wide flattened cylindrical bodies, flat covers w/gold peg finials, angular gold handles, each decorated w/burnished gold designs of stylized floral roundels alternating w/gold panels, artist-signed "MSF," Willets Belleek blanks, ca. 1880-1909, the set (ILLUS.)... **300-400**

American Painted Porcelain Tea Set with Gold Bands & Pink Rose

American Painted Porcelain: cov. teapot, cov. sugar bowl, creamer & round undertray; bulbous bodies w/low domed covers & angular gold handle, each h.p. w/pastel blue border bands above arched angular gold bands separated by delicate pink rose clusters, artist-signed "C.E. Tolehard 1914," MZ Austria factory mark, tray 11 1/4" d., the set (ILLUS.)... **300-400**

Chintz Majestic Pattern Breakfast Set

Chintz China: breakfast set: cov. teapot, cup, creamer, open sugar bowl, toast rack & oblong paneled tray w/end handles; Majestic patt., Countess shape, Royal Winton, the set (ILLUS.) ... **1,750-2,000**

Cliftwood Art Potteries Old Rose Glazed Tea Set

Florence Pattern Stacking Tea Set

Chintz China: stacking-type, cov. creamer, sugar & teapot; Florence patt., Delamere shape, Royal Winton, the set (ILLUS.)... **1,750-2,000**

Cliftwood Art Potteries: cov. teapot, cov. sugar bowl, creamer, cups & saucer & 8" d. plate; the serving pieces w/urn-shaped paneled bodies w/ringed tapering shoulders, each w/a Matte Old Rose glaze, Cliftwood Art Potteries, Morton, Illinois, 1920-40, the set (ILLUS., top of page).. **135-180**

Copeland Spode China: cov. teapot, cov. sugar bowl, creamer, eight 9" d. plates & eight cups & saucers; Classical Revival style, serving pieces of squatty bulbous oblong boat shape w/angled collars & inset domed covers w/button finials, pointed C-scroll handles, each piece decorated w/a dark cinnamon brown band painted w/gilt roses, marked "Spode - Copelands China - England - Tiffany & Co. - New York," ca. 1890s, one plate w/small flake, gilt wear to rims, teapot 5" h., the set (ILLUS., bottom of page) **715**

Copeland-Spode China Tea Set

Doulton-Lambeth Hunting Ware Tea Set

Doulton-Lambeth Ware: large cov. teapot, small cov. teapot, open sugar & creamer; stoneware, Hunting Ware, relief-molded hunt scenes, ca. 1905, the set (ILLUS., above) **600**

German Tea Set in Cheery Chintz Pattern

German porcelain: cov. teapot, cov. sugar bowl & creamer; squatty bulbous bodies, D-form handles, domed covers w/knob finials, Cheery Chintz patt., marked "Er-phila - Warwick - Germany," early 20th c., the set (ILLUS.)... **104**

Grindley (W.H.) & Company: cov. teapot, cov. sugar & creamer; Sheraton Ivory patt., each piece w/a wide low squatty paneled body on tab feet, long pointed handles & low domed covers w/knob finials, decorated w/stylized Art Deco florals, this design was copied by Homer Laughlin China in the U.S., England, ca. 1926, the set (ILLUS., bottom of page)................. **75+**

Grindley & Company Art Deco Style Tea Set

Rare Decorated Handel Porcelain Tea Set

Handel Porcelain: tall tankard-form cov. teapot, squatty bulbous cov. sugar & creamer, small round bowl, larger round bowl w/side handles & oval plate w/end handles; each piece h.p. w/large pink tulip blossoms & green leaves on the white ground, heavy gold rim bands & handles, signed on the base "Handel McMix USA," early 20th c., the set (ILLUS.) **1,725**

Fine Decorated Royal Vienna-style Tea Set

Hutschenreuther Porcelain: cov. teapot, creamer, six cups & four saucers; Vienna-style, each piece decorated w/a wide gold body band finely painted w/a continuous scene of festive children in pastel shades, cobalt blue ground w/elaborate gilt scroll trim, the bulbous teapot w/an upright bail handle w/gilt-bronze figural dolphin supports joined by a porcelain hand grip, artist-signed, impressed monogram & blue beehive marks, Germany, ca. 1900, teapot overall 8" h. (ILLUS.,) **4,465**

Belleek Aberdeen Pattern Breakfast Tea Set

Belleek Hexagon Breakfast Set

Irish Belleek porcelain: Aberdeen breakfast set: cov. teapot, creamer, open sugar & cups & saucers; no tray, D494-II (ILLUS., bottom previous page) **2,200**

Irish Belleek porcelain: Grass teakettle, cov., large size, D751-I (ILLUS. right w/smaller teapot, below) **1,000**

Grass Teapots & Tray

Irish Belleek porcelain: Grass teapot, cov., small size, D750-I (ILLUS. left w/larger teapot) **800**

Irish Belleek porcelain: Grass tray, round, D736-I (ILLUS. with 2 sizes of teapot) **2,000**

Irish Belleek porcelain: Hexagon breakfast set: small cov. teapot, open sugar & creamer, two plates & two cups & saucers, h.p. floral decoration, no tray, D396-II (ILLUS., top of page) **2,600**

Ironstone china: cov. teapot, cov. sugar bowl, creamer, two cups & saucers & rectangular tray; serving pieces w/a flattened moon flask body, stepped rectangular covers w/blossom finials, each piece w/a white ground decorated w/a bold molded cobalt blue-painted stylized flower & leaf branch, the teapot & creamer w/molded figural blue monkey-shaped handles, George Jones, England, late 19th c., chip on one cup, very minor nicks, the set (ILLUS., below) **896**

Rare George Jones Blue & White Ironstone Tea Set

Child's Phoenix Bird Tea Set with Angled Handles

Japanese porcelain: child's size, cov. teapot, cov. sugar bowl & creamer; blue & white Phoenix Bird patt., tapering ovoid bodies & angled handles, marked "Made in Japan," ca. 1930s, teapot 5 1/2" l., 3 3/4" h., the set (ILLUS.)... **130-150**

Child's Phoenix Bird Tea Set with Pointed Handles

Japanese porcelain: child's size, cov. teapot, cov. sugar bowl & creamer; blue & white Phoenix Bird patt., wide squatty bulbous bodies w/pointed handles, marked "Made in Japan," ca. 1930s, teapot 5 3/4" l., 3 3/8" h., the set (ILLUS.)... **135-155**

Phoenix Bird Child's Tea Set with C-form Handles

Japanese porcelain: child's size, cov. teapot, cov. sugar bowl & creamer; blue & white Phoenix Bird patt., wide squatty bulbous bodies w/C-form handles, marked w/a "T" inside a flower above "Japan," ca. 1930s, teapot 6 1/2" l., 3 3/4" h., the set (ILLUS.)... **125-145**

Phoenix Bird Child's Tea Set in a Common Shape

Japanese porcelain: child's size, cov. teapot, cov. sugar bowl & creamer; blue & white Phoenix Bird patt., wide cylindrical bodies w/low domed covers & angled handles, very common type, marked w/Morimura Bros. "M" in Wreath mark & "Made in Japan," ca. 1930s, teapot 6 1/2" l., 3 3/4" h., the set (ILLUS.) **85-105**

Phoenix Bird Child's Tea Set with Ovoid Bodies

Japanese porcelain: child's size, cov. teapot, cov. sugar bowl & creamer; Phoenix Bird patt., bulbous ovoid bodies w/pointed loop handles, marked "Made in Japan," ca. 1920s-30s, teapot 5 1/8" l., 4" h., the set (ILLUS.) **140-165**

Child's Phoenix Bird Pattern Tea Set with Tapering Sides

Japanese porcelain: child's size, cov. teapot, cov. sugar bowl & creamer; Phoenix Bird patt., tapering cylindrical shapes, marked "Made in Japan," ca. 1920s-30s, teapot 5 1/2", 3 5/8" h., the set (ILLUS.) **110-135**

Knowles, Taylor & Knowles Davenport Shape Tea Set

Knowles, Taylor & Knowles: cov. teapot, cov. sugar & creamer; Davenport shape, squatty bulbous body molded w/wide gently swirled lobes below the decorated top border & cover, late 19th - early 20th c., 3 pcs. (ILLUS., above)............................ **500**

Limoges porcelain: cov. tall teapot, cov. sugar, creamer & four cups & saucers; tall urn-shaped bodies w/angular handles, overall gold decoration, signed on the base "Healy Gold 1891," factory mark in green "Limoges CMC France," the set (ILLUS., right)... **800**

All-Gold Limoges Tea Set

Tea Set & Tray Decorated with Clusters of Roses

Limoges porcelain: cov. teapot, cov. sugar bowl, creamer & oblong tray; round bulbous bodies, gold handles & ring finials, h.p. w/clusters of pink & red roses & green leaves, heavy gold trim, factory mark of A. Klingenberg, Limoges, France, ca. 1890s-1910, the set (ILLUS.)............................ **900**

Limoges Tea Set with Roses on a Yellow Background

Limoges porcelain: cov. teapot, cov. sugar bowl, creamer & rectangular tray; squatty bulbous bodies tapering to ruffled bases, rolled slightly ruffled rim, domed covers w/gold loop finials, ornate gold scroll handles, each piece w/a pale yellow background h.p. w/pink roses & green foliage, tiny single-cup teapot, factory mark of Jean Pouyat, Limoges, ca. 1891-1932, the set (ILLUS.)................. **800**

Limoges Tea Set Painted with Images of Cherubs

Limoges porcelain: cov. teapot, cov. sugar bowl & creamer; squatty bulbous bodies, each piece h.p. w/a scene of cherubs, artist-signed "MY" & dated "1904," blank marked by Jean Pouyat, Limoges, France, the set (ILLUS.) **1,500**

Limoges porcelain: cov. teapot, cov. sugar bowl & creamer; squatty bulbous bodies w/gold C-scroll handles, gold serpentine spout & gold loop finials, each piece h.p. w/purple violets & green leaves, factory mark of Jean Pouyat, Limoges, France, ca. 1891-1932, the set (ILLUS.) **800**

Limoges porcelain: cov. teapot, cov. sugar bowl, creamer, tea strainer & round tray; squatty bulbous bodies w/domed covers, finely h.p. w/roses, heavy gold trim, artist-signed, factory mark "Venice - T&V - France," Tressemann & Vogt, ca. 1892-1907, the set (ILLUS., below) **1,900**

Pouyat Tea Set Painted with Violets

Elegant Rose-decorated Limoges Tea Set on Tray

Limoges Tea Set with Popular Violets Decoration

Limoges porcelain: cov. teapot, cov. sugar bowl, creamer & two cups & saucers; footed squatty bulbous bodies w/gold loop handles & finials, h.p. w/popular violets decoration, factory mark of Tressemann & Vogt, Limoges, France, ca. 1892-1907, the set (ILLUS., top of page)..... **600**

Floral-decorated Limoges Set on Tray

Limoges porcelain: cov. teapot, cov. sugar, creamer & round tray; each piece in an oblong upright tapering shape w/oval covers, gold C-scroll handles, h.p. w/colorful florals, factory mark of Delinieres & Co., Limoges, France, ca. 1894-1900, the set (ILLUS.).. **1,500**

Limoges porcelain: cov. teapot, cov. sugar, creamer & round tray; each piece w/a tall tapering waisted body, decorated w/alternating narrow mottled green stripes & stripes w/gold S-scroll bands, ornate gold C-scroll handles, artist-signed, factory mark of Tressemann & Vogt, Limoges, France, ca. 1892-1907, teapot 7" h., the set (ILLUS., bottom of page).. **1,900**

Very Fine Hand-painted Limoges Tea Set on Tray

Limoges Set Retailed by Tiffany & Co.

Limoges porcelain: cov. teapot, cov. sugar, creamer & tray; squatty hexagonal bodies raised on a paneled pedestal base, a wide shoulder tapering to a flared rim, domed covers w/knob finials, white w/gold band decoration, made in Limoges to be retailed by Tiffany & Company, New York, ca. 1900, the set (ILLUS., left) **1,500**

Limoges porcelain: cov. teapot, cov. sugar, tall coffeepot & creamer; teapot, sugar & creamer w/footed squatty bulbous shapes & flared scalloped rims, all pieces decorated w/gold wedding band decoration, Haviland & Co. factory mark, ca. 1876-89, the set (ILLUS., below) **350**

Early Haviland Tea & Coffee Set with Gold Bands

Limoges Set with Teapot, Cups & Saucers & Tray

Rose-decorated Teapot, Cups & Saucers & Dessert Plates

Limoges porcelain: cov. teapot, cups & saucers & round tray; tall urn-form teapot & tall conical cups, each piece h.p. w/bands of pink roses & green leaves, green factory mark "France - PM - De M Limoges" (Mavaleix mark 1), ca. 1908-14, the set (ILLUS., bottom previous page) **600**

Limoges porcelain: cov. teapot, four cups & saucers & four dessert plates; squatty bulbous teapot w/gold C-form handle & loop finial on domed cover, serpentine spout, each piece h.p. w/bands composed of pairs of pink roses & green leafage, factory mark of Jean Pouyat, Limoges, France, 1891-1932, the set (ILLUS., top of page) **700**

Limoges porcelain: one-cup cov. teapot, open sugar, creamer & oblong tray; each piece painted w/colorful roses, a gold wave scroll band around the teapot & creamer neck, gold loop handles & teapot finial, marks of Gérard, Dufraisseix & Abbot, Limoges, France, ca. 1900-41, the set (ILLUS., bottom of page) **900**

Six-cup Limoges Teapot From Set

Limoges porcelain: six-cup cov. footed spherical teapot w/a low scalloped rim, domed cover w/loop finial, serpentine spout & C-scroll handle, h.p. w/lovely shaded red & pink roses & green leaves, gold trim, matching four-cup teapot, cov. sugar, creamer, cups & saucers & an 18" l. double-handled tray, France, late 19th c., the set (ILLUS. of six-cup teapot) **1,400-2,000**

GDA Limoges Tea Set on Tray

Elegant Gold & White Limoges Tea Set on Tray

Limoges porcelain: tall cov. teapot, cov. sugar bowl, creamer, six cups & saucers & a tray; the tall tapering teapot in white w/a scroll gold band around the neck below a wide gold rim band, matching band design on the other pieces, gold handles, spouts & covers, marks for Blakeman & Henderson, Limoges, France, ca. 1890s, teapot 6" h., the set (ILLUS.)..................... **1,500**

Limoges porcelain: tall cov. teapot, cov. sugar & creamer; teapot w/wide rounded bottom & tall tapering sides, each piece in white w/heavy gold trim on spout, handles, rims & finials, green factory mark "France P.M. deM - Limoges," decorator mark of "Coronet France - Borgfeldt," ca. 1908-14, the set (ILLUS. of teapot, bottom of page).. **350**

Majolica: Bamboo & Fern patt., cov. teapot, cov. sugar bowl & creamer; each body molded as a cluster of yellow bamboo w/long green fern leaves wrapping around the lower body, Wardle & Co., England, late 19th c., minor nicks on teapot, mismatched sugar cover, the set (ILLUS. right with Daisy pattern set, page 244)... **308**

Tall Teapot from Three-Piece Set

Fine George Jones Basketweave & Floral Tea Set

Majolica: Basketweave & Floral patt., cov. teapot, cov. sugar bowl, creamer, two cups & saucers & oblong handled tray; serving pieces w/tapering ovoid bodies molded around the bottom w/bands of tan basketweave below a cobalt blue upper body molded w/branches of pink blossoms & green leaves, domed covers w/arched twig handles, brown branch handles & spout, George Jones, England, late 19th c., professional repair to sugar cover rim, one cup & saucer repaired, teapot cover not perfect fit, tray 19 1/2" l., teapot 7" h., the set (ILLUS., above) **3,640**

Majolica: Basketweave & Floral patt., cov. teapot, cov. sugar bowl & creamer; wide squatty bulbous molded pale blue basketweave bodies decorated w/branches of pink blossoms & green leaves, brown branch handles, flattened covers w/white blossom finials, probably England, late 19th c., rim chip on creamer, the set (ILLUS. right with Floral Branch pattern tea set, page 243) **196**

Majolica: Bird & Fan patt., cov. teapot, cov. sugar bowl & creamer; spherical bodies molded w/colorful fans, each w/a flying bird against a pebbled pale yellow background, brown branch handles & spout, probably England, late 19th c., minor spout chip on teapot, the set (ILLUS. left with Cranes pattern tea set, bottom of page)... **308**

Majolica: Bird & Fan patt., cov. teapot, cov. sugar bowl & creamer; spherical body molded w/an open white fan w/flying blue, red & yellow bird, flanked by pink blossoms, all on a pale blue ground, branch spout & handles, Fielding, England, late 19th c., chip on sugar cover, the set (ILLUS. right with Wedgwood Cauliflower tea set, top next page) **392**

Majolica: Blackberry & Basketweave patt., cov. teapot, cov. sugar bowl & creamer; each piece w/a spherical body molded on the lower half w/a band of tan basketweave, the upper half in cobalt blue molded w/blackberry vines in pink & green, brown branch handles & spout, mottled basketweave covers w/ring finials, probably England, late 19th c., the set (ILLUS. right with Oriental pattern tea set, bottom page 245)................................. **364**

Bird & Fan and Cranes Pattern Tea Sets

Cauliflower & Bird and Fan Majolica Tea Sets

Majolica: Cauliflower patt., cov. teapot, cov. sugar bowl & creamer; each piece modeled as a white head of cauliflower w/wide green leaves, Josiah Wedgwood, England, late 19th c., minor spout nicks on teapot, teapot 6" h., the set (ILLUS. left with Bird & Fan tea set w/pale blue ground, above) **924**

Majolica: Cranes patt., cov. teapot, cov. sugar bowl & creamer; spherical bodies molded around the lower half w/a yellow basketweave design, the wide upper band w/a pale blue ground molded w/bands of brown flying cranes, brown twig handles & spout, probably England,

late 19th c., minor glaze nicks, the set (ILLUS. right with Bird & Fan pattern tea set with yellow ground, previous page) **168**

Majolica: Daisy patt., cov. teapot, cov. sugar bowl & creamer; each piece w/a hexagonal body in dark brown, the panels molded w/large white & yellow daisy blossoms & green leaves, angled green branch handles & spout, figural flower cover finials, mark of the Victoria Pottery Company, late 19th c., professional spout repair on creamer, the set (ILLUS. left with Bamboo & Fern pattern set, bottom of page) **784**

Daisy Pattern & Bamboo & Fern Pattern Majolica Tea Sets

Extremely Rare George Jones Drum Pattern Tea Set

Majolica: Drum patt., cov. teapot, cov. sugar bowl & creamer; each piece w/a spherical body designed as a round drum w/wide cobalt blue bands separated by narrow brown bands joined by interwoven rope bands w/buckles, strap & buckle handles & a drum stick spout, very rare design, George Jones, England, late 19th c., teapot 6" h., the set (ILLUS., above) **12,320**

Floral Branch Pattern & Basketweave & Floral Pattern Sets

Majolica: Floral Branch patt., cov. teapot, cov. sugar bowl & creamer; wide cylindrical bodies w/narrow shoulder bands, pale blue background molded w/a large branch w/green leaves & a stylized pink & white blossom, brown branch handles, covers w/flower bud finials, probably England, late 19th c., hairline in creamer, the set (ILLUS. left with Basketweave & Floral tea set) **364**

Majolica: Oriental patt., cov. teapot, cov. sugar & creamer; each piece w/an upright square body w/swelled panels on the sides, each corner w/a pale yellow molded band, cobalt blue ground w/shaded pale green & white swelled panels molded w/an Oriental slender tree w/green leaves & pink blossoms & a perched brown bird, squared pale yellow bamboo handles & a bamboo spout, the low domed covers w/a seated Oriental man forming the finial, probably England, late 19th c., repair to teapot cover finial, teapot 7" h., the set (ILLUS. below with Blackberry & Basketweave tea set, bottom of page)... **364**

Oriental Pattern & Blackberry & Basketweave Pattern Tea Sets

Minton Sevres-style Individual Tea Set

Minton Porcelain: individual-size, cov. tea-pot, cov. sugar bowl, creamer, handled cup & rounded triangular undertray; Sevres-style, each piece in white painted w/a band of pink rose blossoms between turquoise "jeweled" gilt chains, lavender edge bands, Pattern No. A1213, date code for 1853, tray 11 1/4" w., the set (ILLUS., above) **2,868**

Floral-decorated Nippon Tea Set

Nippon Porcelain: cov. teapot, cov. sugar bowl, creamer & six cups & saucers; bulbous bodies on the serving pieces, each h.p. w/stylized pink & yellow floral border bands w/green leaves & gilt trim, unmarked, early 20th c., the set (ILLUS.) **150**

Colorful Noritake Tea Set

Noritake China: cov. teapot, cov. sugar, creamer & oblong undertray; each piece w/a squared tapering body w/gold angled handles, each side decorated w/colorful Oriental floral clusters framed by decorated borders, early 20th c., the set (ILLUS.) **80-100**

Noritake Tea Set

Noritake Porcelain: cov. teapot, creamer, cov. sugar, tray; the teapot, creamer & sugar w/ gold angled loop handles, the 6 x 11" tray w/tab side handles, all in vivid deep orange w/gold & black trim, decorated w/desert scene of robed, turbaned figure against backdrop of palm trees & a tower, the set (ILLUS.) **395**

Lovely Pickard-decorated Porcelain Tea Set

Pickard China: cov. teapot, cov. sugar bowl, creamer & footed compote; serving pieces w/a wide low squatty bulbous body w/looped gold handles & a gold teapot spout, a creamy lower body below a wide middle band decorated w/colorful stylized flowering vines on a white ground, turquoise blue border bands, marked, early 20th c., the set (ILLUS.) **460**

Fine HB Quimper Tea Set with Rouen-inspired Pattern

All Gold Pickard-decorated Tea Set

Pickard China: cov. teapot, cov. sugar bowl, creamer & six 6" d. plates; each piece decorated overall w/a textured gold glaze, the scalloped plates w/stamped floral borders, each marked, ca. 1930, the set (ILLUS.) **201**

Quimper Pottery: cov. tall teapot, cov. sugar bowl & creamer; Rouen-inspired patt., each piece w/blue-trimmed angular handles, domed covers w/pointed finials, each painted w/the figure of a male Breton musician in a landscape, elaborate upper borders of stylized florals in cobalt blue, yellow & red, mark of HB Quimper, only slight glaze wear under sugar cover, France, early 20th c., the set (ILLUS., top of page) **575**

Elaborate Henriot Quimper "Decor Riche" Tea Set

HR Quimper Tea Set with Lobed Bodies

Quimper Pottery: cov. teapot, cov. sugar bowl, creamer & six cups & saucers; Rococo Louis XV-style swirl-molded bodies, all decorated in the "decor riche" patt., each piece w/a color portrait of a Breton peasant w/two musicians on the teapot, dark blue leafy scroll border bands, mark of HenRiot, Quimper, designed by artist LeBorgne, mint except for one glaze fleck on one cup handle, early 20th c., the set (ILLUS., bottom previous page) **2,800**

Quimper Pottery: cov. teapot, creamer, five cups & saucers & an extra saucer; each piece w/a lobed body, each painted w/a figure of a Breton peasant woman or man, stylized floral wreath borders in dark blue, orange & green, ornate blue C-scroll handle on the teapot, mark of HR Quimper, France, early 20th c., teapot 7" h., the set (ILLUS., top of page) **550**

R.S. Poland porcelain: cov. teapot, cov. sugar bowl & creamer; Mold 601, each w/ovoid body, scrolled loop handle, domed lid w/finial, disk foot, decorated w/draping band of shadow leaves in pale blue/green shades & gold trim, early 20th c., the set (ILLUS., bottom of page) **450-500**

R.S. Poland Tea Set

R.S. Prussia Tea Set with Alternating Decorative Panels

R.S. Prussia porcelain: cov. teapot, cov. sugar bowl, creamer & cup & saucer; lobed waisted bodies w/ruffled rims, decorated w/alternating panels of gold floral decoration on cream ground bordered w/green leafy vines & cream flowers on pale blue/grey ground, gold trim over all, the set (ILLUS.)
.... **350-400**

R.S. Prussia Mold 704 Tea Set

R.S. Prussia porcelain: cov. teapot, cov. sugar bowl, creamer, cup & saucer; Mold 704, slender paneled tapering bodies, angled handles, ruffled rims, short feet, decorated w/delicate pink flowers, green vining leaves & Cupids, gold trim, early 20th c., the set (ILLUS.) **300-350**

Royal Bayreuth Child's Tea Set

Royal Bayreuth porcelain, child's, cov. teapot, cov. sugar, creamer, two plates, & two cups & saucers; ovoid bodies, each piece decorated w/a scene of children playing, the set (ILLUS., above).... **750-850**

Royal Bayreuth "Tapestry" Tea Set

Royal Bayreuth Porcelain: cov. teapot, cov. sugar bowl & creamer; each w/a squatty bulbous body & gold handles, "Tapestry" decoration of white mums & purple violets on a pale blue ground, blue mark, Germany, early 20th c., teapot 7" l., the set (ILLUS.).................................... **460**

Royal Bayreuth porcelain: cov. teapot, cov. sugar bowl & creamer; ovoid bodies, the sugar & creamer w/C-scroll handles, the teapot w/overhead fixed handle & serpentine spout, each piece decorated w/a colorful fairy tale scene, the set (ILLUS., bottom of page)...................... **350-400**

Royal Bayreuth Fairy Tale Tea Set

Unusual Cockerel Royal Doulton Tea Set

Royal Doulton Ware: cov. teapot, open sugar & creamer; Cockerel patt., the teapot modeled as a rooster, the sugar bowl as a hen & the creamer as a chick, introduced ca. 1935, the set (ILLUS.)
.... **2,500**

Early Royal Doulton Kingsware Tea Set

Royal Doulton Ware: cov. teapot, open sugar & creamer; Kingsware, each piece w/a different embossed figural scene, introduced in 1902, the set (ILLUS.) **750**

Unusual Russian Porcelain Tea Set

Russian porcelain: cov. teapot, open sugar & creamer, four saucers & four egg-shaped covered cups & two open cups; the teapot & sugar of footed squatty bulbous form w/ornate looping handles w/figural horse heads, the footed open sugar of oblong boat shape, footed cups, each piece decorated w/dark red, yellow & black Byzantine-style panels against the white ground, Kornilov Bros. factory, Russia, ca. 1910, teapot 9" h., the set (ILLUS.) **2,415**

Modern Saenger Porcelain Tea Set

Saenger Porcelain: cov. teapot, open sugar & creamer on oblong fitted tray; teapot w/futuristic squatty bulbous shape w/deep side indentations where creamer & sugar fit in, made by a new artisan in Newark, Delaware, featured in some episodes of "Star Trek: The Next Generation," the set (ILLUS.)
.... **375**

Bleu Nouveau Gilt-decorated Sevres Tea Set

Sevres Porcelain: cov. teapot, cov. sugar bowl, creamer & one cup & saucer; dark Bleu Nouveau ground, the serving pieces w/bulbous ovoid bodies, each piece decorated w/gilt leaf band around the base & a band of stylized blossoms & leaves around the shoulder, further leaf band & gilt line decoration on each piece, various decorator & potter marks, France, mid-19th c., teapot 6 1/4" h., the set (ILLUS.) **2,271**

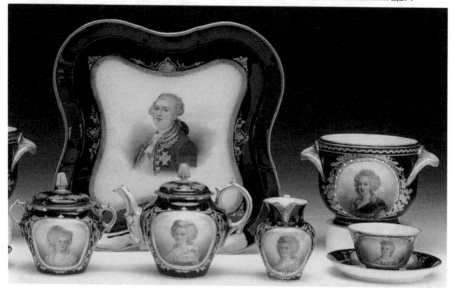

Sevres-style Tea Set with Spurious Factory Marks

Sevres-style porcelain: cov. teapot, cov. sugar bowl, creamer, two cups & saucers & an undertray; the serving pieces w/bulbous ovoid bodies tapering to flat mouths & domed covers w/fluted pointed finials, each w/a cobalt blue ground centered on the front w/a large rounded gold-bordered reserve featuring a bust portrait of a court beauty of the late 18th c., the four-lobed tray centered by a color half-length portrait of Louis XVI, each piece further trimmed w/ornate delicate gold scrolls, spurious Sevres & chateau marks, France, early 20th c., tray 11 7/8" w., the set (ILLUS. of part) **2,350**

Fine Sevres-style Porcelain Tea Set with a Pink Ground

Sevres-style porcelain: tete-a-tete style, cov. teapot, cov. sugar bowl, creamer, two cylindrical cups & saucers & a scalloped round footed undertray; teapot w/ovoid body, creamer w/tapering ovoid body raised on four gold legs, cylindrical sugar bowl, all w/a pink ground elaborately painted w/overall bands of long gold arabesques highlighted w/delicate turquoise blue, deep red & pink "jeweling," spurious gilt interlaced Ls mark, France, mid- to late 19th c., undertray 8 7/8" d., the set (ILLUS.) **3,760**

English Victorian Staffordshire Tea Set

Staffordshire earthenware: cov. teapot, cov. sugar bowl, creamer, two handled cups & saucers & a large undertray; each serving piece of upright diamond shape, each wide side panel decorated w/overall small salmon-colored flowers separated by a narrow panel decorated w/stylized black cranes, blue & black floral neck border, mark of Powell & Bishop, England, second half 19th c., minor gilt wear, small flake on teapot spout, tray 14 x 21 1/2", teapot 5" h., the set (ILLUS.).. **330**

Rare Attwell Child's Three-piece Rabbit Set

Shelley China: child's, cov. teapot, open sugar & creamer; Rabbit Set, teapot in the shape of a duck, the creamer in the shape of a rabbit & the sugar in the shape of a chick, designed by Mabel Lucie Attwell, introduced in 1930, the set (ILLUS.).. **1,700-1,800**

Attwell Boo-Boo Pattern Mushroom Tea Set

Shelley China: cov. teapot, open sugar & creamer; Mushroom Set, Boo-Boo decoration, mushroom-shaped teapot & sugar bowl, figural Boo-Boo creamer, designed by Mabel Lucie Attwell, introduced in 1926, the set (ILLUS.) **1,700-1800**

Miniature Wedgwood Jasper Ware Tea Set

Wedgwood (Josiah): miniature, cov. teapot, cov. sugar, creamer & oval tray; blue Jasper Ware, baluster-shaped pot & squatty bulbous sugar & creamer, all w/white relief Classical figures, modern, the set (ILLUS.) **50**

White Ironstone Napier Shape Tea Set

White Ironstone China: cov. teapot, cov. sugar bowl & creamer; Napier shape, by Bridgewood & Son, England, ca. 1860s, the set (ILLUS.) **600**

Silver - English & Other

Very Rare Hoffmann-designed Austrian Silver Tea Set

Austrian: cov. teapot, cov. sugar bowl, cov. creamer, waste bowl, tongs & oval tray; each piece w/a squatty bulbous boldly lobed shape w/ivory handles & ivory lobed finials, designed by Josef Hoffmann & produced by The Wiener Werkstatte, ca. 1920s, tray 20 1/2" l., teapot 7 3/4" h., the set (ILLUS.) **$71,700**

Rare Wiener Werkstatte Tea Set Designed by Hoffmann

Austrian: cov. teapot, cov. sugar bowl, creamer, teakettle on stand & oval tray; the serving pieces w/upright flat oval bodies w/hinged tapering covers w/brass ball finials, cylindrical rosewood side handles, the kettle on a conforming burner stand w/pierced side holes, designed by Josef Hoffmann, manufactured by The Wiener Werkstatte, tray w/original Wiener Werkstatte lace doily, ca. 1923, tray 14 1/4" l., teakettle & stand 9 1/2" h., the set (ILLUS.).. **53,775**

Victorian English Sterling Three-piece Tea Set

English: cov. teapot, open sugar & creamer; low pedestal base supporting a wide squatty inverted pear-shaped body, all decorated w/overall relief-stamped rococo florals & C-scrolls, C-scroll handles, hinged teapot cover w/figural fruit finial & serpentine spout, Martin Hall & Co., Sheffield, England, 1877, some small dents & creases on each piece, teapot 7 1/2" h., the set (ILLUS.) **805**

Fine Mexican Silver Tea Set

Mexican: cov. teapot, cov. sugar bowl & creamer; each footed piece w/a squatty melon-lobed body, lobed domed covers w/figural flower finials, ornate C-scroll handles, one piece marked "F. Guzman - Mexico," .900 quality, 20th c., the set (ILLUS.) **1,150**

Very Rare Russian Silver & Parcel-Gilt Figural Tea Set

Russian: cov. teapot, cov. sugar & creamer & sugar tongs; each modeled as a cloth saddle bag, decorated w/bold stylized parcel-gilt scrolling foliage within a leaf border, the high-domed caps joined to the bodies w/link chains, similar chains on spouts, marked w/unrecorded Cyrilla workmaster's initials "G.L.," Moscow, Russia, 1896-1908, teapot 8 1/4" h., the set (ILLUS.) **17,925**

Fabergé Russian Silver Tea Set

Russian: cov. teapot, cov. teakettle on stand, open sugar bowl, creamer & tongs; Neoclassical design, each urn-form piece decorated around the body w/wide drapery swags above a fluted design around the lower half, the serpentine spouts w/cast shells at the base, the pots w/angular ivory handles, angular silver handles on sugar & creamer, gilt interiors, mark of Fabergé w/Imperial warrant & the workmaster's mark of Alexander Wakeva, St. Petersburg, Russia, 1908-17, teakettle & stand overall 14" h., the set (ILLUS.) **26,290**

Sterling & Coin Silver - American

Early Tiffany Sterling Silver Tea Set

Sterling: cov. teapot, cov. sugar bowl & creamer; Neoclassical style, each piece w/a tall ovoid body raised on three long scroll legs ending in paw feet, domed cover & arched C-scroll handles, narrow shoulder & cover bands of classical designs, each leg headed by a Bacchanalian mask, mark of Tiffany & Co., New York, New York, ca. 1860-64, teapot 9 1/2" h., the set (ILLUS.)............ **$2,760**

Early Tiffany Sterling Silver Tea Set

Sterling: cov. teapot, cov. coffeepot, cov. teakettle on stand, cov. sugar bowl, creamer, waste bowl & oval tray; ornate rococo designs on the footed squatty bulbous baluster-form bodies, each piece chased w/cornucopias w/fruit, flowers & foliage, a cartouche on each side, pots w/insulator spacers, the tray w/open scroll handles, Reed & Barton, Taunton, Massachusetts, 1946, tray 31" l., teakettle overall 13 1/2" h., the set (ILLUS.) **$22,705**

Various Materials

Child's Blue & White Graniteware Tea Set

Graniteware: child's size, cov. teapot, four cups, four saucers, creamer & cov. sugar bowl; white w/blue design, teapot 3 1/4" d., 5 1/4" h., the set (ILLUS.) **$450**

Large Oriental Lacquer Tea Set

Lacquerware: two cov. teapots, cov. sugar, creamer, six cups & saucers, six small plates & six small bowls w/spoons; ovoid & bulbous black bodies decorated w/designs of dragons in orange & gold, gilt interiors, Oriental, early 20th c., the set (ILLUS.).. **196**

English Art Deco Silver Plate Tea Set

Silver plate: cov. teapot, cov. sugar, creamer & rectangular tray; Art Deco style, each piece w/a squatty slightly flaring rectangular body & wide tapering shoulder, low domed cover w/reddish amber rectangular Bakelite finials, teapot w/angled Bakelite handle, tray w/cut corners & matching Bakelite squared end handles, England, ca. 1925, tray 15" l., the set (ILLUS.).. **196**

Tea Sets - 1950-2000

Ceramic

Lefton China Elegant Rose Three-piece Tea Set

Lefton China: cov. teapot, cov. sugar bowl & creamer; Elegant Rose patt., oval upright cylindrical ribbed bodies, decorated w/clusters of large red roses & green leaves on a white ground, sponged gold trim, ca. 1955-65 (ILLUS.)................. **$200-250**

Lefton China: cup & saucer; Violets patt., funnel-shaped cup, No. 2300 (ILLUS. front with Lefton teapots, bottom of page)... **35-40**

Lefton China: teapot, short, round w/swirled rib design, Violets patt., No. 20610 (ILLUS. left with other Lefton pieces, bottom of page)................................... **75-95**

Lefton China: teapot, tall w/gently lobed pear-shaped body w/scroll handle, Violets patt., No. 092 (ILLUS. right with other Lefton Violets pieces, bottom of page)...... **75-95**

Lefton China: 9" d. plate, Violets patt., No. 2910 (ILLUS. back with Lefton teapots, bottom of page)..................................... **30-35**

Lefton China Violets Pattern Tea Set Pieces

PART IV

RARE IRISH BELLEEK TEAWARES

It is hard to believe that Belleek produced such a wide range of tea sets, which included teapots. Depending on where one draws a line, there are some 38 known distinctive shapes and, when colors and sizes are taken into account, the variations exceed 100.

The patterns can be divided into four main design groups, with two misfits (Chinese and Mask do not fit into any group): Marine (Echinus, Neptune, etc.), Geometric (fan, scroll, etc.), Floral (Shamrock, Lily, Grass, etc.), and Celtic. The make-up of the individual sets differs enormously. The smaller sets consist of the basic necessities for serving a cup of tea on a tray: tray, cup and saucer, small teapot (enough for one cup) cream and sugar. Other sets have a much wider range of pieces.

Many of these sets also included either a teakettle or coffeepot. Belleek distinguished its teakettle by a handle over the top of the base, as opposed to the side handle like the teapot. Coffeepots, like teapots, had their handles on the side, but were taller in design.

Most of these sets, including the teapot, were introduced in the late 1st period early 2nd period. Some of these teapots have been reproduced within the last five years at the Pottery without much change in the design, which goes to prove what great designs were made at the beginning.

Other teapots have been slightly modified. For example, the Lace, Limpet and Shell teapots lost their feet in later designs. These modifications were mostly implemented to help with the production, making it speedier and, therefore, saving costs. The spout on other teapots including the Tridacna pattern was shortened, again to prevent damage whilst being shipped.

It is worth the collector's while to study the teapots because the more rare examples are highly sought after and worth a great deal, whereas the more common teapots, although still highly collectible, are not so looked for.- Lady Marion LanghamUnless otherwise noted, all the following are "teapots." Teakettles are identified by the handle formed "over the top" as opposed to being attached to the side.

The "bracketed" range of prices given is based on period (of manufacture), size and decoration.

All pricing given here is for the earlier Black Mark periods, i.e., 1st Period (ca. 1863-1890), 2nd Period (ca. 1891-1926) and 3rd Period (ca. 1926-1946)

Belleek produced many of its teapots, but not all, in three sizes, these identified, of course, as small, medium and large.

Known tints are Pink, Green, Blue and Orange. Decoration may be a "heavy" application of a mixture of the tints (refer to example of Footed Echinus) or more elaborate such as hand painted flowers or scenes. Eugene Sheerin, Belleek's most famous artist, once painted an entire breakfast set utilizing the Ring Handled Ivory Pattern, with each piece of the set displaying a different Irish scene. — Del Domke

All photos courtesy of Lady Marion Langham.

Undecorated Erne Pattern Tea Set

Unnamed Belleek Pattern with Celtic Design & Green Trim

Tea set: cov. teapot, creamer & cup & saucer; Erne patt., undecorated, 2nd period, creamer $220-260; cup & saucer, $260-320; teapot only (ILLUS. of group, bottom of previous page) **$700-800**

Tea set: cov. teapot, creamer & two cups & saucers; unnamed pattern w/Celtic design trimmed in green, 2nd period, creamer, $300-400; each cup & saucer, $300-400; teapot only (ILLUS. of group, top of page)............................... **600-800**

Low Lily Tea Set with Green Tint & Gold Trim

One Version of the Rare Chinese Tea Urn

Tea set: cov. teapot, open sugar & creamer & two cups & saucers; Low Lily patt., green tint w/gold trim, 2nd period, creamer & open sugar, $400-500; cup & saucer, $260-320; teapot only (ILLUS. of set, bottom of previous page) **700-800**

Tea urn, Chinese (Dragon) patt., fancy dark pink, black & heavy gold trim, 17" h., 1st period (ILLUS., above)............... **18,000-25,000**

Extremely Rare Decorated Chinese Pattern Tall Tea Urn

Tea urn, Chinese (Dragon) patt., fancy pale pink, black & heavy gold trim, 17" h., 1st period
(ILLUS.)... **18,000-25,000**

Grass Pattern Teakettle with Multicolored Decoration

Teakettle, Grass patt., multicolored decoration w/gold, 1st period (ILLUS.) **600-1,000**

Gold-trimmed Ringhandle Teakettle

Teakettle, Ringhandle patt., undecorated except gold trim, 3rd period (ILLUS.) **1,000-1,400**

Aberdeen Pattern Teapot with Cob Decoration

Teapot, Aberdeen patt., Cob decoration, 2nd period (ILLUS.).. **700-800**

Decorated Artichoke Pattern Teapot

Teapot, Artichoke patt., green decoration w/gold trim, 1st period (ILLUS.).......... **800-1,000**

Teapot, Bamboo patt., undecorated, 1st period (ILLUS. right with decorated Echinus teapot, pg. 273).................................. **800-1,000**

Blarney Pattern Teapot with Green Tint & Gold Trim

Teapot, Blarney patt., green tint & gold trim, 2nd period (ILLUS.) **700-800**

Unique Unrecorded Belleek Bone China Teapot with Maroon Trim

Teapot, Bone china unrecorded shape, maroon trim, unique piece (ILLUS.) .... **Price unavailable**

Rare Chinese Pattern Decorated Teapot

Teapot, Chinese (Dragon) patt., multicolored decoration with gold, 1st period
(ILLUS.)... **1,600-2,800**

Cone Pattern Teapot with Orange Tint & Gold Trim

Teapot, Cone patt., orange tint & gold trim, 2nd period (ILLUS.)... **600-800**

A Decorated Echinus and Undecorated Bamboo Teapot

Teapot, Echinus patt., footed, blue & pink decoration w/gold trim, 1st period (ILLUS. left with Bamboo
teapot) **800-1,200**

Early Echinus Teapot with Pink Tint & Gold Trim

Teapot, Echinus patt., footed, pink tint & gold trim, 1st period (ILLUS.) **700-800**

Fan Pattern Teapot with Pink Tint & Gold Trim

Teapot, Fan patt., pink tint & gold trim, 2nd period (ILLUS.)... **600-1,000**

Multicolored Finner Pattern Teapot

Teapot, Finner patt., mulitcolored decoration, 2nd period (ILLUS.) **1,000-1,400**

Grass Pattern Teapot with Color Decoration

Teapot, Grass patt., multicolored decoration, 1st period (ILLUS.) **600-800**

Hexagon Pattern Teapot with Pink Tint

Teapot, Hexagon patt., pink tint, 2nd period (ILLUS.) **500-700**

High Lily Teapot with Green Tint

Teapot, High Lily patt., green tint, 2nd period (ILLUS.) **700-800**

Lace Pattern Teapot with Chocolate & Gold Decoration

Teapot, Lace patt., chocolate decoration & gold trim, 2nd period (ILLUS.) **1,000-1,400**

Early Undecorated Lace Pattern Teapot

Teapot, Lace patt., undecorated, 1st period (ILLUS.) **800-900**

Limpet Footed Pink Tint 2nd Period Teapot

Teapot, Limpet patt., footed, pink tint, 2nd period (ILLUS.) **600-800**

Pink & Gold-trimmed Limpet Teapot

Teapot, Limpet patt., pink tint w/gold trim, 3rd period (ILLUS.).. **300-400**

Low Celtic Pink Tint Teapot

Teapot, Low Celtic patt., pink tint, 3rd period (ILLUS.) **800-1,200**

Undecorated Mask Pattern Teapot

Teapot, Mask patt., undecorated, 3rd period (ILLUS.)... **400-500**

Neptune Pattern Teapot with Pink Tint

Teapot, Neptune patt., pink tint, 2nd period (ILLUS.)... **400-600**

Ringhandle Teapot with Celtic Decoration

Teapot, Ringhandle patt., Celtic decoration, 3rd period (ILLUS.) **800-1,000**

Shamrock-Basketweave Teapot with Standard Decoration

Teapot, Shamrock-Basketweave patt., standard decoration, 3rd period (ILLUS.)................... **400-500**

Shell Pattern Teapot with Pink & Gold Decoration

Teapot, Shell patt., footed, pink & gold decoration, 1st period (ILLUS.) **800-1,000**

Sydney Pattern Teapot with Pink Tint

Teapot, Sydney patt., pink tint, 2nd period (ILLUS.) **600-800**

Early Undecorated Thistle Pattern Teapot

Teapot, Thistle patt., undecorated, 1st period (ILLUS.) **600-800**

Gold-trimmed Thorn Pattern Teapot

Teapot, Thorn patt., gold trim, 1st period (ILLUS.).. **600-1,000**

Early Tridacna Teapot with Gold Trim

Teapot, Tridacna patt., gold trim, 1st period (ILLUS.) **400-600**

Victorian Pattern Teapot with Gold Trim

Teapot, Victoria patt., gold trim, 2nd period (ILLUS.) **800-1,200**

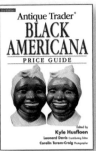
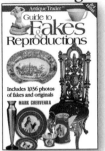
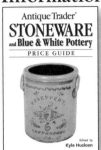
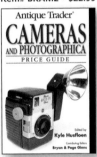
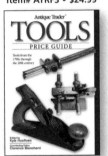
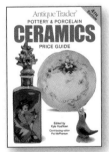

Warman's® Field Guides Redefine *Resourceful*

Warman's® Star Wars Field Guide
Softcover • 4-3/16 x 5-3/16 • 512 pages
300+ color photos
Item# SWFG • $12.99

**Warman's® Depression Glass
Field Guide**
Softcover • 4-3/16 x 5-3/16 • 512 pages
500 color photos
Item# DGPG2 • $12.99

Warman's® Jewelry Field Guide
Softcover • 4-3/16 x 5-3/16 • 512 pages
400+ color photos
Item# ATFG2 • $12.99

Warman's® Bottles Field Guide
Softcover • 4-3/16 x 5-3/16 • 512 pages
300 color photos
Item# BTFG • $12.99

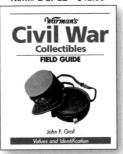

**Warman's® Civil War
Collectibles Field Guide**
Softcover • 4-3/16 x 5-3/16 • 512 pages
300 color photos
Item# CWFG • $12.99

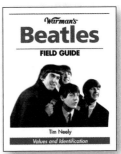

Warman's® Beatles Field Guide
Softcover • 4-3/16 x 5-3/16 • 512 pages
300+ color photos
Item# BTLFG • $12.99

Warman's® Toys Field Guide
Softcover • 4-3/16 x 5-3/16 • 512 pages
275 color photos
Item# TOYG • $12.99

Warman's® Bean Plush Field Guide
Softcover • 4-3/16 x 5-3/16 • 512 pages
1300 color photos
Item# BNSFG • $12.99

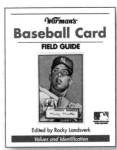

Warman's® Baseball Card Field Guide
Softcover • 4-3/16 x 5-3/16 • 512 pages
512 color photos
Item# BCFG • $12.99

To order call 800-258-0929 Offer BAB5
M-F 7am - 8pm • Sat. 8am - 2pm, CST

Mail order form to:
kp books
an imprint of F+W Publications, Inc.
Offer BAB5
P.O. Box 5009, Iola, WI 54945-5009

Shipping & Handling: $4.00 first book, $2.25 each additional. Non-US addresses $20.95 first book, $5.95 each additional.

Sales Tax: CA , IA, IL, KS, NJ, PA, SD, TN, VA, WI residents add appropriate sales tax.

Satisfaction Guarantee: If for any reason you are not completely satisfied with your purchase, simply return it within 14 days of receipt and receive a full refund, less shipping charges.